BUILD YOUR SHOPIFY BRAND

A BLUEPRINT FOR CRAFTING YOUR CUSTOMER JOURNEY TO MAXIMIZE SALES

SHOPIFY MADE EASY 2023
BOOK 2

VERONICA JEANS

CONTENTS

Introduction	v
1. Visual Branding	1
2. Shopify Brand Setting	45
3. Structure Your Pages	51
4. Store Information Pages	83
5. Storyboard Your Customer Journey	132
6. Create Effective & Converting Product Pages	147
7. Gift Cards	231
8. Collections	245
9. Navigation & Menus	271
10. Shopify Theme	299
11. Virtual Store Front	362
12. Apps & Sales	387
About the Author	395
Acknowledge	397

Copyright © 2022 by Veronica Jeans

All rights reserved.

No portion of this publication may be reproduced, distributed, or transmitted in any form or by any means, including photocopying, recording, or other electronic or mechanical methods, without the prior written permission from the publisher or author, except in the case of brief quotations embodies in reviews and specific other noncommercial uses as permitted by copyright law.

The information provided within this book, Shopify Made Easy - Build Your Shopify Brand - book 2, is for general informational purposes only. While the authors try to keep the information up-to-date and correct, there are no representations or warranties, express or implied, about the completeness, accuracy, reliability, suitability, or availability with respect to the information, products, services, or related graphics contained in this book for any purpose. Any use of this information is at your own risk.

Any advice provided in this book is based on the authors' experience and does not reflect the opinion of Amazon or Shopify. All opinions expressed in this book are solely the opinion of the authors.

I have made every effort to contact all copyright holders.

Published by Veronica L. Jeans

VeronicaJeans.com

INTRODUCTION

There are really only 3 simple rules to remember when you set up your online store.

3 Rules for eCommerce:

Rule 1. Create a product they want

Rule 2. Get people to know it exists

Rule 3. Persuade people to buy your product

This is **not** a guide on making millions through specific sales techniques or strategies. Instead, the focus is on setting up your **sales engine** effectively to **achieve successful product sales.**

Here is the secret to a successful business…

- Learn from other people's experiences.
- Create a plan and goals and stay focused.
- Follow the plan and do not get distracted.
- Build a team.
- Be passionate about your product.

I will try to help you set up your business for success.

Through this book, I will share my experience with you, create a plan, and work together to complete your store setup, enabling you to start selling your products. We will work as a team and remain focused on achieving this goal. With this approach, your brand and store will hopefully showcase your passion for your products.

In this particular book, I have incorporated my extensive experience in technology, business, financing, and eCommerce, both from my own business and from clients, to provide you with an edge in your online venture.

The primary focus of this book is to help you establish a memorable brand and a successful customer journey that encourages visitors to return and purchase your products repeatedly.

Neil Patel, SEO strategist, and speaker, says, "According to one academic study, 94% of the time, someone's first impression is based on design, and it only takes 50 milliseconds for that split-second decision to get made."

UNDERSTANDING "THE BRAIN THING" IN CONSUMER BEHAVIOR

Consumer behavior is a complex process involving many factors, including personal beliefs, experiences, and emotions. In recent years, researchers have explored how the brain processes information during the buying process, a phenomenon often referred to as "The Brain Thing."

According to research, shopping activates specific regions of the brain. Some brain areas are responsible for emoting happiness, while others are responsible for pain or discomfort. It is no surprise that the parts of the brain involved in buying create a range of emotions. Our brains make several instant decisions while buying a product, including whether we like it, whether it will help us, and how much it costs.

Additionally, people have biases when making purchasing decisions and understanding how preferences can deliver insights into why consumers choose different products and brands. The overall message should answer the question, "What's in It For Me?" from the customer's perspective.

In summary, understanding "The Brain Thing" is essential for businesses seeking to improve their marketing strategies and consumer engagement. By tapping into the emotional aspects of consumer behavior, businesses can create memorable and engaging shopping experiences that resonate with their target audience.

The bottom line is:

The overall message should answer = WIIFM (What's in It For Me - for the customer)

WHY I WROTE THIS BOOK

The purpose of writing this book is to help entrepreneurs like you establish an online presence and initiate product sales with ease, without having to spend excessive time learning new skills.

My Shopify books to simplify the process of setting up your Shopify store, covering the essential tools required to get started. For more advanced information, I will refer you to my other books or tools.

With thousands of illustrations and links to helpful internet tools and apps, this authoritative guide provides a comprehensive blueprint for building a successful eCommerce business using Shopify, the leading eCommerce platform.

This book is not about the products you sell; it concentrates on building a solid foundation for your business to ensure smooth operation and profitable product sales. By now, I assume you have a product or idea in mind for your online store.

WHAT MAKES THIS BOOK SPECIAL?

I update my books annually to keep up with the constant changes in Shopify. There is an abundance of information available on Shopify's blogs, which can be overwhelming, making it difficult to set up and optimize your online business.

Setting up your Shopify store has never been easier with the step-by-step blueprint and screenshots in this book, allowing you to follow along without needing technical expertise.

Using the methods I teach my clients and students, I walk you through each step of setting up a Shopify store, drawing on my experience owning Shopify stores in the USA and internationally.

Each chapter of the book focuses on a specific subject or setting within the Shopify setup, accompanied by step-by-step instructions and screenshots of your Shopify dashboard, and includes numerous tips based on my experience assisting other Shopify owners in building their successful eCommerce businesses.

It is impossible to include all the necessary information in one book; therefore, this book focuses on building the foundation of your ecommerce store.

This book is about setting up theme implementation, product uploading, and creating navigation and information content.

It is not about setting up social media channels and marketplaces like Amazon or optimizing your store for conversions.

To ensure your Shopify setup is not overwhelming, I have created the Shopify Made Easy book series, with each book taking you further in optimizing your Shopify store.

SHOPIFY MADE EASY SERIES

Book One

Start Your Online Business

A Step-by-Step Guide to Establishing a Profitable eCommerce Business with Shopify

Book Two

Build Your Shopify Brand

A Blueprint for Crafting Your Customer Journey to Maximize Sales

Book Three

Grow Your Shopify Business

A Comprehensive Guide to Boosting Your E-commerce Sales and Growing Your Business

HOW THIS BOOK WORKS

In this book, I provide you with the location of each dashboard section in Shopify and guide you on the necessary steps to set up your store.

INTRODUCTION

For further information, each chapter includes a reference section with links designed for easy comprehension, making them effortless to read and understand.

All the links are with my domain. ***https://veronicajeans.online/subject*** instead of this very long confusing URL (browser link) example: [*https://app.ahrefs.com/site-audit/3401207/25/data-d0f4-11e7-8ed1-001e67ed4656&filterCollapsed=true*]

Throughout this book, I incorporate quotes from Shopify to provide additional verification for the steps you are executing, enhancing their reliability.

To ensure the accuracy of the information presented, I also include quotes from reliable sources.

All the images in this book are screenshots of the Shopify dashboard and have been optimized for printing.

Once you have set up your Shopify store, this book will serve as an excellent reference, as it can be challenging to remember where all the settings are if you do not use them regularly. This book will simplify the process for you.

WHY SHOPIFY?

One question I am frequently asked is, "Do I need a website if I have a shopping cart?"

The answer is no; if you have a shopping platform like Shopify, you do not require a separate website. Shopify is an all-in-one shopping platform that includes your website, store, and blog, making it a complete web application for building and managing your online store.

One of the most significant advantages of Shopify is its user-friendliness. Even if you are not tech-savvy, you can easily set up your Shopify store.

With Shopify, you get a website, store, and blog all in one package. If you register your domain with Shopify, you will also receive alias email addresses.

NOTE: Shopify is not a hosting email provider.

Shopify enables integration with various marketplaces and social media platforms, such as Facebook, Instagram, Amazon, eBay, Walmart, Pinterest, TikTok, Etsy, Raku, and many others, continually expanding its reach.

INTRODUCTION

With Shopify, you can directly integrate with other vendors to source, dropship, or print-on-demand products from China, Europe, and the United States.

Setting up payment options in Shopify is easy and convenient, with built-in payment systems that allow you to set up your payment merchant account by simply adding your information to the Shopify admin. Additionally, Shopify permits the acceptance of multiple currencies, making it a genuinely international shopping cart with several payment options.

Order processing and shipping can be conveniently managed within your Shopify admin, where you can generate shipping labels, invoices, tracking, and more with ease.

While Shopify can host your domain name, you also have the option to use a domain name hosted by a third-party provider. If you have your domain name with a third-party hosting company, you can connect it to your Shopify store.

Why would you register your domain with Shopify and not with a third-party domain host?

- It's easy to use and has many features that can help you grow your business.
- Shopify hosts it, so you don't need to worry about setting up and maintaining your website server.
- It's a hosted platform that can be accessed and managed from anywhere worldwide.
- It comes with SSL encryption (HTTPS), so you don't have to set that up separately
- You get privacy protection for free from Shopify.

As a guide to all of my books, I have developed a free bonus course that provides downloadable worksheets, bonus video content, and access to all the resources and links referenced in this book.

Here is a link to my RESOURCES & TOOLS page:

https://veronicajeans.online/resources

Bonus tool: There is also my onboarding worksheet that you can use to add all your store, social, and password information.

BUILD THE KNOW, LIKE, TRUST & BUY FACTOR

You want to build the 'KNOW - LIKE - TRUST - BUY' factor on all your online store pages.

Customers need to know you, like your products, and trust your store. Then, they will buy from you.

Do you know what sells products? INFORMATION...and more information. Information creates knowledge, likes, trust, and buying.

The more information in your ecommerce store, the better. Here is the secret sauce for any ecommerce store - CREATE ENOUGH INFORMATION for a visitor to become a customer!

Have you ever felt frustrated with a store that fails to provide enough information when you are researching products? Providing sufficient information is how you can gain an advantage over your competitors in the ecommerce arena.

WHY VISITORS LEAVE A WEBSITE

It's important to understand why visitors may leave your online store and to address any issues that may cause them to do so. This can help improve the user experience and increase the likelihood of visitors returning to your store in the future.

Some common reasons for visitors leaving a website include:

- **The design is outdated:** An outdated design can negatively impact the user experience and give the impression that the store is not up-to-date with current trends. Investing in a modern and visually appealing design can help attract visitors and build trust with potential customers.
- **The content is difficult to read:** Content that is difficult to read or understand can cause frustration and lead to visitors leaving the website.
- **The content or products don't live up to promises on landing:** Content or products that fail to live up to the promises made on the landing page, will make visitors feel deceived and lose trust in the store.

- **The store relies on outdated plugins:** Outdated plugins can cause technical issues and potentially harm the website's functionality.
- **There are too many ads or videos on auto-play:** Too many ads or autoplay videos can be overwhelming for visitors and detract from your content and products.
- **The navigation structure is unclear:** Unclear navigation can cause frustration and make it difficult for visitors to find what they are looking for.
- **The website is slow to load:** Slow-loading negatively impacts the user experience and may cause visitors to leave before making a purchase.
- **Offers aren't relevant or appealing:** Offers that are not relevant or appealing to visitors will decrease the likelihood of a purchase. Understanding the target audience and tailoring offers to their preferences can help increase engagement and sales.
- **The product benefits are unclear:** Unclear product benefits can lead to confusion and cause visitors to leave without making a purchase.
- **There is no call-to-action:** A lack of call-to-action can cause visitors to leave the website without completing a purchase.
- **The website is not mobile-friendly or does not display well on the visitor's device:** A website that is not mobile-friendly or does not display well on certain devices will cause frustration.
- **The site is not secure or appears not trustworthy:** A lack of security or an appearance of being untrustworthy can cause visitors to leave without making a purchase.
- **The payment methods are not clear:** Clearly outlining payment methods and providing a range of options will help increase the likelihood of a successful sale.

As you develop and add information and content to your online store, the above reasons will be resolved for your online store.

With Shopify themes, you will not have a problem with an outdated design or your site not being mobile-friendly. Shopify also has all your secure environment automatically set up, and your payment methods and checkout are designed with the customer journey in mind.

So the foundation of your tasks is **identifying the information** and **content relevant to your niche** and products and adding it to the correct areas of your store.

TECHNOLOGY

What technological requirements do you need before starting your online store?

To ensure that your product images appear great, you may need a laptop or computer to bulk upload your products. It is recommended that you have a laptop with at least 16GB of memory. This will make it easier to create images and videos, and bulk upload.

You have the option of running your store from a mobile device or an iPad/similar device using the Shopify App, but it is recommended to use a laptop or desktop computer to add products and information efficiently.

You can connect to a regular printer or label printer to print shipping labels and invoices as needed.

CHAPTER 1
VISUAL BRANDING

 "Products are made in the factory, but brands are created in the mind." – Walter Landor

THIS CHAPTER WILL INTRODUCE you to the WHAT, HOW, and a little bit of the WHY of branding, covering all aspects of the subject. While branding is a broad topic, this section specifically focuses on branding your store. By applying the knowledge you gain from this section, you can establish a strong and cohesive branding identity for your store.

WHAT TO EXPECT IN THIS CHAPTER:

- *Develop Your Brand Strategy*
- *Identify Your Ideal Customer*
- *Create a Custom Persona (Your Customer)*
- *Create Your Own Branding*
- *Brand Your Store*

DEVELOP YOUR BRAND STRATEGY

To start, let's discuss the fundamentals of branding and its significance. Without a clear understanding of the basics, it is challenging to position your brand effectively to attract potential customers.

Shopify - The Future of Commerce Trend Report 2022: *"Fifty-two percent of shoppers are more likely to purchase from a company with shared values, and 53% of brands are creating products in 2022 that align with their values. Be consistent. If you take an ethical stance on social or environmental issues, demonstrate how those values run through your brand, from the top of the business to your customer service representatives."*

What Is the Difference Between a Brand, Branding & Brand Strategy

Wikipedia says: *"A brand is a name, term, design, symbol or any other feature that identifies one seller's goods or service as distinct from other sellers."*

A brand is how a company or individual is perceived. It's an emotional connection that a customer has with the brand. It's the reputation of a company that is an asset for the business.

Branding is the ongoing process of building that connection through various marketing channels and touchpoints.

Brand strategy is the plan that guides how a company will build and maintain its brand to achieve its goals.

Here are some examples of a brand:

Coco-Cola has built a brand that is more than just the product. Coke is described as bringing family and friends together, encouraging sharing, and bringing happiness rather than just a soda. And they protect that brand fiercely all over the world.

IKEA - "To create a better everyday life for many people."

Patagonia - "We're in business to save our home planet."

The first impression matters - As Jeff Bezos, CEO of Amazon, says, "*Branding is what people say about you when you're not in the room."*

"To succeed in business, knowing who you are and what you want to be is vital."
Veronica Jeans

There's a reason why every great business leader has been able to convey their story and influence other people. These leaders all understood what they wanted out of their lives and could successfully tie their vision in with their business strategy. They knew a strong brand was more than just a logo or slogan.

Here are key ingredients to think about to create your message and make it very clear, concise, and understandable to your visitors as soon as they land on your online store.

Here are the 4 key ingredients for building your brand:

- Establish your vision & mission - why people should buy from you; this is your slogan and short description in your brand settings.
- Establish your uniqueness - what makes you different from your competition.
- Determine who your target audience is - who your customer is.
- Create your visual branding - cohesive visual assets your customer will recognize.

Establish Your Vision & Mission

You will frequently hear entrepreneurs say they started their businesses because they wanted more freedom, money, or influence.

Most small business owners start because they've identified a market opportunity or are passionate about a product or service. However, not many have a clearly defined vision of their business.

An old saying goes, "if you don't know where you're going, how do you know when you have arrived?"

Businesses must have a compelling purpose and clear reason for being if they are to gain the advantage needed in today's competitive environment. It's not enough to know what you do (the what), or how you do it (the how), you need to understand why you do it - your purpose and passion.

 People don't buy what you do, they buy why you do it.

Step 1: Define Your Vision

Why do you need your vision?

Before deciding on your goals, you must understand why you are in business.

You need to know your purpose, why you got into the business, your vision, and where you see yourself and your business in the future.

Here are a few reasons why you should have a vision statement for your business:

- Builds an image of what your business will look like in the future.
- Provides an objective for you and your business, which you can use to make strategic decisions.
- Attracts people who share your values.
- Makes your brand communication consistent across all types of media.
- Distinguishes you from your competitors by displaying your hidden value.

If you do not define your why or your passion when times get tough, as they inevitably will, it will be hard for you to keep moving forward. However, your vision will help carry you through the hard times. A purpose keeps you moving forward.

Most of the reasons mentioned can be solved by answering the WHY! And it starts with your vision statement. I will quote Simon Sinek, who makes you think about your why and why you need it.

"Very few people or companies can clearly articulate WHY they do WHAT they do. By WHY I mean your purpose, cause, or belief - WHY does your company exist? WHY do you get out of bed every morning? And WHY should anyone care? People don't buy WHAT you do, they buy WHY you do it," Sinek explains in the book "Start with Why: How Great Leaders Inspire Everyone to Take Action."

Your vision plays a highly pivotal part in your strategic planning process -- or at least it should. Without a sense of purpose and direction, it's nearly impossible to thoughtfully prepare for the future, let alone determine what campaigns you should run each month.

Your vision statement should be inspirational enough for you and your team to find purpose and direct enough to serve as a filter for making important business decisions. Additionally, your mission statement should encapsulate the product or service you deliver, the audience you provide it to, and the problem it solves.

 People don't buy what you do, they buy why you do it…

they buy your story.

They will become your best ambassadors if they believe in your 'why'. For example, Meg Staples, the HerTribeAthletics.com owner, is growing her business by inspiring her ambassadors, and they are growing her business organically by promoting the products to their friends.

Lindsay Taylor, the owner of NaughtyGoodBites.com, has this vision on her website: *"Regardless of how we each grew up, or the women we have become today, we are all joined together as dreamers. Women are dreaming of creating our most intentional lives, making an impact, and setting an example for the little girls to follow. Here, at NaughtyGood, I strive to do just that. I dream of a room full of women empowering, celebrating, and honoring each other. I believe greater things can happen if we continue to stand together, laugh together, cry together… and eat chocolate together!!!."*

This is powerful, and would you not buy chocolates from her?

> Pro Tip: I read somewhere - imagine you are pitching to Shark Tank – they have no patience for BS.

Step 2: Summarize and aim for impact - keep it simple.

Suppose you know your WHY – great! But sometimes our whys change. They are fluid and move as we do. So allow yourself to check in with yourself every so often. Ask yourself: Is my why still my why?

If you don't know your WHY, take some time out of your busy schedule to consider it. Remember, this is about what motivates you at a very deep level.

Don't be surprised if it takes some time for you to formulate your answer. Once you have done that, write down your WHY, the deep-seated reason you started your business. Make sure it is visible in your workspace so that it will remind you of what drives you every day.

Make sure it has these components:

- It should be inspiring.
- It must not be selfish.
- It cannot be against someone or something.
- It should be constructive rather than self-destructive.
- It must be feasible in practice.

- It shouldn't just be an idea but something that will keep you going when the going gets tough.
- When you think about it, you should feel happy.

Here are some questions you can ask yourself:

- Can you describe what you would like your business to become? (the best in..., recognized for...., a leader of/for...)?
- What would you like to see your business achieve (What reputation, What level of excellence)?
- How do you envision the future of your business?

Now create one to three sentences of the 3 answers you have.

There is no hard or fast rule for how long any vision or mission statement is. However, the rule of thumb is that it should be easy for your employees to be able to repeat without hesitation.

Here are some ideas from well-known brands:

Shopify: *"To make commerce better for everyone. Then they promote the reason why they're driven to remove the hassle and complications of managing an eCommerce website: so businesses can focus on what's most important to them."*

Mission - *"To make commerce better for everyone."*

Tesla: *"To create the most compelling car company of the 21st century by driving the world's transition to electric vehicles."*

Mission - *"To accelerate the world's transition to sustainable energy."*

Nike: *"Our mission is what drives us to do everything possible to expand human potential. We do that by creating groundbreaking sports innovations, by making our products more sustainably, by building a creative and diverse global team, and by making a positive impact in communities where we live and work."*

Mission - *"To bring inspiration and innovation to every athlete in the world."*

Starbucks: *"To establish Starbucks as the premier purveyor of the finest coffee in the world while maintaining our uncompromising principles while we grow."*

Mission - *"to inspire and nurture the human spirit – one person, one cup, and one neighborhood at a time."*

Step 3. Develop Your Mission Statement

Next, we start working on your mission statement - the WHAT, WHO, and HOW!

Why do we need a mission statement?

A mission statement explains your company's values and purpose. A strong mission statement is about two to three sentences explaining what the business does, who is involved in it, and **how it does it**. Your mission statement is not just a slogan but your roadmap to your goals.

Your mission statement will direct your strategy and focus, and goals.

Your mission statement will look like this:

- What do you do or sell?...your products or services.
- What problem do you solve? How do you solve the problem?
- Who are your customers?
- What do your customers value most?
- How do you use your products and services to reach our goals?
- What differentiates you from your competitors?
- What kind of image do you want to convey to the outside world?

Here is an example of the 'How' do you do what you do:

NaughtyGoodBites.com: *"I will deliver each package in less than 12 hours, partner only with local artisans and small business shops, and commit to all recycled materials for packaging."*

Thinking about the 'how' at this stage of your strategy will make it much easier to create content and connect to what your customers need.

Here is an example of 'What' you do for your customers?

"Provide chocolate boxes that spread love and include locally-sourced, high-quality items made within the community."

 Your vision is what drives you.

Your mission is your roadmap.

Your mission will help you focus on what you need to work on and how you will deliver maximum value and impact.

It is easy to confuse people in the marketplace. But checking on big brands will give an idea of the difference.

How to write a mission statement?

Write about what your business does.

- List some of your core values.
- Write a sentence about how your business does what it does.
- Write a sentence about who is part of your business.

Please look at the three sentences and combine them to make a straightforward, clear statement.

Here are some tips:

- Be accurate and only mention things that pertain to your business.
- Be realistic. To achieve your vision, you must make this part of your goals. You should be able to accomplish it.
- Be unique; don't copy what your competition does. I know it is extremely difficult to be different when you start. But as you grow, your uniqueness will appear more apparent.
- Do not use words that sound good or bland; use valuable words for your business.
- Do not get stuck in the "I have the best customer service" trend - instead, think of how you will deliver the best customer service. Cut out as many buzz words as possible.

If you have difficulties, content creator copy.ai (https://veronicajeans.online/copy-ai) can help you create your brand mission and vision.

I have created some quick examples for Kalahari Gold - we only have one type of product.

Vision - *"Through our dedication to ethical sourcing and promoting economic growth, we aim to inspire and empower women everywhere, one drop of Marula oil at a time."*

Mission - *"Kalahari Gold is dedicated to empowering women, preserving the environment, and promoting well-being by importing premium-quality, eco-friendly Marula oil from Namibia to the USA. We are committed to fostering economic growth in local communities and providing our customers with a natural, organic solution for healthier skin, hair, and nails."*

The best way is to read many other mission statements to get ideas. Then, write, rewrite, and improve your mission statement because it will not be perfect the first time. Ask for help!

IDENTIFY YOUR IDEAL CUSTOMER

To create a brand, you need to first understand your target audience (customers. Understanding this will help you develop a **brand positioning statement** and messaging that resonates with your customers.

Next, you need to create a **visual brand identity** that includes a logo, colors, typography, and other visual elements that will help customers recognize and remember your brand.

You also need to create content and messaging that aligns with your **brand values** and resonates with your target audience.

Finally, you need to consistently communicate your brand messaging and visual identity across all marketing channels and touchpoints to build brand awareness and loyalty.

That is exactly what we will be doing in this book.

I will give you the steps to create your branding identity and tools so that you can successfully launch your Shopify store. This will help you establish how you want your store to look and feel.

> Pro Tip: Your brand can change anytime. Consider it a relaunch when you rebrand, making it new and exciting for your customers.

My brand has changed since I started and will change again. My point is, don't fret over deciding what your brand will look like now. Make a decision and start your store.

Whatever you visualize as your branding, the bottom line is that it must be relevant to your products and customers. If it is not, then it will be difficult to create a connection between your brand and your customers, and your brand will ultimately fail.

Let's identify your perfect customer. The first step is to brainstorm all the information you know about them, including their age, location, occupation, and any problems our products can help solve. In addition to brainstorming, we can conduct research to gain more insight into our idea customer's lifestyle and interests. This enables you to create a **custom persona** to guide your branding strategy.

Being specific about your ideal customer is important because it will make it easier to create relevant content, descriptions, images, and other assets that speak directly to them.

For example, if you are targeting women aged 50+, you would not use images of young women on your website. Similarly, if you are targeting rugby fans, you would not feature images of business suits on your website.

So, if you are selling baby gear, think of your customer who is going to be a mom, her age, where she lives, does she have a job, how she feels with the new baby coming.

We also need to know where she spends her time online, whether it's TikTok, Instagram, or Facebook.

Sometimes it can be challenging to be specific about your one ideal customer, especially when you feel that everyone could benefit from our products or services.

However, it's crucial to avoid the spaghetti analogy of throwing everything at the wall and seeing what sticks. Instead, we should create **ONE customer persona** because once you have identified that one perfect person, you will find many others who look just like her.

CREATE A CUSTOM PERSONA (YOUR CUSTOMER)

Even if you do not have customers yet, you know approximately who your customer is that would buy your product.

Step 1. Define your product.

Look at your products and answer these questions:

- What problem does your product solve?
- What needs does it satisfy?
- How does your product improve your customer's life?
- Why did you create your product?
- What was the situation when you realized your product?
- What is the purpose of your product?

Step 2. Identify who your product helps.

Answer these questions:

- Age
- Gender
- Income
- Ethnicity
- Marital/Partner Status
- Education
- Children.

List out the answers. These will create a clear picture of your ideal customer.

Here is a fun way of thinking about who your customer is.

Imagine your perfect customer's experience with you one year from now.

Take a few minutes to close your eyes and imagine someone discovering your brand online. At first, they are intrigued by one of your posts or ads. Next, they take action to get some of your free content, more information, or a low-cost product. Imagine their experience. Imagine the excitement or relief when they read your words or watch your video.

Now, imagine yourself presenting your paid product. Picture yourself in their shoes as they hear your offer. What are they hoping you will say? What fears or doubts do they have? What do they think as they stare at the 'buy' button? This is the moment that you have been building towards. All of your hard work is about to pay off. You are about to turn a total stranger into a happy and loyal customer. This is a win-win situation for you and them, resulting from their perception of your brand.

They believe in the promise of what you are offering and are inspired to take action. Now, write out the thoughts going through your customers' heads as they click the 'Buy' button. What are they telling themselves as they pull out their credit card? What are they hoping will happen after they pay?

Next, write out the thoughts that they will have after they purchase your product or service. Imagine them looking at your reviews page and thinking about what they will write when they begin to type out their 5-star review.

Step 3. Find your customers.

When you are starting to distribute your content online, you need to know where your customers are visiting on the internet, for example, social media, blogs, news, etc.

Here is how to find them:

Join groups - online or offline. Participate and engage in the right kind of group by answering questions, joining the chat, and showing up consistently. A great way to find your people is to check into groups where you know they might be.

Donna, the owner of themissingpiecepuzzle.com, started joining all the puzzle groups on Facebook. Not only did she find her customers, but she also found a way to communicate with prospective customers by answering their questions. A bonus was creating blogs from some questions to drive more traffic to her store through her blog.

Social Media Analytics will give you a lot of information as well. Look at the following:

- Your audience demographics
- Content formats that get the most reach and engagement (i.e., text, images, videos, or links)
- Most popular topics
- Most popular social networking sites for your audience

This information will also give you an idea of what to write, post, and use in your advertising to attract the right customer.

Step 4. Get into the mindset of your customers.

Here are more examples of how to find prospective customers:

- Talk to people
- Conduct one-on-one interviews
- Use Customer Surveys

Write down all the information you gather. Your ideal customer profile, the groups where you have found them, the questions and interviews, the questions in the groups and your answers, etc.

You can use all this invaluable information in your FAQ content, website and product description, and content for marketing.

Step 5. Gather your information.

Creating a spreadsheet or document with your answers is a great idea.

This exercise will help you build your assets to attract your ideal customer to your store.

Get some information about your competitors' customers, set a Google Alert on their name to see when & where they are mentioned. Check out their website to see who they target in their images, content, and descriptions.

Create a Google Alert with your keywords so you can get daily, weekly or monthly alerts to questions.

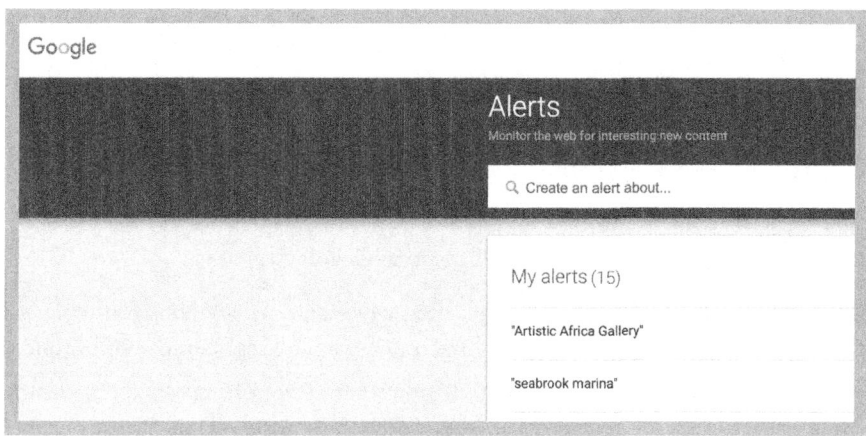

[4.10.1]

The previous image shows my Google alert, and I have my client's websites, Shopify, my name, etc. If there are any mentions, Google will send me an email with the alert.

Step 6. Create different types of customers.

Start with step one and create another type of customer. Most eCommerce businesses have different customers but solve the one problem they have or are perceived to have.

So TheBoneLock.com has pet owners that can use his product, but he also has new parents with babies with no pets.

The one customer is trying to keep one or other pet out of the room and not with a typical pet gate. And the other customer wants to ensure the door stays open to hear the baby but keeps the door secure so it does not slam closed.

TheMissingPiecePuzzle.com has different target audiences - parents with small kids, puzzle lovers, people looking for gifts for grandparents, and brides looking for unique guest books. There are several more, but these are her main audiences. She created her visual assets to suit every special occasion and different products and images for each of her different types of customers. For instance, one type of puzzle has 2 or 3 different product pages. Each of these pages will be a landing page for her posts or ads that she creates.

Create a document outlining each customer type, which will help build the visual assets you need for your online digital marketing and store.

Now you are ready to create your brand.

CREATE YOUR OWN BRANDING

The basics of your branding for your store are the tone of your colors, the look of your store, the fonts you use, and the images you choose.

Creating a branding storyboard that will give you an overview of your colors, fonts, and basics is a great idea. Then you don't have to search for your brand information continuously. You will have it at your fingertips.

You can see in the following image how I set up my brand elements in a Google document. My profile image, links to my social pages, brand colors, brand fonts, icons, and background images.

[2.11.0]

Only you can visualize your brand. Most of the time, explaining your vision of your brand to somebody else will disappoint you because it is never what you have envisioned in your head.

The following exercise will help you visualize the appearance and tone of your brand. Once you have completed this exercise, describing your vision to a designer will be easier.

Step 1. Find 5 - 10 brands you like and list parts of their branding you want.

Things you want to start to take note of as you do your research:

- What colors and fonts are they using?
- Do they have a logo, or do they use a font for the brand name?
- What do their social media channels look like?
- Do you feel personally connected to them? Why? How?
- What media do they use to showcase their products? Audio, video, photo, text?
- How do they introduce themselves and explain their business?

Step 2. List the characteristics of your favorite brands.

List 10-20 words that come to mind when you think of these brands. For example, Success, Sincere, Caring, Posh, Ambitious, etc.

I recommend using a combination of nouns and adjectives that pop into your head within the first few seconds of looking at their websites, watching their videos, or viewing their social profiles.

Step 3. Decide how YOU want your brand to be perceived.

Before creating a logo, choosing your fonts and colors, or setting up your online presence, you must clarify how you want people to perceive your brand.

You have already accelerated this process by describing the brands you want to emulate. Your job right now is to take the best characteristics of your favorite brands and mold them into your brand.

This is my list:

EXPERTISE: Innovative, Smart, Knowledgeable, Experienced, Visionary.

CHARACTER: Professional, Trustworthy, Caring,

DRIVE: Inspiring, Exciting, Motivated

When you start writing your story and product descriptions, this exercise will benefit you in creating your store and your brand.

The next step is to prepare your branding, see the colors and font, and know the store's voice you want to present to the world.

BRAND YOUR STORE

According to HubSpot, 46% of people rank the website's design as the number one factor determining a company's credibility.

Here are a few things you need to prepare and have ready to customize your Shopify theme.

- Branding Colors (4 max)
- Logos
- Favicon (Browser tab logo)
- Fonts
- Images & Photos

VISUAL BRANDING

- Create Your Own Custom Product Photos
- Videos

In the next few steps you will be able to prepare and create your own branding tools for your Shopify store.

> Pro Tips: If you don't know anything about branding and need help, there are several ways to get something done cheaply but with good value for money. The cheap route would be Etsy. Quite a few branding companies will create a quick branding package. Your logo (or a couple of options), colors, and fonts will be included.

NOTE: *I know great agencies with excellent branding packages that won't break the bank. With this option, there will be more opportunities to change to get what you want.*

BRANDING COLORS

The color choices on your website and how dated they feel have a more significant impact on visitors than you might realize.

The following image shows you a dated store.

[2.11.1]

And here is an up-to-date website with full-width images and visual appeal.

[2.11.2]

Research shows that people judge products within **50 milliseconds of exposure** — 94% of that judgment is based on color alone. Choosing the right colors can enhance readability by 40%, increase comprehension by 73%, and improve learning by 78%.

Colors are one of the essential elements that add credibility to your website.

The University of Toronto conducted a study on colors and how individuals experience them. The results were very interesting. They determined that most people prefer combinations of simple colors. In most cases, just two or three colors were perceived as appealing.

That's why sticking to a color palette is so important to the success of your site and, ultimately, your business.

Three (3) colors on your color palette should probably be the max for your website. If you use2 more colors, use shades of the primary 3 or 3 colors. Colors should be used as accents and also to emphasize. And part of the main colors is for your buttons.

Have fun choosing.

Tools:

Here is a color pallet to choose from:

https://coolors.co/

http://colormind.io/

I found these tools with a quick search on Google.

LOGOS

Your logo is an essential part of building a successful brand identity. It is a visual representation of your brand that helps to differentiate you from competitors and makes it more recognizable to customers.

Step 1. Design your logo

Keep your logo simple.

Here are some tips:

- Your logo should be visible on mobile, so resist adding your slogan below the logo.
- Don't add too many details or text to your logo. The effectiveness of your logo will be lost on your website/store or mobile.
- Print the logo onto a business card to see how the details will show.
- Make the font readable for a website and mobile.

Next, I will show you some examples of brand logos.

Here is a logo with a simple design:

[2.11.3]

The following logo was designed for a retail store sign and not adjusted for the online and mobile stores. It is very cute with the spider and the text 'boutique'. Under the logo is 'Baby Children & Tween', which is barely visible. The logo on the website shows that the text under the logo is not very clear, as you can see in the following image.

[2.11.4]

And viewing the small text on mobile really takes up valuable real estate.

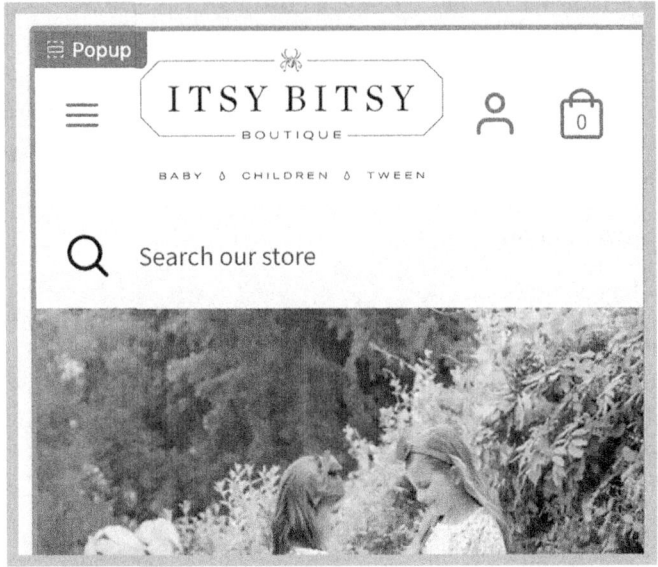

[2.11.5]

Step 2. Create different logo variations

Create different variations of your logo - a square logo for your profiles on social media and a horizontal logo for your website/store.

I usually experiment with different sizes and see what size logo is most visually appealing.

Here are some examples of different types of logos for one brand:

For the website:

[2.11.6]

For a social profile:

[2.11.7]

For the label of a bottle:

[2.11.8]

Default logo: Types of images you can add - HEIC, PNG, or JPG. The recommended width of the logo: is 512 pixels minimum.

Square logo: Used by some social media channels. It may be cropped into a circle.

Types of images you can add - HEIC, PNG, or JPG. The recommended size of the logo: is 512×512 pixels minimum.

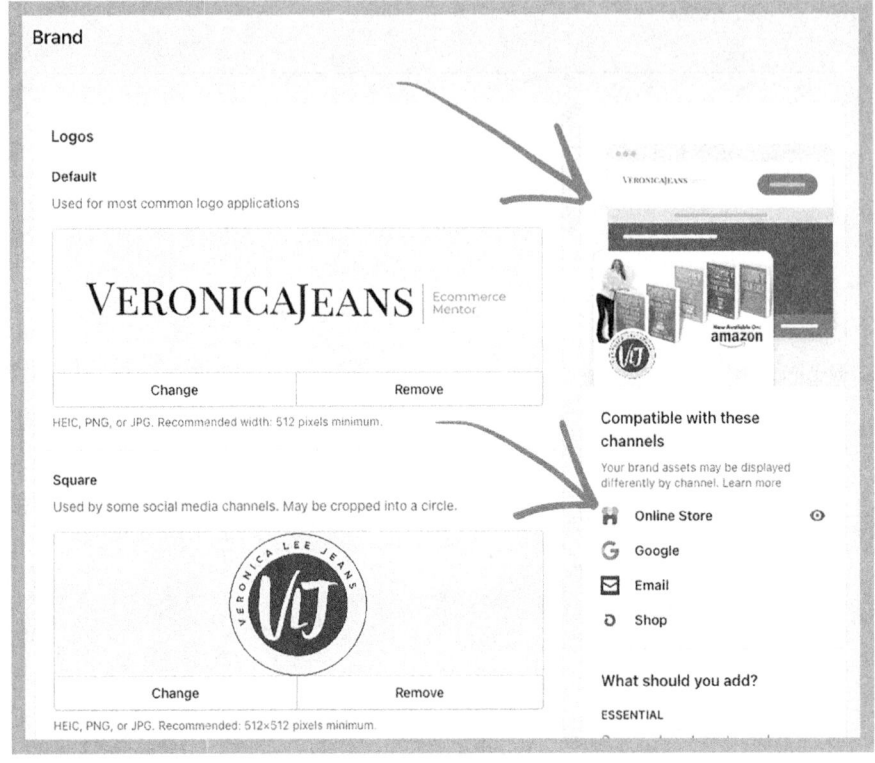

[2.10.2]

> 💡 Pro Tip: The ideal measurement of your store's logo is found in your theme under 'Customization.'

FAVICON

What is the favicon? And why do we need a favicon?

Wikipedia says: *"A favicon, also known as a shortcut icon, website icon, tab icon, URL icon, or bookmark icon, is a file containing one or more small icons associated with a particular website or web page."*

Where do you see the favicon? It is the tiny little logo on the browser tab when you open the website.

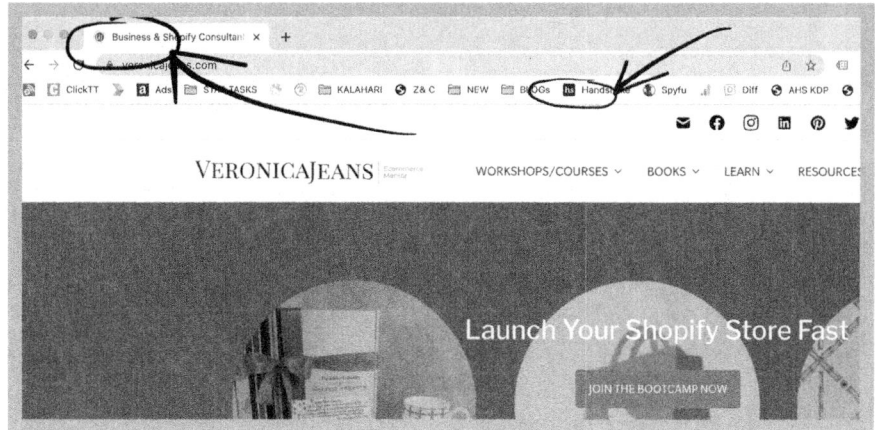

[2.11.10]

It personalizes your website/store, looks professional, and is tactical. So, if somebody bookmarks your website, your mini logo will also be bookmarked.

Step 1. Size your favicon

The size of the image has to be 32 x 32 pixels. Create a PNG (which means that the background is transparent). Don't add too much information to this image.

Strip your logo to the essential details and test it in your store when you open a tab in your browser.

In the first image (2.11.11), there is too much in the background,

[2.11.11]

The second image is nice and clean, and distinct. Remember, the image is super small, so details will be lost.

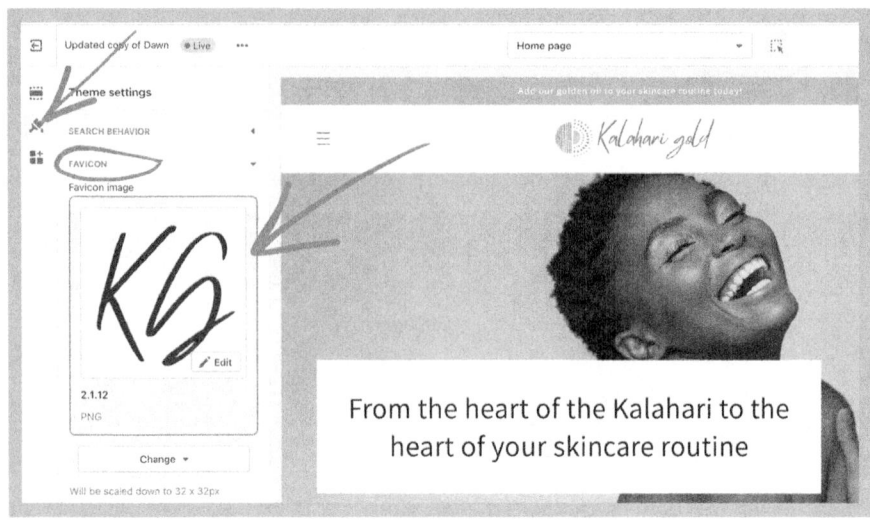

[2.11.12]

Tools:

Canva.com is a great tool for logos

Shopify logo creator

(https://www.shopify.com/tools/logo-maker0

FONTS

In each theme, you will get a selection of fonts to use with the theme. If the font is unavailable on the Shopify themes, you can upload your font in your Shopify store's 'Edit Code' section.

Here are some basic rules:

- Choose a maximum of 2 fonts - one for your headers and one for your body text.
- If your font is highly stylized, use it sparingly on the store pages.
- Your font needs to suit your brand.

> 💡 Pro Tips: Do not use a fancy font for your body text. All of your fonts have to be readable in any browser. Make sure you test your fonts on a page to see what they will look like. It is easier to keep to the standard basic fonts.

And here, in the following image, the font in the logo is part of the heading in NaughtyGoodBites.com.

[2.11.15]

Here is an example of a font that is part of the logo and is repeated the title or heading on the page in the following image.

[2.11.16]

The following image shows a basic font in a paid Shopify theme. We stuck to 'Avenir', and 'Lato' makes the menu more readable.

Headings: Avenir Next Semi Bold

Main menu and buttons: Lato Medium

Regular text: Avenir Next

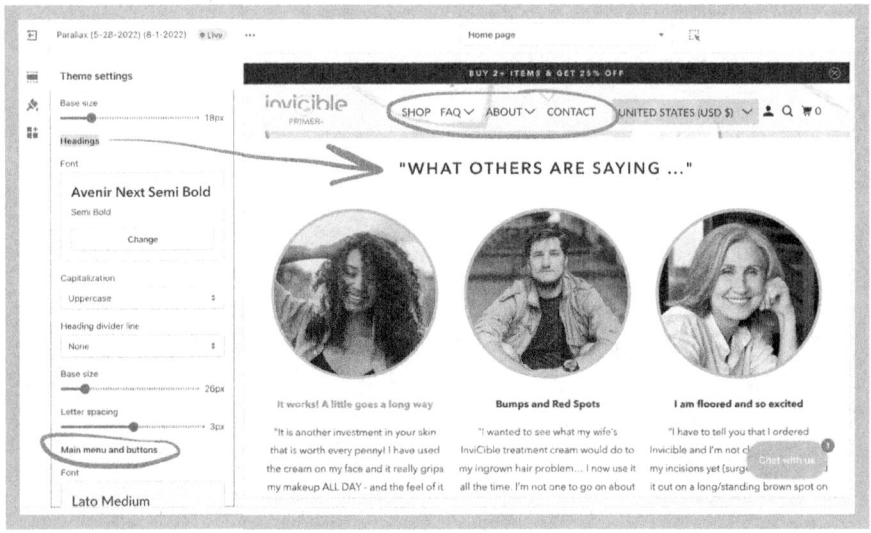

[2.11.17]

And in your description, you can use different sizes or capitalization to draw attention.

[2.11.18]

> Pro Tip: Don't go too fancy or drastically artistic with your fonts. There are several reasons why. The main issue is readability. Make it as easy on the eyes as possible. Remember, it will be tough to read a fancy font on mobile.

Fonts to avoid: Cursive, curls, or Times New Roman (this looks good on paper but not on the web) and other serif fonts. Test fonts on friends and family.

As I told one of my students, "Get it done, and don't get too complicated and stuck on the little things."

IMAGES & PHOTOS

Customers can't smell or taste your products, so making your visuals incredibly delicious and tempting is crucial. Your goal should be to make your potential customers feel hungry just by looking at your product photos.

You have to present the best photos to fire their imagination and make them want to buy your products. It's all about your images which should be bright, CLEAR, and beautiful.

Here are some small facts:

- 60% of people engage with photos.
- 90% of the information is transmitted to our brain visually.
- 93% of consumers consider images essential in purchasing decisions.

The difference between images and photos:

Image - Any visual object modified or altered by a computer or an imaginary object created using a computer.

Photo or photograph - Anything taken by a camera, digital camera, or photocopier.

In the world of ecommerce, product photos or images can be categorized into two types. It's important to distinguish between these two types:

Professional photos or images supplied by a manufacturer, drop shipper. or professional photographer. Professional photos are not always necessary unless you sell food or fashion products. It's highly recommended to have professional photos taken for food or fashion products, as these types of products require specific expertise and editing to make them look appealing. Professional food photos are doctored in surprising ways to make the food look appetizing, which is difficult to replicate on your own.

Photos or images created by you. Many ecommerce owners make mistakes when creating their own product photos. This is often due to a lack of funds to hire a professional photographer or assuming that taking photos themselves will be good enough.

> Pro Tip: Investing in a professional photographer can save you a lot of trouble in the long run.

Next, I will show you some tips for creating great product photographs on your own.

Types of Images

Part of your branding will be to decide the size, look of your images, and style.

There are different types of images for a website and store with different names.

- Hero image
- Panoramic image
- Sliders
- Product Images
- Collection Images
- Blog Images

The **hero, panoramic, and slider images** convey your message visually to your visitor, whether it is what you sell or a promotion. In your Shopify theme, you can add relevant text on top of the image to reinforce your message.

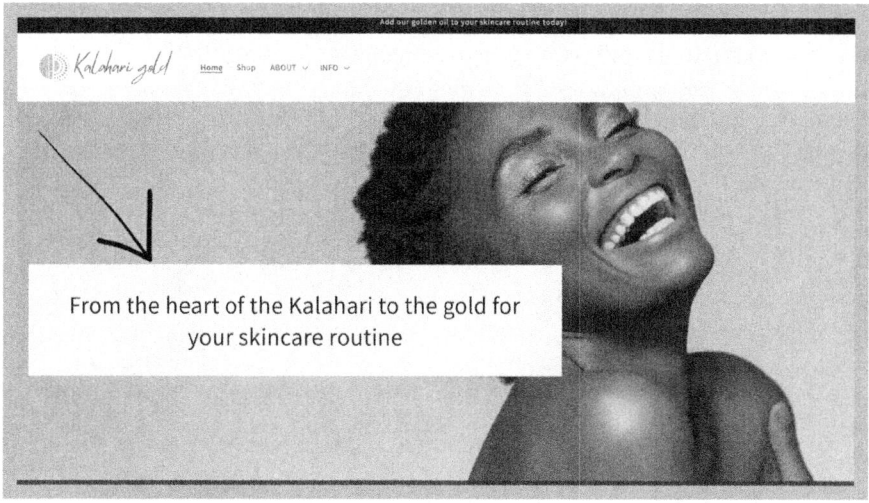

[2.11.28]

If these are at the top of your page, ensure the message is visible on all devices. In some themes, the image will show first, and the text will be below the image in a mobile view.

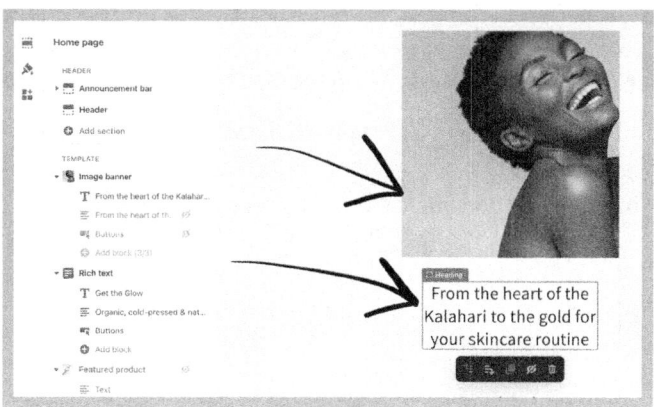

[2.11.29]

> Pro Tip: Do not add text directly on the image when you create the image. The text will not show or be cut off on a mobile device, and you will lose the impact of your message.

As you can see in the following image, the top text is added to the theme, and the text at the bottom is added directly to the image, and the text is cut off.

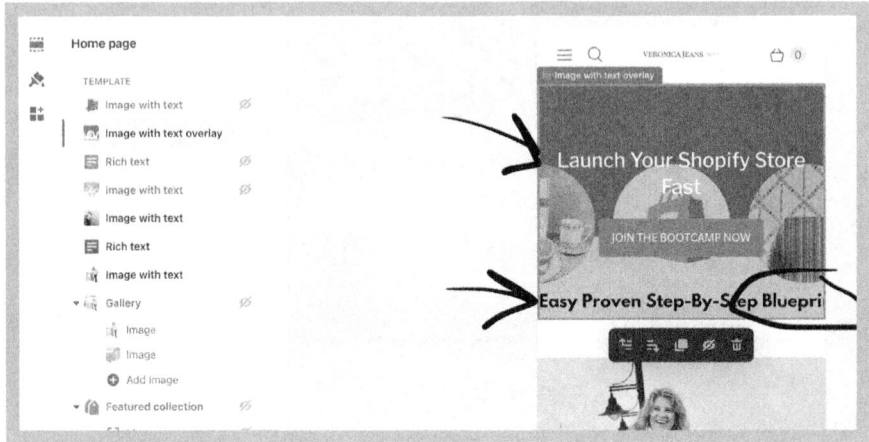

[2.11.30]

Shopify themes are optimized for all devices, so images and text will resize per device.

Product images will show the dimensions you chose.

The height of the images can vary to match the visual look you want to achieve in your store. For example, you want tall images for fashion images. We also used them in the sculpture gallery store MoyoCollections.com:

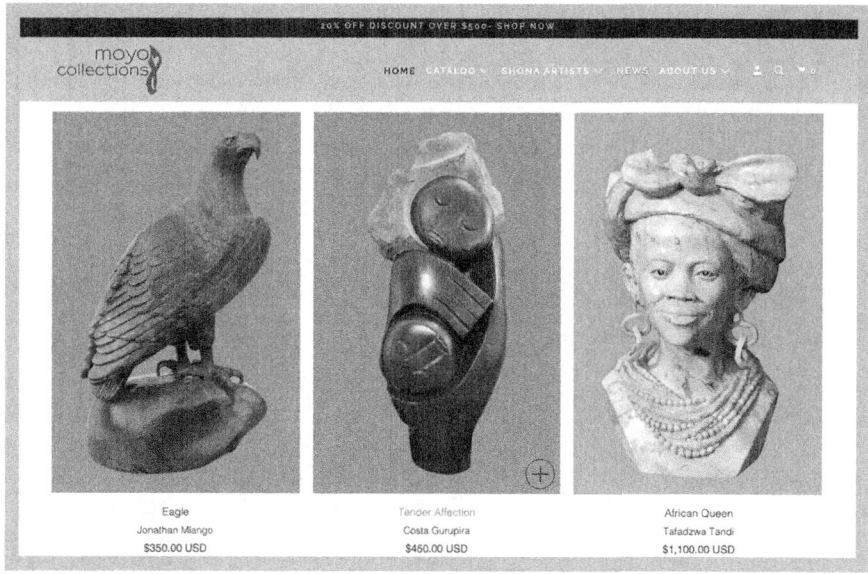

[2.11.26]

Or rectangular images, as in TheMissingPiecePuzzle.com - her puzzles are rectangular, and she shows the exact size of the puzzle.

[2.11.27]

Square images are pretty much the standard for most eCommerce stores. The images you choose really depend on the product and also the brand. Again, keep every image the same size throughout your store.

Collection images are much the same as product images. Again, you dictate what your brand should look like.

Blog images can be treated like your hero images. You choose any size image for your blog. But sometimes the image does not size correctly in the browser, as shown in the following image. The Shopify theme determines the position size and you need to adjust the banner image sizes by testing the outcome.

[2.11.31]

The important factor is all your images should be visually appealing.

> Pro Tip: Create a custom size for your standard images like a product, banner, social, etc., in Canva.com or a photo software, so you can quickly create the same size images. If you have an odd size for the image, you can add that to the appropriate template or frame; you will then get a consistent look for all your images.

Image Sizes

Suggestions for image sizes:

These are suggested sizes for your Shopify store. Typically, your theme will indicate the size image you should upload.

Hero image, sliders, or panoramic images:

Size: 1600 x 600

This is a nice size to fill up the whole browser window width-wise.

Collection images:

Size: 1000x1000pixels or 480x480 pixels

> Pro Tip: The image size depends on how many collections you have on one page and also how big your collection images on your homepage will be.

Your images will resize to the collections you have in one row.

Amazon Requirements for image sizes:

The main image size has to be 1000x1000 pixels with a white background. You can also add lifestyle photos as additional images.

Product images:

1000/1084 x1000/1084 pixels. Or if you have long (horizontal) images, 'width' x 1000 pixels.

> Pro Tip: Why do I mention 1000 pixels? It is an Amazon requirement, so it is worth creating your images only once if you want to add your images to Amazon.

Stock Photos & Your Own Photos

Having your own photos for products, banners, or collection images is always preferable. However, there may be situations where having your own photos is not feasible, and you have to resort to using stock photos to get your store up and running.

It's important to remember that stock photos tend to have a generic look, and if you use free stock photos, it's likely that someone else has used them as well. One option to consider is purchasing stock photos still available on other stock photo websites but are not as widely used as free stock photos.

If you sell products from other vendors or brands, having amazing photos may not always be possible. Nevertheless, you can still try to personalize your store as much as possible by incorporating your own images. By doing so, you can create a unique and distinctive visual identity for your store that sets you apart from other online retailers.

> Pro Tip: Don't copy images online because the photos/images could be copyrighted. If you snag a copyrighted image, you can be sued for damages.

FACT: *It happened to one of my customers who has a personalized puzzle store - she displayed a photographer's work as one of her photo puzzles. It cost her $5000 just for infringing on one photo.*

Free Stock Images

If you want free stock photos, here are excellent websites offering free stock photos. Make sure you can use the images for commercial use.

Websites to check for free images:

- Unsplash
- Startup Stock Photos
- New Old Stock
- Wikimedia Commons
- Super Famous
- Little Visuals
- Death to the Stock Photo
- Pexels
- Pixabay
- Compressor.io
- Shopify Burst

CREATE YOUR OWN CUSTOM PRODUCT PHOTOS

You don't need a high-end camera, just a mobile phone, to create your product photo. It is easy to take amazing photos with most mobile phones these days. Many mobile phone apps can edit and manipulate photos. Test these out and see which ones you like to use. But remember, you have to get to your desktop computer to upload your images.

> Pro Tip: Ensure the RAW feature (you can think of a RAW file as the raw "ingredients" of a photo that will need to be processed in order to bring out the picture's full potential) is enabled on your mobile device. The biggest advantage of RAW is its ability to recover highlights and shadows in post-processing without adding grainy noise. Underexposed or overexposed areas can be easily corrected in RAWs.

The following are tips for photographing and creating products photos and images:

1. Center a product photo: The product should be in the center of your photo because it is the most important part of the image. The product should be large enough in the photo to dominate the space.

2. Use natural lighting: Take your photo in the sunlight hours but not in direct sunlight. Find a great window with good light (sunshine) from the outside - lovely bright sunshine. Morning light is the best to take photos of your products. If you are using a photo box, make sure the lights are strong enough so you don't get blue-toned photos.

3. Create lifestyle product photos: Lifestyle photos show how your product can be used or in an environment that is relevant to the product. These photos can be used on your product pages or as the main featured images on your homepage.

> Pro Tip: Create photos with the product in various positions but with enough space around the product. Adding background details to a lifestyle image is very difficult if you want to use it in other areas of your store.

The image can be manipulated with your image tool editor in your Shopify product dashboard, to use in various areas in your store. For example, the image can be cropped to make the product larger. Or the image can be used as a header or hero image on your home page.

For instance, in the following example, there is no option to create a square product image because of a wood background. It is not easy to recreate the background unless you are an expert in photography.

[2.11.19]

Here you can see what happens to the product if we try to create a square image.

[2.11.20]

In the following photo, the product is centered, and now we can create several different-size images.

[2.11.21]

4. Create consistent-sized images: All your product images should be consistent in your store. What I mean by that is either tall images or square images I would suggest square photos unless you are doing fashion photos, but it is your choice. Nothing is worse than going to the website store where the images are different sizes. It really looks like you don't care. I have added an image size section in this chapter for you.

5. Lighten the images if they are even a little bit dark, but generally, if you take your photos in the correct light, they will be perfect.

> Pro Tip: Add your photos to Canva.com, and you can adjust your photo's lighting and shadows, take out the background, etc. If you cannot do the editing yourself, I suggest trying out Pixelz.com. They will enhance your photo overnight.

6. Keep the look of your store consistent. If you are showing images on a white or colored background, make sure all your first images are the same. If you want lifestyle images to be your first look on your product pages, keep that style of an image on the first image shown. Again, keep the images the same size. It looks sloppy if you don't, and it seems you don't care.

[2.11.23]

7. Less background distraction: Do not add too much background detail. You want your product to pop out of the image in the center of the background. For instance, if you create a lifestyle photo with props or nature, try only to have one or two small props in the background. Your product has to be front and center.

8. Create one image with a plain or white background without any distractions in the background for your product page. This product image shows off your product without any distractions.

> Pro Tip: In Canva, you can add different colored backgrounds or shadows to your product. I created the 3D look of my books in SmartMockups (some of the mockups are available in Canva), removed the background, and added shadows to both my profile and the books.

[2.11.22]

9. Images must be low resolution (for a website) - at least 70 PPI resolution. **The reason?** Your website will load quicker, especially when viewed on a mobile phone. 76% or more buyers shop on mobile phones all the time.

> Pro Tip: Canva.com does a great job of creating low-resolution or compressed images for your website.

[2.11.24]

> 💡 Pro Tip: Do not use images of small size or with a low resolution and create larger images. The image will be pixelated (very grainy) and blurred, meaning it will not be clear when you view it on your computer. If your images are grainy, they don't make a good impression!

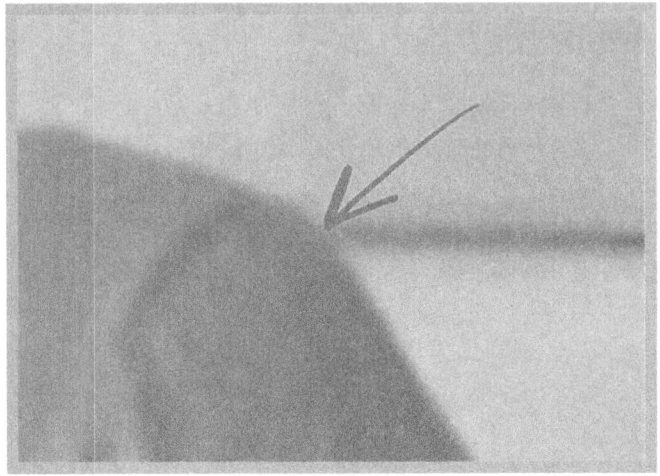

[2.11.25]

VIDEOS

Add some videos to really make a good impression with your customers. It's a simple matter of logic to predict that video marketing and live streaming will be increasingly popular shopping methods in 2023.

Today, almost everyone has a social media account. With the ascent of TikTok, Instagram, Snapchat, and YouTube, people are becoming more accustomed to short videos of their favorite products or services.

Video marketing and streaming are shaping and evolving eCommerce globally. They will continue to create a smooth customer shopping experience across multiple platforms and provide a more personal touch with each purchase.

Over 50% of consumers will watch a product video before they buy. Brands on Amazon have increased sales by 3.6x with a product video.

With Livestream selling, brands are experiencing conversion rates of up to 30% and lower product return rates.

Your eCommerce business will significantly benefit from including videos to engage your customers and increase customer engagement.

You can immediately get a visual, personal connection with your audience when including videos in your store and using them for social posts to attract more visitors.

Two big things I have been harping on for years for eCommerce entrepreneurs is - **Start blogging consistently** and **create Live videos**. Both are not the easiest to think about when running a business.

Livestreaming" is one of the buzziest terms of the moment in retail, but the live shopping concept has actually been around for decades, popularized in the 1980's by TV shopping networks like QVC and HSN. But the media has changed — instead of television sets, landlines, and remote controls, live shopping is now happening on computers, tablets, and smartphones.

Coresight Research estimates that the livestreaming market in the U.S. will reach $11 billion this year and continue to grow steadily, accounting for $35 billion in sales and 3.3% of all U.S. eCommerce by 2024. Of course, that's just a drop in the bucket compared to the livestreaming market in China, which Coresight predicts will reach $300 billion in sales this year.

Self-hosting allows brands to offer replays after the live event has aired. This is an important capability; research shows that 70% of sales from livestreaming happen after the event, on replay. Where brands seem to be having the most success today is hosting their livestreams on their owned site and simulcasting onto social platforms. As soon as Kelli from ParisiansPure.com started doing Livestreaming, her sales increased.

Here are a few quick facts:

245 million people in the U.S. watch online videos every day.

Merely mentioning the word 'video' in an email subject line, the click-through rate **increased by 13%**.

62% of users report increased **interest in a product after viewing** a related Facebook video.

Your engagement will increase by 12% **on Facebook.**

Nearly 65% of all video is viewed on a **mobile device**.

Internet video traffic will account for **95% of all consumer Internet traffic.**

Videos **up to 2 minutes long** get the most engagement.

Types of Product Videos

- The 'how-to' video
- The 'product in use' video
- The 'close up' video
- The 'installation' video
- The 'unboxing' video
- The 'story' video
- The 'thank you' video

Some Tips for Creating Videos:

1. CAMERA or MOBILE PHONE

Whether you use a proper camera, or a mobile phone, invest in QUALITY equipment either way! A few hundred dollars extra can mean the difference between an amateur-looking video and something that looks professional, crisp, and clean. When in doubt, invest in an excellent camera. If you have the resources, I recommend paying a bit more to get a decent phone or camera and a tripod to keep your videos stable. Record your videos on your phone as a vertical video, or better, make the video horizontal. If you record your videos on any other equipment, create the size and format suited to your audience and media.

2. Invest in a good MICROPHONE.

While the visual quality of smartphone cameras is pretty good these days, the audio is not always the best, depending on your type of mobile phone. Your video can be grainy, but the audio has to be top-notch. This is the best investment you can make for creating videos if your phone audio is not good enough.

3. LIGHTING

Lighting is the big difference between poor quality and great quality, especially if you're shooting indoors. Position yourself or your product in an area with plenty of natural or artificial light from the front and sides for optimal lighting. If you're showcasing a product, it's best to have light coming from the top and sides to highlight its features. Additionally, make sure your lens is focused on the product to ensure it's in clear focus.

4. SCRIPT your videos.

You need a script even if you are recording any of the product-related videos I mentioned before. Remember to keep your story short and concise. If you skip this step, you'll find yourself editing more than you need to, releasing a video longer than it should be, and probably losing your audience along the way. Start your script or blog posting with an outline. List your key points and order them logically. Please do not write it all out because you want to sound natural and not scripted. But this will keep your video logical and on task. It's important to strike a balance, as you don't want your videos to come across as overly scripted or commercial. Your personality should still shine through, and the message you're conveying should feel authentic and relatable. Ultimately, the decision to edit your videos should be based on what will best serve your goals and connect with your audience. Once you have a script, create the blog post to add more value to your video. This step creates AMAZING SEO for you as well.

5. POSITIONING

To ensure that your face is captured clearly, position yourself in the center of the frame while recording. The space above your head is valuable real estate that can be used to showcase your face but avoid having too much headroom in the shot. Before recording, conduct a test to check for distractions, such as messy hair or unwanted objects in the background. It's common for people to focus on their own faces, but it's important to look at the camera lens instead. By doing so, you'll look directly at your audience and make a more meaningful connection. Avoid positioning your phone or camera below your face, as this can show too much of your nostrils. Instead, aim to keep the camera at eye level or slightly above it for a more flattering and engaging perspective. When shooting a product, ensure your product is centered and not cut off. It is easier to have more space on the sides. You can create other sizes and formats for your videos.

6. LOCATION, LOCATION, LOCATION!

The background can either enhance or detract from the focus of your video, whether it's showcasing a product or presenting yourself as a speaker. If the background is cluttered, messy, or unappealing, it can distract from the main subject of your video and make it difficult for viewers to focus on your message. The location of your video can also influence your footage's acoustics and sound quality. A noisy or echo-filled location can make it difficult for viewers to hear and understand your message; a quiet and controlled environment can make your audio sound clear and professional. Avoid blending in with your surroundings, and ensure you or your product are the shot's focus. Following these tips ensures that your videos are visually appealing and engaging.

7. Do you need to EDIT your videos?

Editing can help you tailor your video to your target audience and convey your message effectively. Whether you need to edit your videos depends on the video's purpose and the platform on which it will be shared. If you're creating a video for your website or online store, editing can help you achieve a more professional and polished look. Editing allows you to cut out unnecessary footage, adjust the pacing, and add special effects or transitions to enhance the overall quality of the video. It also allows you to correct any mistakes or errors that may have occurred during filming.

> Pro Tip: Add the Reactive Live Shopping App to your Shopify store and start showing off your products. More about the app in our Apps & Sales chapter.

RESOURCES

Wave has royalty-free stock music and some great templates and stock videos.

Check out CANVA.com - great for video creation and music!

I have added a lot of tools for your store on my resources page on my website - www.veronicajeans.com.

https://veronicajeans.online/resources

You will find some:

- Equipment recommendations
- Video camera recommendation
- Video lighting equipment list
- Video creation resources
- Video creation tools & resources
- Amazon links

CHAPTER 2
SHOPIFY BRAND SETTING

 "Design is the silent ambassador of your brand." -Paul Rand.

**WHERE TO FIND THIS IN SHOPIFY? SETTINGS > BRAND

NOW THAT YOU have the brand identity and tools for branding your Shopify store, we will add them to your dashboard's 'Brand' setting.

WHAT TO EXPECT IN THIS CHAPTER:

- *Brand Setting Implementation*
- *Logo*
- *Brand Colors*
- *Cover Image*
- *Slogan*
- *Short Description*
- *Social Links*

BRAND SETTING IMPLEMENTATION

Shopify has automatically enabled your branding identity and tools to be added to themes, apps, and sales channels. All the information you add to the

'**Brand**' settings will be automatically synced. However, you can override the default brand settings in any application.

The following brand elements will be added automatically:

Some Apps and Social Media channels - Compatible with these channels

- Online Store
- Google
- Email
- Shop

NOTE: Not all themes are integrated with the 'Brand' setting. You can manually pull the assets into your theme if your Shopify theme does not synch with the 'Brand' setting. This is especially for paid Shopify themes.

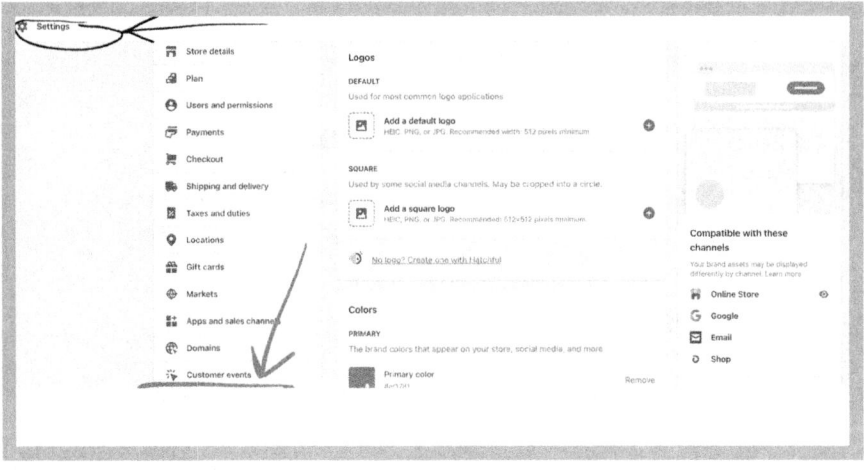

[2.10.1]

Step 1. Add your logo.

Add your logo in the appropriate sections.

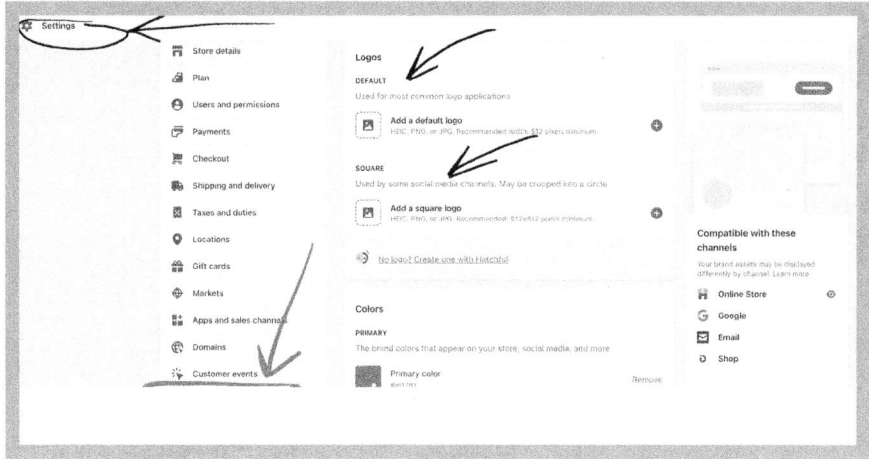

[2.10.1a]

Preview your logo: Square, Circle, Favicon. Then, click on the dropdown to view your logo. You can still manually override these images when adding them to your theme.

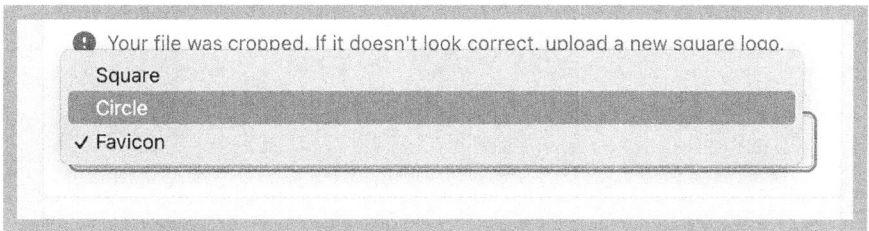

[2.10.9]

Step 2. Add your brand colors.

There are Primary colors and Secondary colors. The Primary colors are for your store, social media, and more. The Secondary colors are for accents and additional details.

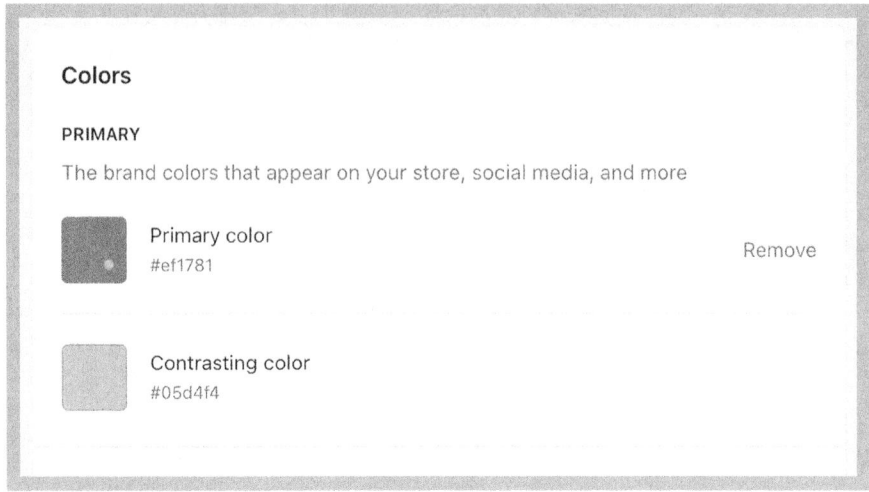

[2.10.4]

Step 3. Add your cover image.

Add an image that reflects your store and products. Your cover image is 1920 × 1080 pixels, which shows up in profile pages and apps.

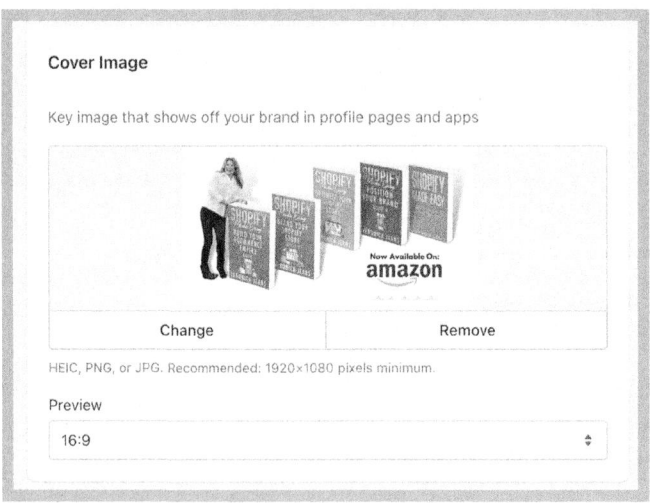

[2.10.5]

Step 4. Add your slogan.

This is your vision statement that you have already established in Chapter 1. This has to be short and snappy.

This is a brand statement in Shopify that can only be 80 characters.

[2.10.6]

Step 5. Add your short description.

Your mission statement is your short description in this section. Now we can add the information about the company and the products. What makes you unique from other brands - what benefit will your product be to your customers?

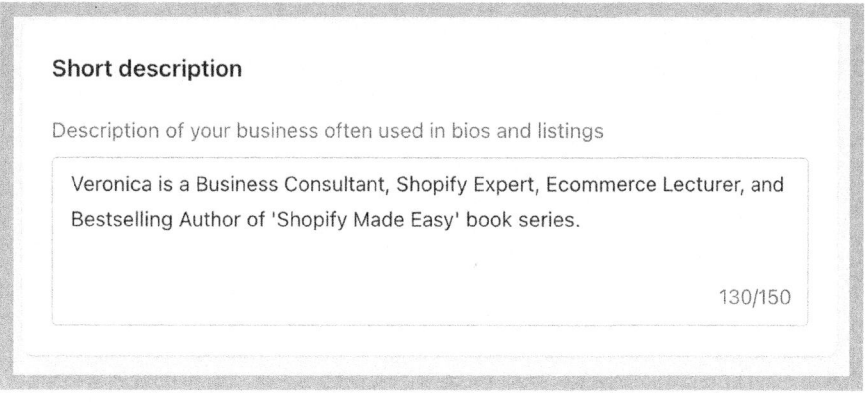

[2.10.7]

Step 6. Add your social links.

These links will be added to the social icons at the footer of your store and on your product pages.

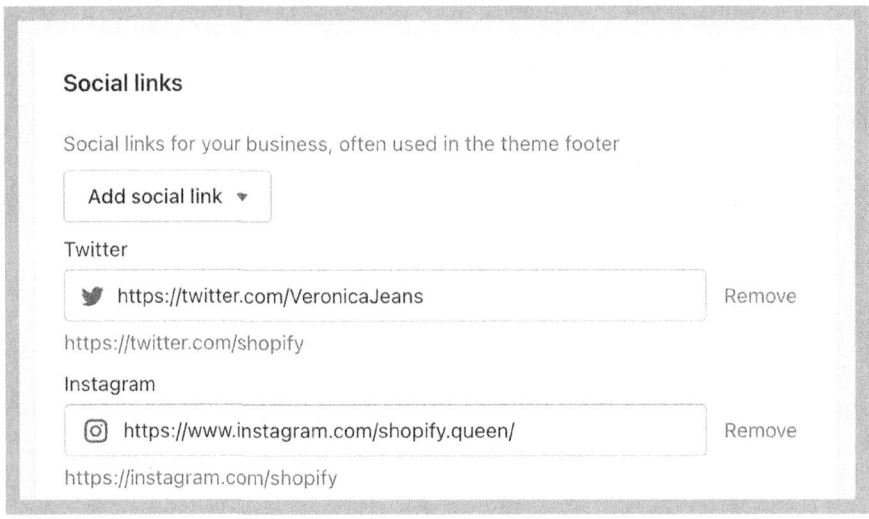

[2.10.8]

RESOURCES

Check out CANVA.com - great for creating logos.

ChatGBT – great for creating descriptions and slogans.

CHAPTER 3
STRUCTURE YOUR PAGES

 "In less than 50 milliseconds, visitors decide whether they'll stay or leave your website." Javier Bargas-Avila, Senior User Experience Researcher at YouTube UX Research

**WHERE TO FIND THIS IN SHOPIFY? ONLINE STORE > PAGES

STRUCTURING website pages correctly is often overlooked and essential to your page layout.

We form first impressions of the people and things we encounter in our daily lives in an extraordinarily short timeframe. We know the first impression a website's design creates is crucial in capturing visitors' interest. In less than 50 milliseconds, users build an initial "gut feeling" that helps them decide whether they'll stay or leave. This first impression depends on many factors: structure, colors, spacing, symmetry, amount of text, fonts, and more.

In other words, users strongly prefer website designs that look both simple and familiar. That means if you're designing your store look, you'll want to consider both factors.

WHAT TO EXPECT IN THIS CHAPTER:

- *The Importance of Structure*
- *Structuring Your Pages in Shopify*
- *Formatting Your Pages*

THE IMPORTANCE OF STRUCTURE

The structure of each page is very similar, but there are exceptions, for instance, the 'About' page or the 'FAQ' page.

Structure is often overlooked and essential to your page layout. There are a lot of boring pages online that have no images and are not formatted for easy consumption for a website visitor. Visitors will not linger and identify with your brand if something is hard to read and digest.

Did you know, according to one academic study, 94% of the time, someone's first impression is based on brand, and it only takes 50 milliseconds for that split-second decision to get made?

You worked hard to get somebody to your page, so let them have the **best experience** ingesting your information.

Here are some tips on how to format and structure content on your page:

1. Do not have a wall of content without any breaks or sections. Keep your paragraphs short. 2 - 4 **short** sentences are sufficient. Most people read the information on their smartphones. Short paragraphs are easier to read on your phone than long ones.

2. Make your sentences short and readable. Readers want information in a straightforward way. Remember, people are reading content not on their PCs but on their mobiles. Sentences should not be a whole paragraph.

3. Do not use complicated language, but make sure a 10-year-old can read it. Make your language easy to read. No technical jargon unless it is for a White Paper (this is a research-based report focused on complex issues), which is the opposite of what your normal reader wants.

4. Insert headings and subheadings to make your content skimmable. Create different sections within the text and divide them into paragraphs, each relating to a specific idea or subject. Allow your visitor to switch to the next paragraph if they find the current topic irrelevant.

5. Make your fonts readable. I recommend using a font that is not a script, typewritten, or condensed style for your main content. Writing for the internet is opposite to what you have learned about writing. Test your font on your phone to see how it would appear. Simple is best.

6. Avoid using too much CAPS (capital letters) in your main content. CAPS are meant to stop the flow of reading. Rather highlight the important work with bold text.

7. Avoid using more than 2 types of styles for your font. This is important for your complete online store branding. Too many styles look messy.

8. Be consistent with your font style, sizing, and spacing.

Check for grammar mistakes and use appropriate software. There are a few that are good. Errors will still creep in but ask somebody to check for you.

> Pro Tip: Remember, you are writing for the internet, and short, fluffer-free content is what visitors want. Your visitors want coherent, relevant, clear, easy-to-follow content.

STRUCTURING YOUR PAGES IN SHOPIFY

The first part of structuring your page is to know how to use the information and content. The main structure of the pages in the store only has to be set up once for the whole store.

Once you create a page, the page you create will fit under the main top area of the store, which has the logo, menu, shopping cart icon, search icon, and maybe some social icons. The bottom of your page is called the footer.

The page is added automatically to this position once the page is created. All your information and content with text, products, images, etc., will appear in the middle of the page.

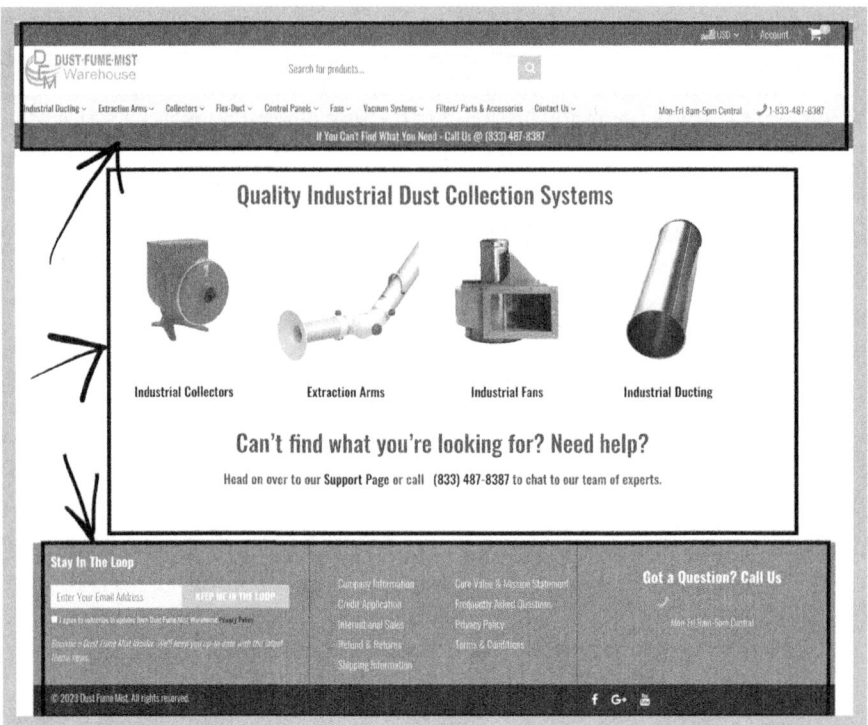

[2.8.14]

Here are some general items to add to a page before we format the page.

Step 1. Add a Tagline

Your tagline should be right at the top of the page, preferably on a banner image, to give it more impact. Visitors who pop into your store need to know immediately what you do or sell for each page. For this reason, make each tagline for each page different.

Why do we need a Tagline or USP?

A clear, compelling message can turn an unaware visitor into an excited prospect.

This message will be reflected throughout your store, social media, and print. This can identify you and make you different from your competition.

This is what you need to think about when creating your USP (Unique Selling Proposition). A unique selling proposition (USP) statement is what differentiates you and your company from other vendors. Its primary value is to create competitive differentiation.

For online retailers, a unique factor could be excellent customer service (i.e., Zappos), free or timely shipping and handling (i.e., Amazon Prime)

Of course, there are many more.

Handmade in America, organic, durable, etc.

When creating your USP, try to answer these questions:

- What is your client's most significant pain or frustration?
- What is your solution to their problem?

Here are some formulas for adding a tagline or USP to each of the ecommerce pages, using the given characteristics above (handmade in America, organic, durable) as examples:

Collection page:

Formula: [Product category] that's [unique characteristic] for [target audience]

Example: Handmade in America jewelry that's durable and stylish for modern women

About page:

Formula: We [what you do] because we believe in [what sets you apart]

Example: We create organic skincare because we believe in the power of nature for healthy, glowing skin.

Community page:

Formula: Join our [community type] for [benefit or solution to pain point]

Example: Join our sustainable living community for tips on living a green lifestyle without sacrificing quality.

Team page:

Formula: Meet our [team name] - [what they do] to [solve client's pain point]

Example: Meet our customer service team - we're here to help you find the perfect, durable products for your home.

Sustainability page:

Formula: We're [brand name], committed to [sustainability goal] to [benefit for customers and planet]

Example: We're GreenLiving, committed to using only organic, sustainable materials to create long-lasting, eco-friendly products.

Remember to keep your tagline or USP focused on your customers and their needs. Use the given characteristics as a way to differentiate yourself from competitors and provide a solution to their pain points.

Outline only one possible solution for one problem. Don't try to explain everything to everybody!

Step 2. Highlight the main products, services, or points of interest

As with the tagline, each page will have a different focus. Do not confuse your visitors with too many different topics on one page.

Here are some rules to follow:

- Insert headings and subheadings, and assign a hierarchy to the content.
- Harness the power of bulleted lists.
- Give your text blocks a breather—play with line and letter spacing.
- Break up text uniformity.
- A long wall of text without interruptions or sections is the main obstacle in reading content.

The first rule of thumb is to **create different sections within the text and divide them into paragraphs** (even sub-paragraphs, if necessary), each relating to a specific idea/subject.

This way, you'll get three results:

- Lighten the visual impact of your page or email text.
- Allow visitors to switch to the next paragraph if they already know or find the current topic irrelevant.
- Speed up the overall reading of the text, making it easier to scan the page.

Step 3. Visual branding

We are in the social visual age….it is all about images and videos! Your eCommerce store's visual branding must reflect your products and your customer.

So wherever possible, add your media to any page. But it has to be relevant to the topic, which might not need images like a 'FAQ' or 'Refund' page.

Step 4. Add testimonials

Include customer testimonials on as many pages as possible.

Use quotes and images to highlight positive feedback from your customers.

Step 5. What's Next?

Add a 'Call to Action'. Use a clear and persuasive call to action: Encourage your visitors to make a purchase, sign up for your newsletter, or follow you on social media with a clear and persuasive call to action.

FORMATTING YOUR PAGES

Formatting content is a crucial aspect of website design that can greatly affect the readability and accessibility of your website's content. Proper formatting helps to organize and present information in a clear and logical manner, making it easier for users to find and understand the information they are looking for.

What does formatting your page mean?

Page formatting refers to arrangement and visual organization of its elements of a page on your website. This addresses aspects like font selection, font size and presentation (like bold or italics), spacing, margins, alignment, columns, indentation, and lists.

Here are some easy ways to format your web page:

- Use H2 or H3 for the headings in your text where necessary: Headings are important for structuring your content and guiding readers through your website. Use H2 or H3 tags to indicate major sections or subheadings within your content.
- Use H3 or smaller for subheadings: Subheadings are useful for breaking up longer sections of text and providing a visual hierarchy of

information. Use H3 or smaller headings for subheadings within your content.
- Use either numbered lists or bulleted lists, but not too many: Lists are a great way to present information in a concise and organized manner. However, using too many lists can make your content look cluttered and hard to read. Use either numbered lists or bulleted lists sparingly and only when necessary.
- Highlight or bold important text in a paragraph, but not too much: Emphasizing key points in your content can help draw readers' attention and make your message clearer. However, using too much bold or highlighted text can be distracting and make your content harder to read. Use only where it is necessary.
- Add alt text to all your links and images: Alt text is a brief description of an image or link that is displayed when the image cannot be downloaded, or the link cannot be accessed. Alt text is important for accessibility and can help users with visual impairments or slow internet connections understand the content of your website. It also adds SEO which is search engine optimization.

> Pro Tip: Before you add your images to your store (while they are on your computer), rename your images and add a description to the image including a keyword that is relevant to the image and content of the page.

HOW TO USE THE RICH TEXT EDITOR IN SHOPIFY

The tool to help you structure and format your pages is the 'Rich Text' editor in Shopify. Unless you are familiar with the editor, I have included a full explanation of how to use it. First, let's show you how to use the editor in your store before we start on the page's structure.

The Rich Text Editor is available in all your Pages, Product, Collection, and Blog dashboards to help you add information to your online store. The editor is pretty easy to use. I have added this guide to help you identify all the icons in the editor.

Here is a quick reference for each section:

1. Formatting Options
2. Bold Text
3. Italicize text
4. Underline text
5. Create a bulleted list
6. Create a numbered list
7. Indent text
8. Unindent text
9. Align text
10. Change text and background colors
11. Insert links with the rich text editor
12. Link to a file in the page content
13. Insert tables with the rich text editor
14. Upload & edit images
15. Insert videos with the rich text editor
16. Insert audio files with the rich text editor
17. Clear formatting in the rich text editor
18. Add HTML content

In Shopify, there are 2 different Rich Text Editor types:

The following image is for 'Pages' and 'Blogs'.

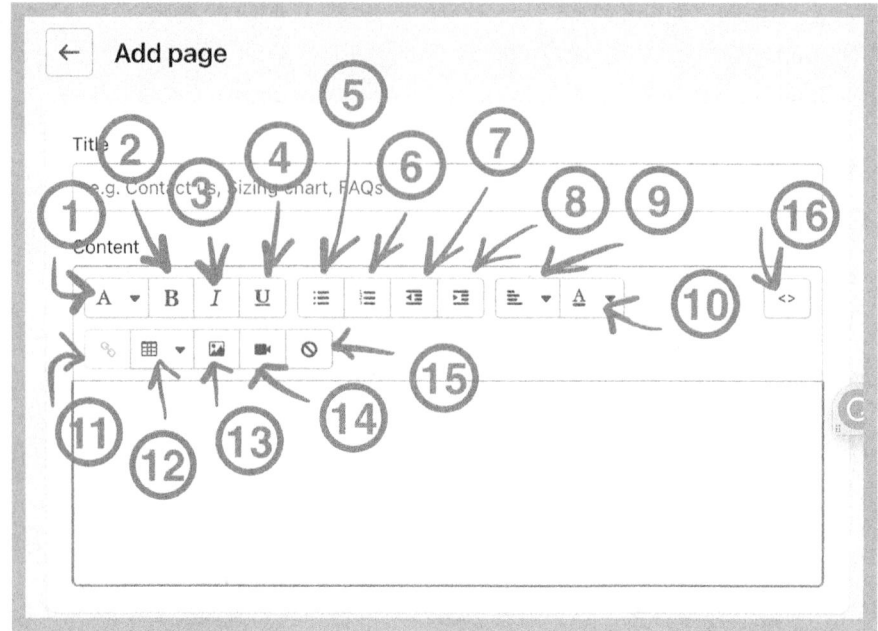

[2.9.1a]

In the next image, this type of editor is in 'Product' and 'Collection' pages.

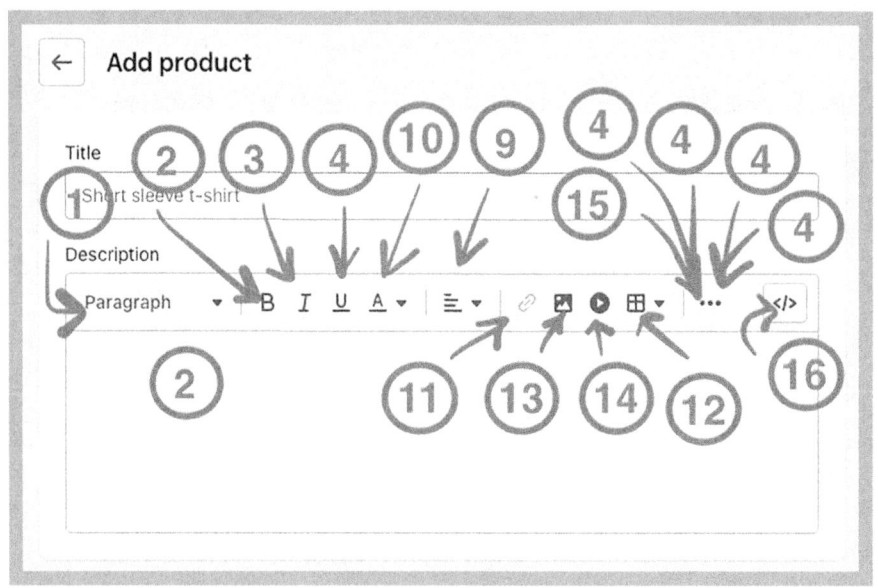

[2.9.1b]

STRUCTURE YOUR PAGES

The following will show you how to use each section in the 'Rich text editor' as shown in the image 2.9.1a for 'Pages' and 'Blogs'.

1. Formatting options

Paragraph - Most of the content of your website is paragraph text. Paragraph text usually has a font size of 10–12 pt (points), but some themes use different font sizes. If you want to separate the paragraphs and sub-titles in your description, highlight the paragraph and choose 'paragraph' in the editor section. This will add a space before and after the paragraph.

Heading (1-6) - Headings are used to format content. There are 6 heading levels. Heading 1 is the most important level, and Heading 6 is the least important. Shopify shows you in the editor what the different sizes look like.

Blockquote - A block quote is used to show text that is attributed to someone else, like a quotation or an excerpt from a book or website.

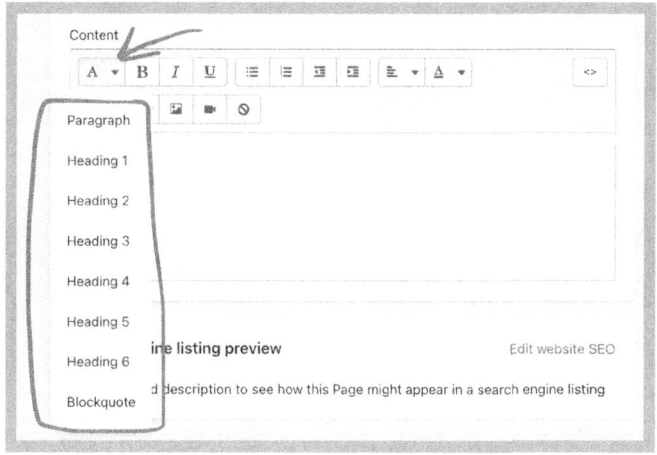

[2.9.2]

2. Bold text

To make the text bold, highlight the text and click the 'Bold' button.

3. Italicize text

To make the text italic, highlight the text and click the 'Italic' button.

4. Underline text

To make the text underlined, highlight the text and click the 'Underline' button.

4. Bulleted list

To create a bulleted list, click the 'Bulleted list' button. You can type to create bulleted list items. To create new list items, press the enter or return key. To finish the list, press the enter or return key twice.

5. Numbered list

To create a numbered list, click the 'Numbered list' button. You can type to create numbered list items. To create new list items, press the enter or return key. To finish the list, press the enter or return key twice.

6. Indent text

To indent a paragraph, click the 'Indent' button. Indenting a paragraph increases the margin on the left side.

7. Unindent text

To unindent or outdent a paragraph, click the 'Outdent' button. 'Unindenting' a paragraph removes any indented margins that it has.

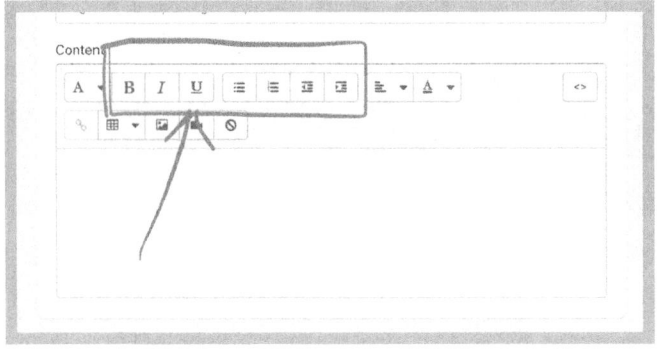

[2.9.3]

8. Align text

To align text, select the text, click the 'Alignment' button, and choose 'Left align', 'Center align', or 'Right align'.

STRUCTURE YOUR PAGES

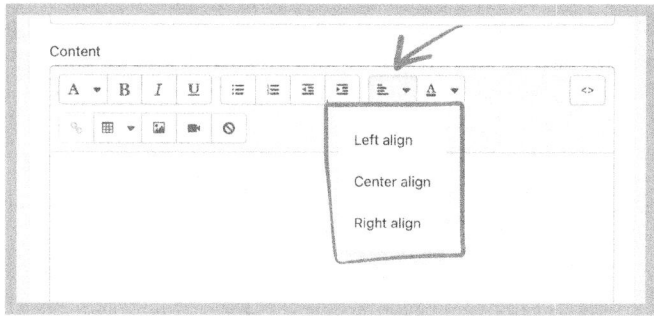

[2.9.4]

9. Color of Text & Background

Change text colors - Highlight the text and click the 'Color' button. Click a color to change the highlighted text to that color.

Change text background colors - Highlight the text and click the 'Color' button. Click 'Background' color. Click a color to change the highlighted text's background to that color.

[2.9.5]

10. Insert links with the Rich Text Editor

You can insert links (hyperlinks) in blog posts, pages, product descriptions, and collection descriptions with the rich text editor. You can add links that direct customers to pages within your Shopify online store and to other websites. You can also add links that open email messages or make phone calls, to help customers contact you.

Step 1. Highlight the text or image that you want to turn into a link.

Step 2. Click 'Insert link'.

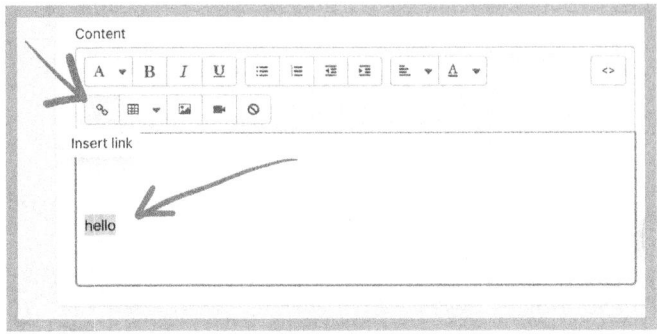

[2.9.6]

Step 3. Enter the destination URL for the link in the 'Link to' field. To link to an external website, not on your Shopify store, enter 'https://' followed by the web address, for example, 'https://www.example.com'.

Step 4. To link to a page within your Shopify online store, enter the short URL, for example, '/collections/summer-collection'.

Step 5. To create a link that opens an email message, enter 'mailto'. followed by the email address, for example, 'mailto.example@example.com'.

Step 6. Enter a **short description** of the link in the 'Link title' box.

Step 7. Choose how the link will open with the 'Open this' link in the menu. 'The same window': The link will open in a user's existing browser tab or window. 'A new window': The link will open in a new browser tab or window.

Step 8. Click the 'Insert' link to convert your highlighted text into a link.

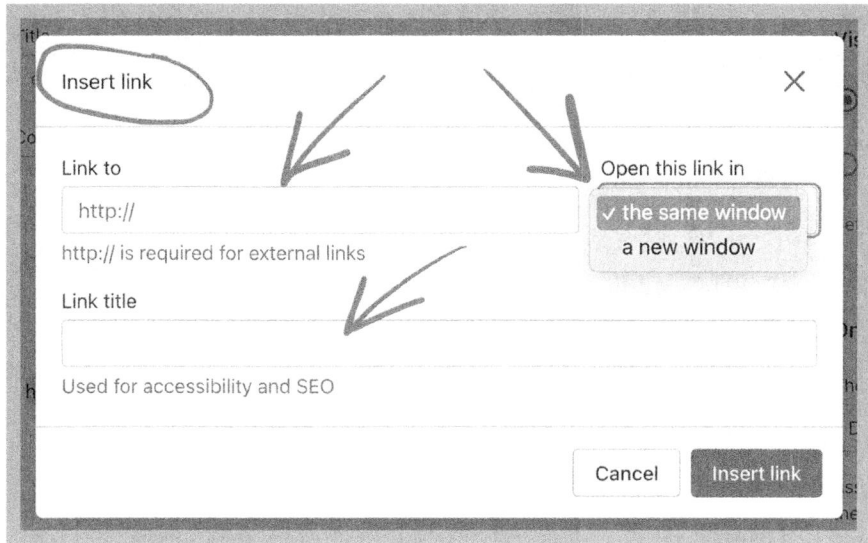

[2.9.7]

11. Link to a file in the page content

After you upload a file, you can link it to content in the rich text editor to make it available for download from a product or collection description, webpage, or blog post.

From your Shopify admin, go to Settings > Files.

Step 1. Copy the URL for the file that you want to link.

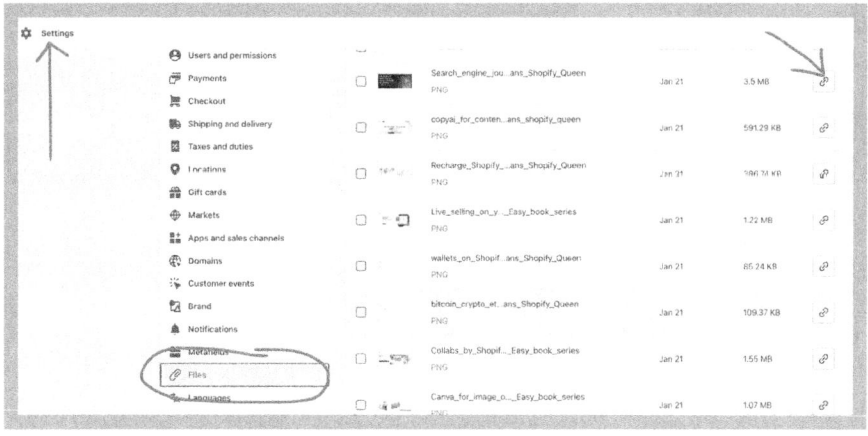

[2.9.8]

Step 2. In your Shopify admin, click the product, collection, webpage, or blog post where you want to add the file.

Step 3. In the rich text editor, enter or choose link text. For example, you might add a link to a PDF size chart from the link text; click here to download our sizing chart.

Step 4. Select the link text.

Step 5. Click 'Insert link'.

Step 6. In the 'Link to the field', paste the URL for the file you want to link.

12. Insert tables with the Rich Text Editor

With the rich text editor, you can insert tables in your blog posts, pages, product descriptions, and collection descriptions. You can place text, images, or even videos into a table after you create it.

Step 1. In the rich text editor, click the Insert table button.

Step 2. Click 'Insert table' to insert a table. This creates a table with one row and one column.

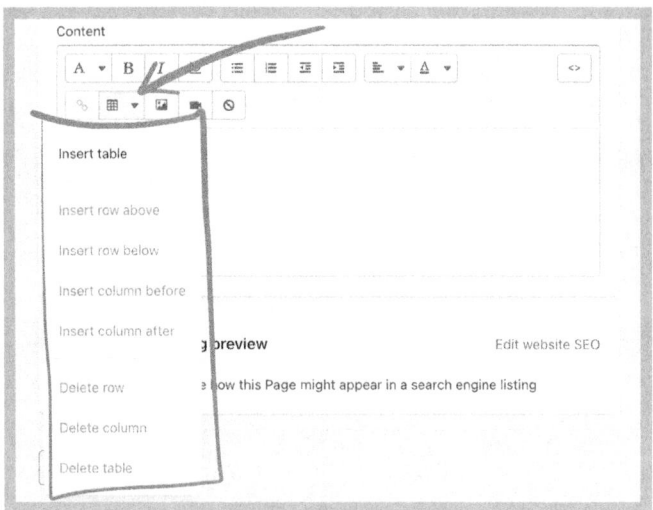

[2.9.9]

Step 3. When you have created a table, click the 'Insert table' button again to modify the table's rows and columns.

STRUCTURE YOUR PAGES

Step 4. Insert row above. Place your cursor in a row and click this button to insert a new row above.

Step 5. Insert row below. Place your cursor in a row and click this button to insert a new row below.

Step 6. Insert column before. Place your cursor in a column and click this button to insert a new column before that column.

Step 7. Insert column after. Place your cursor in a column and click this button to insert a new column after that column.

Step 8. Delete row. Place your cursor in a row you want to delete, and then click this button.

Step 9. Delete column. Place your cursor in a column you want to delete, and then click this button.

Step 10. Delete table. Place your cursor anywhere in the table and then click this button to delete the entire table.

13. Upload & edit images

Step 1. In the rich text editor, click the 'Insert image' button.

Step 2. In the 'Insert Image' dialog, click the 'Uploaded images' tab.

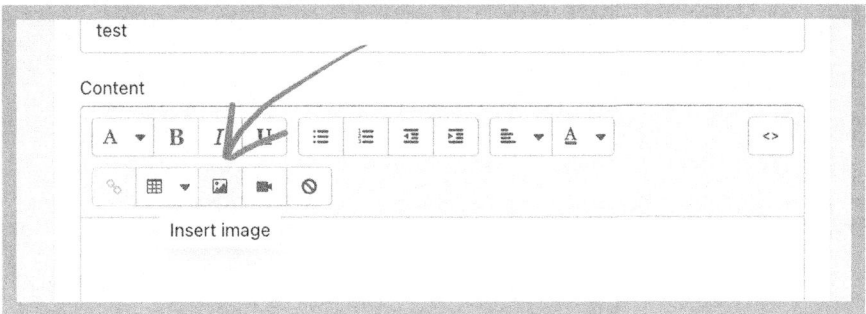

[2.9.10]

There are 3 choices to upload images:

- Uploaded images
- Product images
- URL images

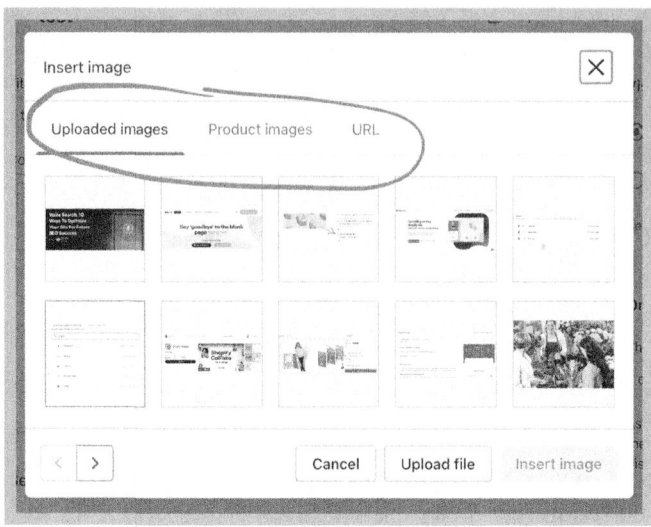

[2.9.11]

Uploaded Images - These are images either in your store already or you can upload an image from your computer.

Step 1. Click Upload file.

Step 2. Choose a JPG or PNG image file from your computer.

Step 3. Once the image is uploaded, click the image you uploaded to select it.

More options will open up - 'Image alt text' and 'Size'

Step 4. Add your image alt text. 'Image alt text' is the description of your image. Alt text makes images more accessible to everyone, including people with visual impairments. It is a great SEO (Search Engine Optimization) tool.

STRUCTURE YOUR PAGES

[2.9.12]

Step 5. From the 'Size' menu, select the image's display size. You can select 'Original' to insert the image without altering its display size, or any of the other sizes, and your image will change dimensions to suit your choice.

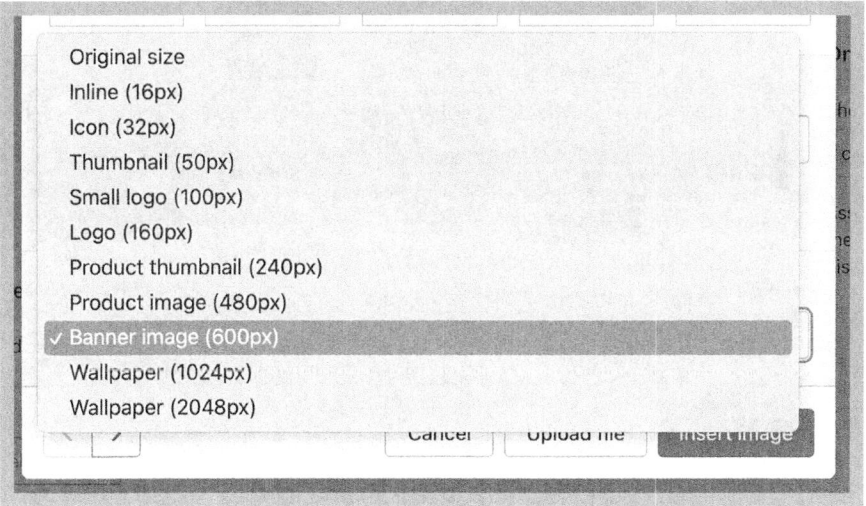

feature image I use 1000px x 1000px

> 💡 Pro Tip: Choosing a size for your image doesn't overwrite the original size of the image. You can insert the same image on different store pages in different sizes.

Product Images – these images are already in your Shopify store. If the image you want is not included in this view, you need to go back to 'Uploaded images' tab to upload your product image.

Step 1. Click 'Insert image' to place the image into the rich text editor.

Step 2. In the 'Insert Image' dialog, click the 'Product images' tab. Choose an uploaded image from product images. Click the image that you want to insert. If you don't see the product image you want to insert, you can use the arrow buttons to look on different pages.

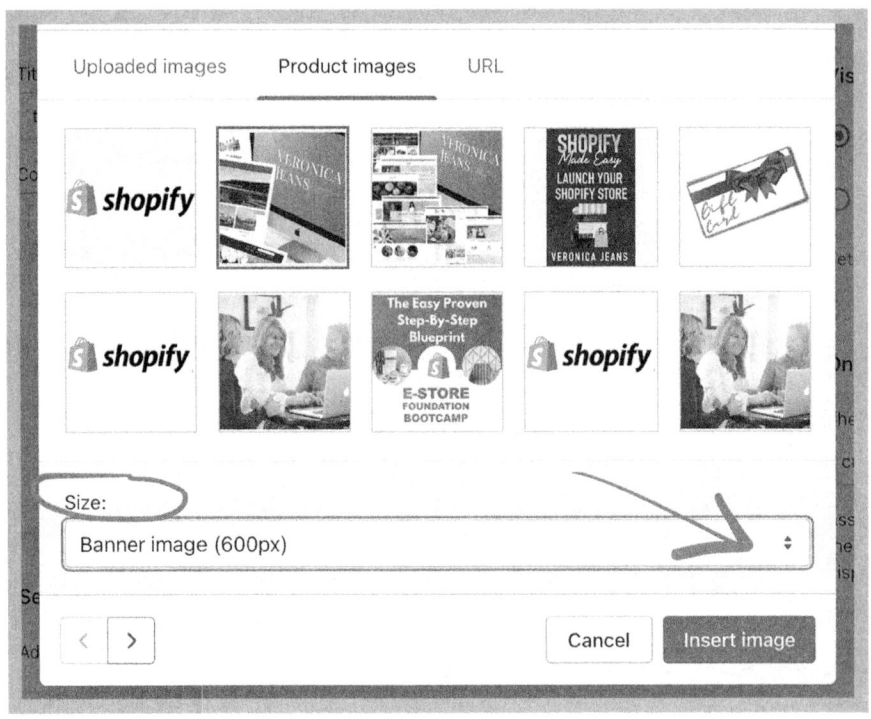

[2.9.14]

Step 3. From the 'Size' menu, select the image's display size. You can select 'Original' to insert the image without altering its display size.

STRUCTURE YOUR PAGES

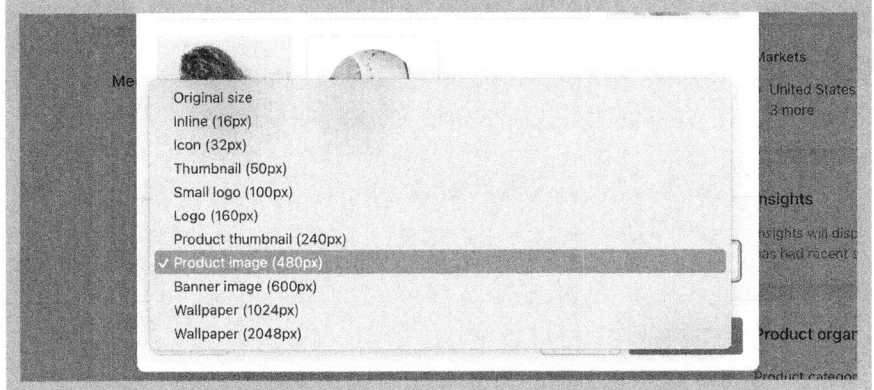

[2.9.14a]

Step 4. Click 'Insert image' to place the product image into the rich text editor.

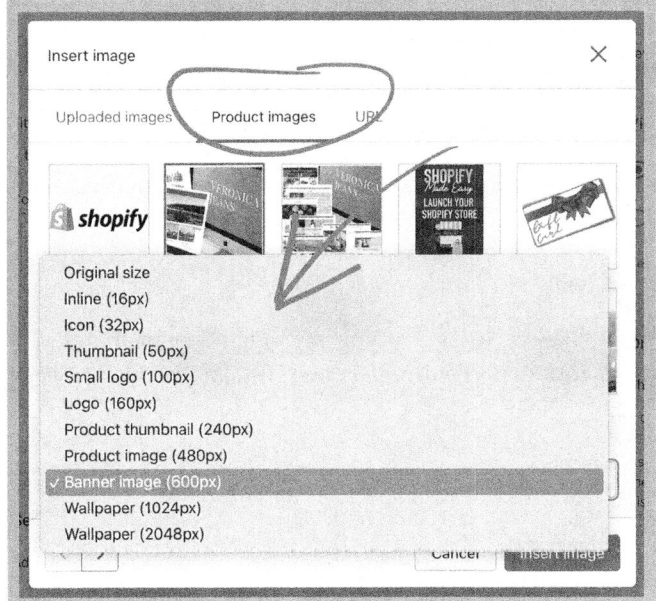

[2.9.15]

> Pro Tip: Choosing a size for your image does not overwrite the original size. You can insert the same image on different store pages in different sizes.

URL images - You can add an image by using a public URL.

Step 1. In the rich text editor, click the 'Insert image' button.

Step 2. In the 'Insert Image' dialog, click the URL tab.

Step 3. Enter the publicly accessible URL of your image file.

[2.9.16]

Step 4. Click 'Insert image' to insert the image in the rich text editor at its original size.

Upload & edit images

You can change the size, text wrapping, and alignment of an image within the rich text editor. You can also edit the image URL or add or edit image alt text.

STRUCTURE YOUR PAGES

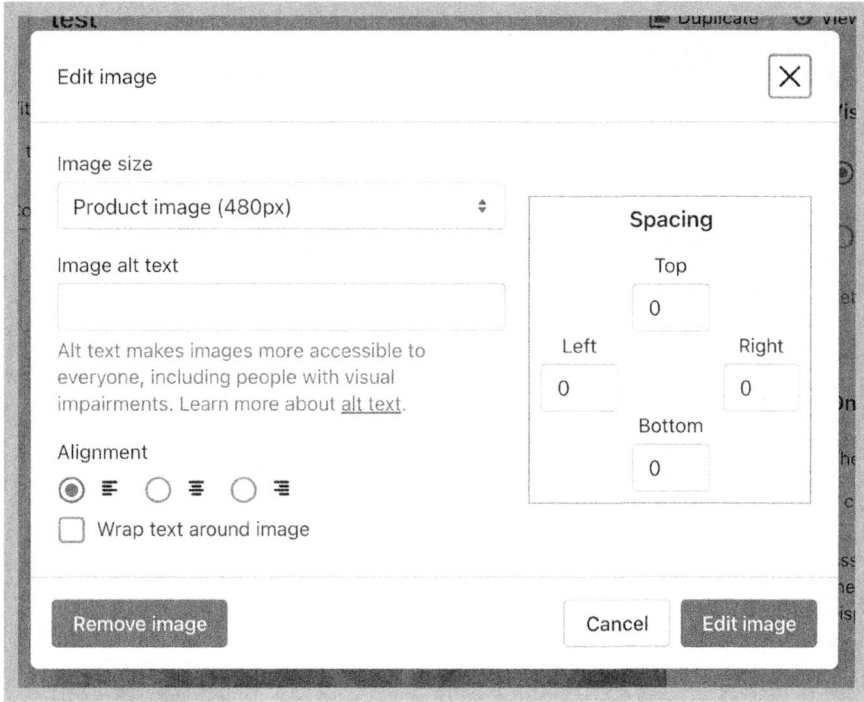

[2.9.17]

Step 1. Double-click the rich text editor image to open the Edit image dialog.

Step 2. Use the size and alignment options to edit the image.

Step 3. To change the size of the image, select a size option.

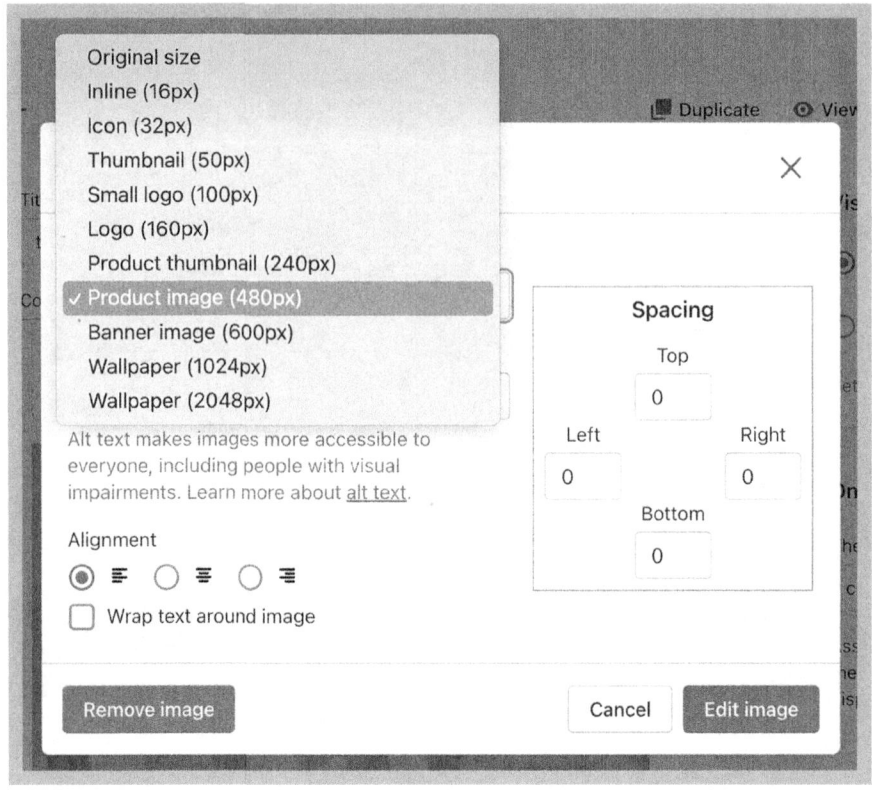

[2.9.18]

Step 4. 'Image alt text' is the description of your image. To improve your online store's SEO and accessibility, add or edit image alt text.

Step 5. To add spacing for the image, enter the number of pixels of space that you want on each side.

STRUCTURE YOUR PAGES

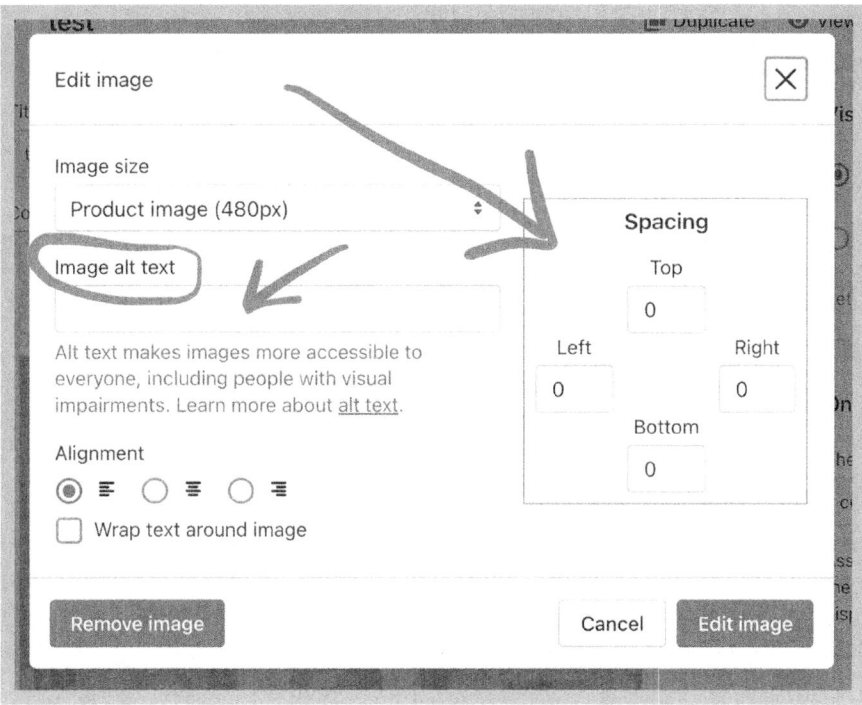

[2.9.19]

Step 6. Align text around the image. You can add text to wrap around the image. Check 'Wrap text around the image'; the text will flow to the right or left depending on how you align your image.

Step 7. Select from the icons representing the left, center, or right alignment to change the image's alignment. The image will either float to whatever you choose. This will determine where you add the spacing - if the image is to the left, your spacing will be on the right and the same for the other side.

> Pro Tip: I normally add about 25px to either left or right, so there is spacing between the image and the text if the text is going to float next to the image.

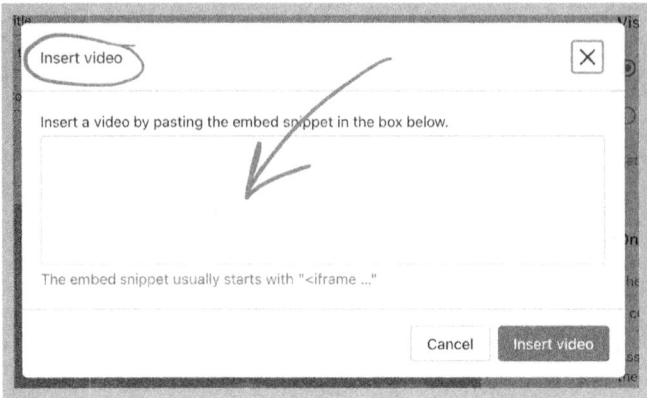

[2.9.20]

14. Insert videos with the rich text editor

You can insert and embed videos in blog posts, pages, product descriptions, and collection descriptions using the rich text editor. You can also add a video to display your products with your 'Media' options in your product dashboard with a direct upload or a URL address.

[2.9.23]

Here are two ways to upload your video:

- Videos hosted on Shopify
- Video hosted off Shopify

Videos hosted on Shopify - The only to use these links is to the 'Media' option on the product page or in 'Customize' for all pages. The file must be under 2MB (megabyte), so there is a restriction to adding videos to your store.

Step 1. Add your video to Shopify in 'Settings' and 'Files'.

Step 2. Copy the link as shown in the following image.

Step 3. Open the rich text editor from the 'Online Store' section for the page or blog post you want to feature the audio file.

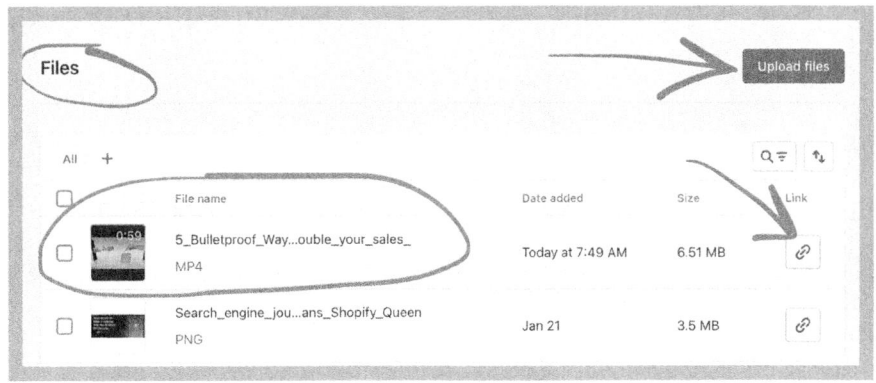

[2.9.22]

Step 4. Add the link to your product page 'Media' option or the 'Customize' dashboard.

Video hosted off Shopify - When you are hosting your video off the Shopify platform, you can use them in all descriptions in all pages. There is no file size restriction.

Step 1. First, upload your video to a streaming site such as YouTube, Vimeo, Wisteria, or Wave.video. There are some other sites, but these are the ones I use. Then grab the URL link or the **embed code** to add it to Shopify.

Step 2. Copy all of the code inside the 'Embed code' box.

Step 3. In your Shopify admin, click the 'Insert video' button in the rich text editor.

Step 4. Paste the embed code into the box in the 'Insert video' dialog.

Step 5. Click 'Insert video'.

Step 6. Click Save when you are finished to save your changes to the item you were editing.

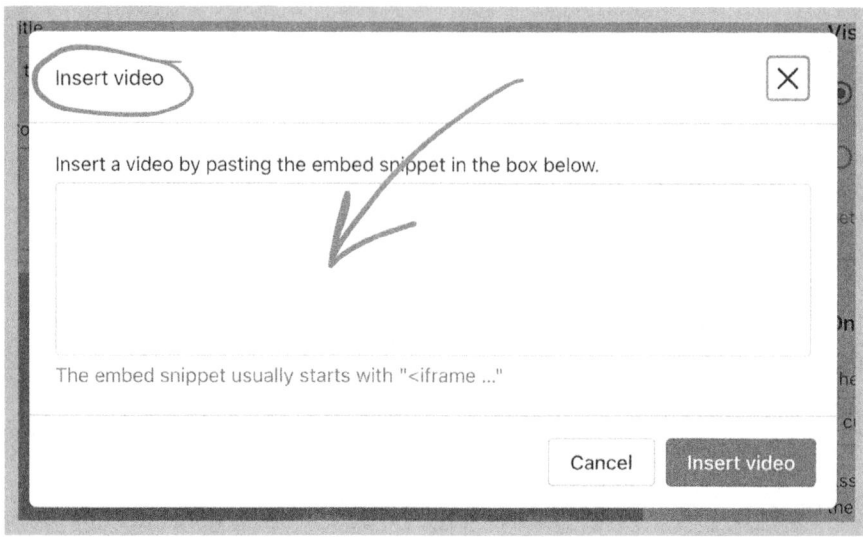

[2.9.21]

> Pro Tip: If the video is from YouTube and you want to show only related videos from the same YouTube channel, then find the video's URL in the embed code. Copy and paste [?rel=0] at the end within the quotation marks.

NOTE: *You can generate embed code directly from YouTube, but the embedded video won't be as responsive to different screen sizes.*

Your Shopify theme will automatically make your embedded videos responsive.

> Pro Tip: If you cannot find the embed code for your video, grab the website address of the video, and visit https://embedresponsively.com. Embed Responsively is a tool that will give you an improved embed code for your video.

NOTE: *You might encounter playback issues on certain iPhone models when vertically viewing videos that were embedded using code from Embed Responsively.*

STRUCTURE YOUR PAGES

On Embed Responsively, click to select the video website where your video is located.

Paste the video's URL that you copied into the 'Page URL' box on Embed Responsively.

Click 'Embed'. Embed Responsively will create the embed code for you.

Insert audio files with the rich text editor

The rich text editor can insert or embed audio files on or off Shopify in blog posts, pages, product descriptions, and collection descriptions.

Audio file on Shopify

Step 1. From your Shopify admin, click 'Settings', then click 'Files'.

Step 2. Copy the link as shown in the following image.

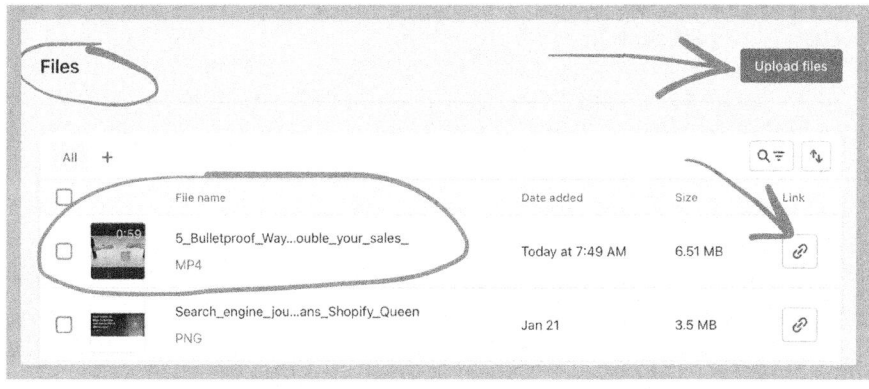

[2.9.22]

Step 3. Open the rich text editor from the 'Online Store' section for the page or blog post you want to feature the audio file.

Step 4. Add the link to your product page 'Media' option or the 'Customize' dashboard.

Audio file off Shopify

Step 1. Click 'Upload files' to upload the audio file you want to insert or embed in your store.

Step 2. Open the rich text editor from the 'Online Store' section for the page or blog post you want to feature the audio file.

Step 3. Copy <div id="player"><audio controls="controls">, then paste the code in the rich text editor to embed an audio player on your page.

Step 4. Copy the following code.

[<source src="https://cdn.shopify.com/s/files/1/0220/2378/files/example.mp3" type="audio/mpeg"/>]

Step 5. Paste this code in your rich text editor after the code for the audio player, and then replace https://cdn.shopify.com/s/files/1/0220/2378/files/example.mp3 with the URL you created for your audio file when you uploaded it to Shopify. You can find your audio file's URL at any time on the Files page.

Step 6. Click View to make sure your audio file plays correctly.

15. Clear formatting in the rich text editor

To remove formatting from text or images, highlight the content and then click the 'Clear formatting' button.

[2.9.26]

Add HTML content

NOTE: *Only attempt to change or add HTML code if you are proficient.*

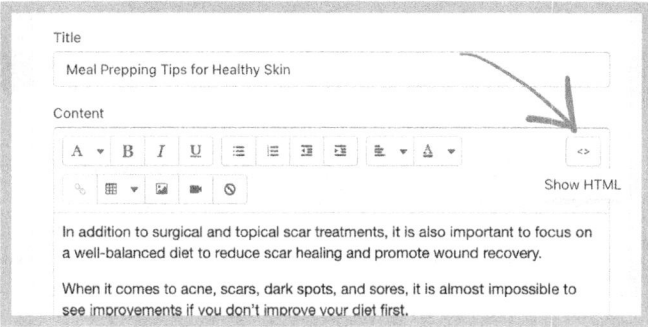

[2.9.25]

You can enter HTML content for your blog posts, pages, product descriptions, and collection descriptions with the rich text editor.

Step 1. Click the 'Show HTML' button to view the HTML code for the content inside the rich text editor.

Step 2. In the HTML view, you can make any changes to the content in the rich text editor. You can add images, videos, or tables using HTML and debug or fine-tune the layout and content style.

[2.9.26]

Pro Tip: Add or remove internal comments in the rich text editor in your HTML code.

You can use comment tags <!-- and --> for the internal text you don't want to publish to your store.

To add an internal comment, enclose the text that you want to keep hidden within <!-- and -->. For example. <!--yourtext-->.

The enclosed HTML tags within the comment tags are saved as internal text. For those HTML tags to work properly, you need to remove the comment tags <!-- and --> around them.

CHAPTER 4
STORE INFORMATION PAGES

 'People buy from people they like and trust.'

**WHERE TO FIND THIS IN SHOPIFY? ONLINE STORE > PAGES

PROVIDING your customers with comprehensive information about your store and products is crucial. This includes details on product usage, shipping, and delivery, as well as information about your store and your business. By doing so, you can establish trust with your customers and demonstrate that you value their experience with your brand.

WHAT TO EXPECT IN THIS CHAPTER:

- *Types of Pages for Your Store*
- *How To Add Pages & Content to Your Store*
- *How to Use Pages & Blog Dashboards*
- *Build Publishing, Editing, or Deleting*
- *Optimize Your Pages in the Shopify Theme*
- *Creating Your Pages*

You need customers, and when they visit your online store, you want them to buy!

Treating every page in your online store as the most important page is crucial. Customers must trust you enough to purchase your products, and the way to build that trust is by providing them with enough information to make informed decisions.

You want to build the 'KNOW - LIKE - TRUST - BUY' factor on all your online store pages. Customers need to **know you**, **like your products**, **trust your store,** and then **they will buy** from you.

Do you know what sells products? INFORMATION…and more information. Information creates knowledge, likes, trust, and buying.

The more information in your ecommerce store, the better. Here is the secret sauce for any ecommerce store - CREATE ENOUGH INFORMATION for a visitor to become a customer!

Have you ever felt frustrated with a store that fails to provide enough information when you are researching products? Providing sufficient information is how you can gain an advantage over your competitors in the ecommerce arena.

I will go through each type of page and the information and content you will adapt to your store and show you how and where to add it. But first, let's see what types of pages we need for your store.

TYPES OF PAGES FOR YOUR STORE

There are different types of pages with relevant information for each in your online store. Here are all the most essential pages for your store:

Company: Contact, Reviews, Community, About Us, Blogs.

Legal: Refund Policy, Terms of Service, and Privacy Policy.

General: Shipping, Returns, FAQ (Frequently Asked Questions). Some more ideas for pages depending on the products you sell:

- Ingredients
- Specifications
- Monogramming
- Sizes/Sizing
- Community

- What Makes Us Unique
- Online Ordering
- Pricing and How to Pay

Shopping Cart: Checkout page, Thank you page, Order page, etc.

eCommerce Brand: Home Page, Collection pages, Product pages.

HOW TO ADD PAGES & CONTENT TO YOUR STORE

There are 3 major actions to adding information to the store:

- Add content to your Shopify store.
- Structure your pages in Shopify.
- Optimize your pages in your theme.

The methodology of adding the content or information is the same for each page in your store, except the products page dashboard offers more options to add or choose from.

Customizing your content for your Shopify store, is how you optimize your pages with your Shopify theme which essentially means adding more useful content for your customers to each type of page.

In the 'Customize' setting, you can add images or videos, and text to any of your pages, depending on your Shopify theme. I will show you how to optimize your pages in your 'Theme' settings for each different type of page in chapter - Shopify Themes.

Add Content to Your Shopify Store

Shopify has different page dashboards for pages, products, collections, and blogs.

**Where to find this in Shopify? Online store

Most of your pages for your store are in the 'Online store' setting in your Shopify dashboard.

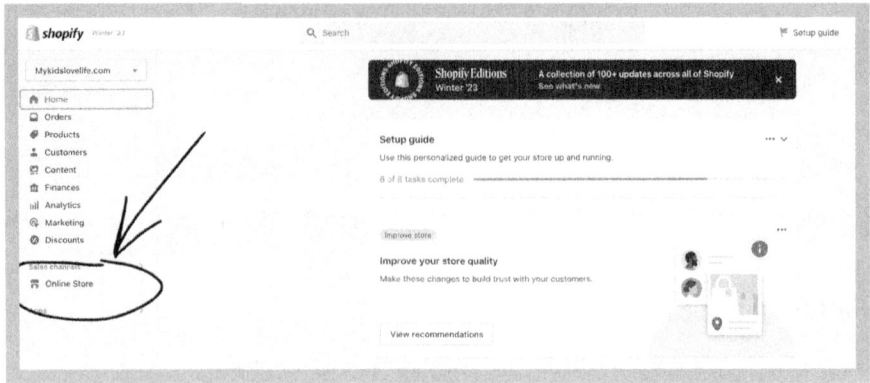

[2.8.1]

Once you click on 'Online store' setting, you can see your themes, pages, blogs, navigation and preferences.

The 'Themes' setting is immediately visible once you open the 'Online store' setting.

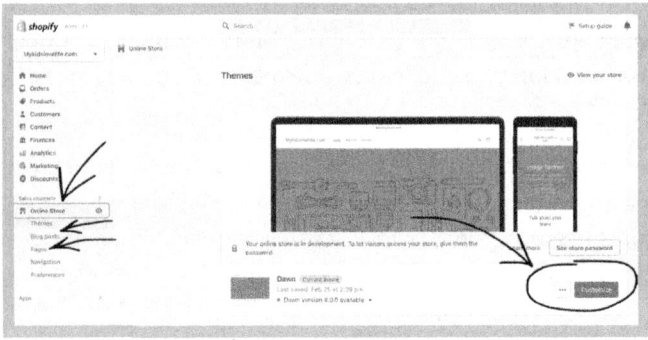

[2.8.2]

Pages:

**Where to find this in Shopify? Online store > Pages

Most of the information for the company and general information is in the 'Pages' setting.

STORE INFORMATION PAGES

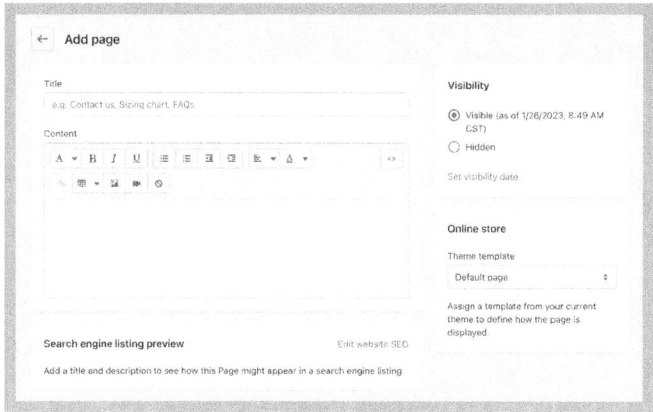

[2.8.4]

Blog Posts:

**Where to find this in Shopify? Online store > Blog posts

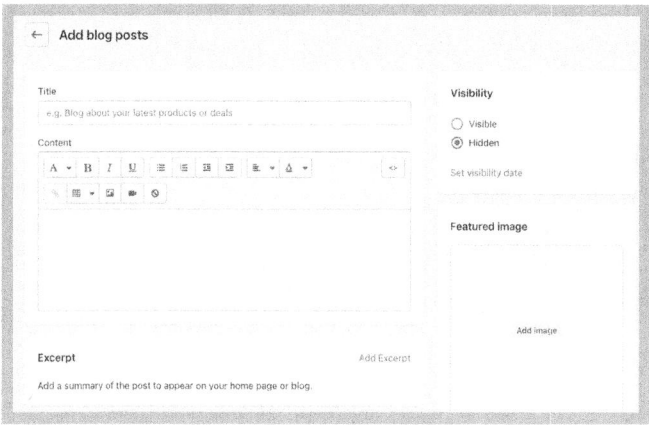

[2.8.5]

Following are the different setups on the pages for the Ecommerce page in Shopify. These pages have different detailed requirements, which are covered in the Product and Collections chapter.

Product:

**Where to find this in Shopify? Products

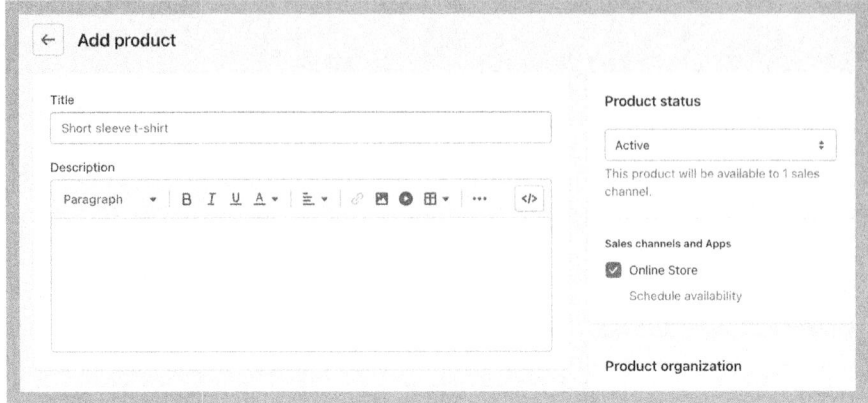

[2.8.6]

Collection:

**Where to find this in Shopify? Products > Collections

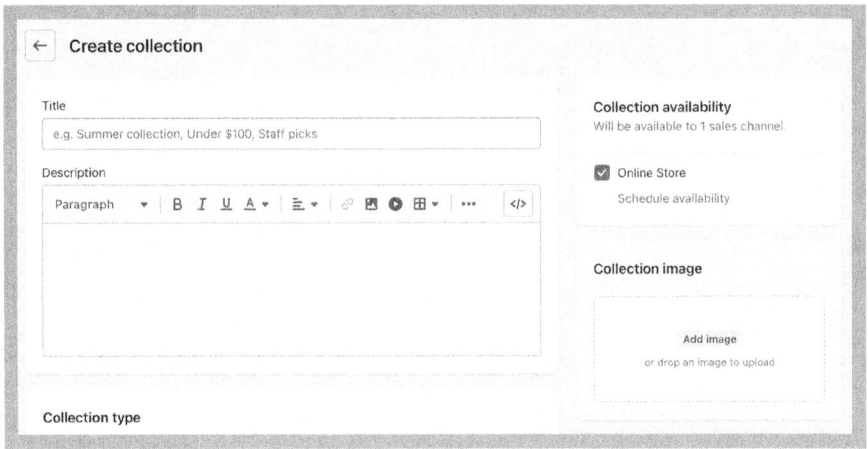

[2.8.7]

LEGAL PAGES:

**Where to find this in Shopify? Settings > Policies

Legal pages are all created from templates that can be edited. But some steps are not necessary, like the title for the page. The content can be improved with the suggestions of how to format and structure your page.

My suggestion is not to change the sentences in the Privacy and Terms of Service content. You can make the headings larger, but it is unnecessary.

HOW TO USE PAGES & BLOG DASHBOARDS

Next, I will show you how to use the 'Page' and 'Blogs' dashboards to add your information and content. Products and collections will be discussed in each different chapter for products and collections.

The general dashboard of each page is:

- Title
- Content
- Visibility
- Online store: Theme Template
- Search Engine Listing

Differences will be explained in the relevant type of page.

Here are the steps to add information and content for the different sections on a page.

Step 1. Title

The title for your page about the company or general information is usually very brief but descriptive.

Here are some ideas:

- The 'Contact Us' page is not typically changed.
- Reviews can change to 'What our customers say' or 'Customer Testimonials'.
- The Community page can show your mission for what you support. For example: Zappos is 'Zappos for Good', or Nespresso has several - Community, Sustainability, and Recycling. As you can see, you can add very simple titles to these pages. The most important part is you know what information they want to convey with each page.
- The 'About' page can change to 'Our Story' or 'My Story.' Here you can be a little bit different. People love stories.

For any other pages, add a descriptive title so your customers will understand and recognize when they need the information.

How to write a good title for your products.

- Watch your title length.
- Give every page a unique title.
- Your title font and size are determined by your Shopify theme and can only be changed in the code.

NOTE: *Your page will not save unless you have a title. You do not need to add a description or content to your page to save the page.*

Step 2. Description - Content & Information

Your page dashboard's 'Content' area is where you add all your information. Use your editor tools to organize your content in the 'Content' area. This will help you create a professional-looking page.

> Pro Tip: Always research what other pages look like and see if you can replicate the same or similar look.

The easiest way to start adding content to your pages is to add your content without formatting. After you have edited the content for grammar and spelling mistakes, you can format your content.

Here are the essentials on every page:

- Add images to reflect the content. Try not to use too many stock photos because everybody else is using them, which will dilute your brand.
- Add a video that relates to the content (not necessary but is a good idea).
- Link content pages to each other. A page that is too long will not keep the attention of your visitors. Break the content into a main page and several sub-pages to expand your information.
- Always add a 'Call to Action' (CTA) to prompt your visitor to take the next step, whether to read more, join the newsletter, or buy something.

You have to lead your visitor to become a customer or a repeat visitor.

NOTE: *The following chapters will cover the different types of pages and what information and content to add to the pages.*

STORE INFORMATION PAGES

Step 3. Visible

You can see the 'Visibility' option on the right of your page dashboard. Your pages are automatically visible on the internet. Select the 'Hidden' option if you want to hide your pages. You can also hide your page and make it visible on a specific date - schedule your page going live.

[2.8.8]

Step 4. Online store - Theme template

Templates are different types of pages you can create depending on the theme you use. The following image shows the two templates available in a free Shopify theme.

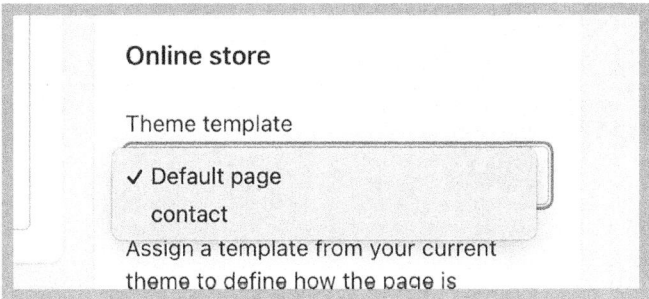

[2.8.9]

For instance, the 'Contact' template will have a form on the page already created for your use. All you need to change is to add the 'contact' template and the contact form is on the page automatically.

[2.8.10]

NOTE: *When you view this in your rich text editor, the content is in the editor's code.*

The page template will only show the content you add, not the contact form. The following image shows the information above the contact form I added to the page in the rich text editor.

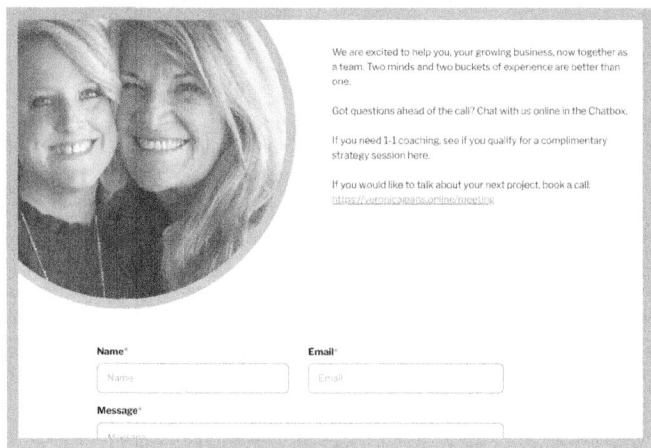

[2.8.11]

You can also create different page templates in the 'Theme' settings in 'Customize'. This is a different way of structuring your page without the knowledge of HTML. There might be more page templates if you have a paid Shopify theme.

Step 5. Search Engine Listing Preview

Shopify will automatically create your page title, description, and URL (Uniform Resource Locator - which means the web address of your page) for the 'search engine listing preview' when you add your title and description at the top of the page.

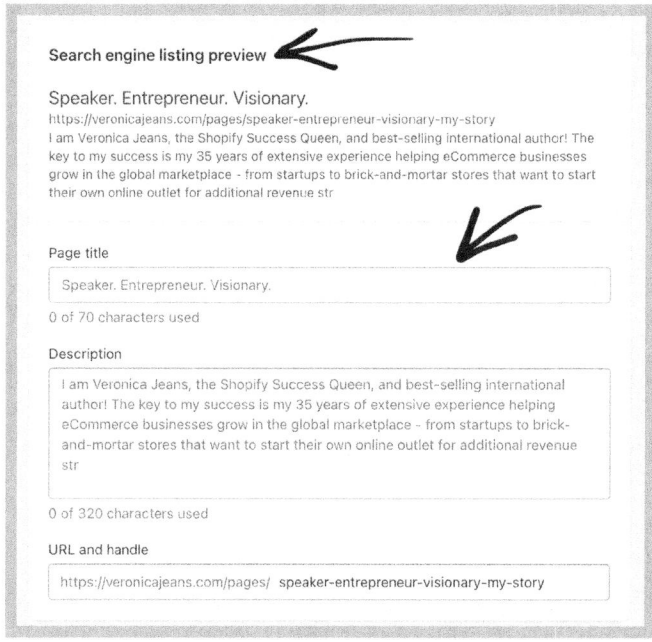

[2.8.12]

You need to change your information to your best advantage to show in the search engines. As you noted, Shopify adds all your content to your SEPL, but all the content will not show up in Google search. It will be truncated if it is too long.

BUILD PUBLISHING, EDITING, OR DELETING

When you open your 'Pages,' you can see all the pages you have created.

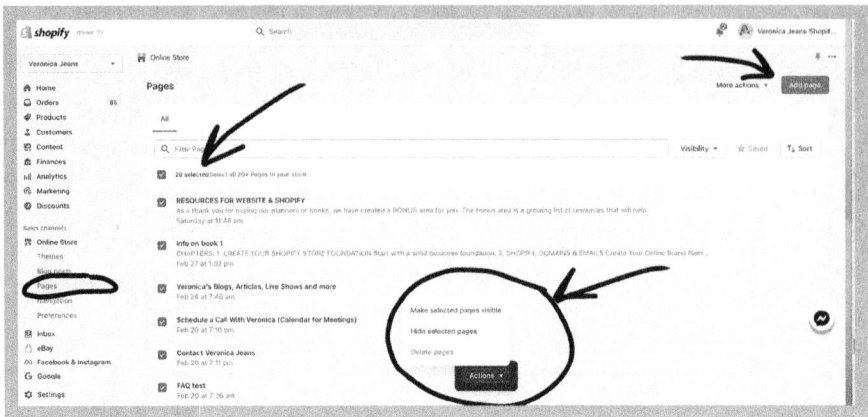

[2.8.13]

To delete or publish your pages in this view, you need to select your page or pages. At the bottom of the page, an edit popup will appear. Click on 'Actions' and you can either make some of the pages visible or hide, or delete the pages you selected.

> 💡 Pro Tip: if you cannot see all the information, put your mouse pointer on the edge of the box. A plus sign will pop up. Hold your mouse down and drag the plus sign. That will open the section where your information is hidden.

TOOLS

Here are some tools for checking grammar and spelling mistakes.

- A handy tool to use is Grammarly, which you can add as an extension of Chrome. Grammarly will help you with grammar and spelling mistakes.
- Chrome extension 'Wordtune' is a great tool to improve your sentences.
- Copy.ai is a fabulous extension to your content for your pages and information - https://veronicajeans.online/copy-ai
- ChatGPT - https://chat.openai.com/
- WordTune - Chrome extension - https://app.wordtune.com

OPTIMIZE YOUR PAGES IN THE SHOPIFY THEME

There are different reasons to optimize your page. For instance, you can improve your page in the 'Rich Text' editor without knowing more about HTML coding. Now, doing it in your 'Theme' settings is much easier. We have already identified all the different features and sections in the Shopify theme settings.

Step 1. Create a page

**Where to find this in Shopify? Online store > Pages

If you want to customize your pages, first add a page in the 'Page' setting.

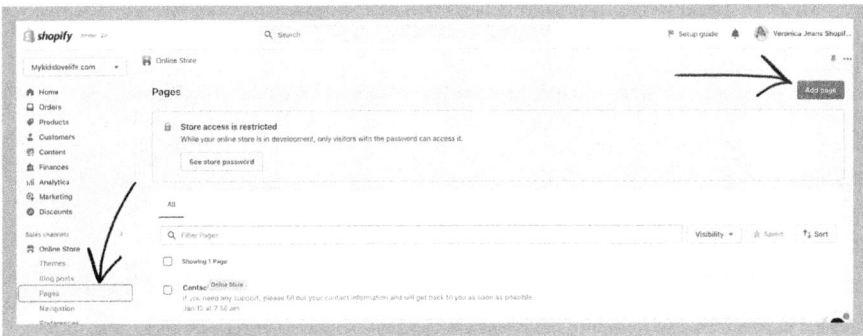

[2.13.0]

The 'Page' editor will open with a blank page. Add the title of the page for the page. Now you can add the relevant information for the page. The automatically allocated template will be the 'Default template'.

[2.13.5]

Step 2. Customize the page

Where to find this in Shopify? Online store > Themes > Customize

Now, navigate to the 'Theme' setting and click on the 'Customize' button.

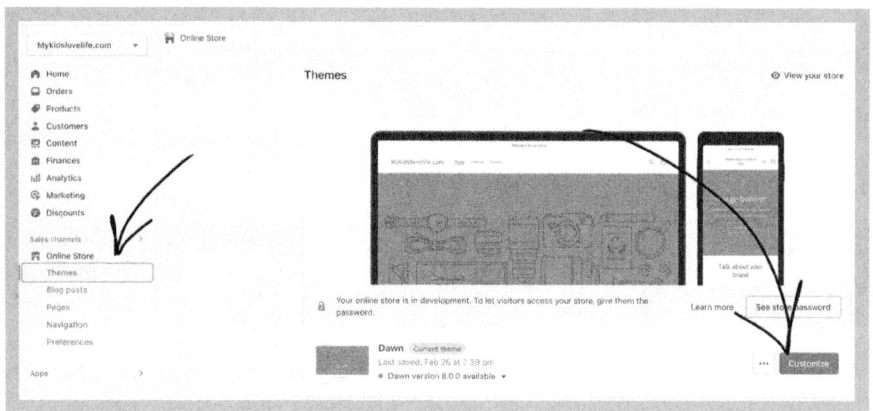

[2.13.6]

In the dropdown box at the top of the dashboard in the 'Customize' editor, navigate to the Pages option and the second-tier page dropdown. This will show you the 'Default' and 'Contact' page templates. These are automatically created by your Shopify theme.

STORE INFORMATION PAGES

[2.13.7]

Step 3. Create the new page template

In the second-tier pages dropdown, choose '+Create template'.

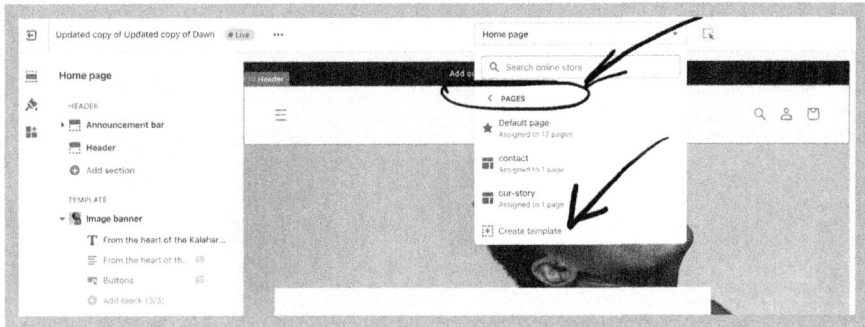

[2.13.8]

Name your page template with either the default theme template or it can also be a new template. This can only be created in the 'Edit code' section, and this is an expert setup. For this lesson, I would stick to the default which covers most of what you need. Each page template must have a unique name that is not duplicated anywhere.

Step 4. Select a page for the template

On the left side of the dashboard of the newly created theme template, the page allocated will be the 'Default' theme template. If the page is not the one you have already set up, then change the page to select another page.

[2.13.10]

Step 5. Assign the template to the selected page

At the top of the left side of the dashboard, you can see if any pages have been assigned to this template. As seen in the following image, there are no pages assigned.

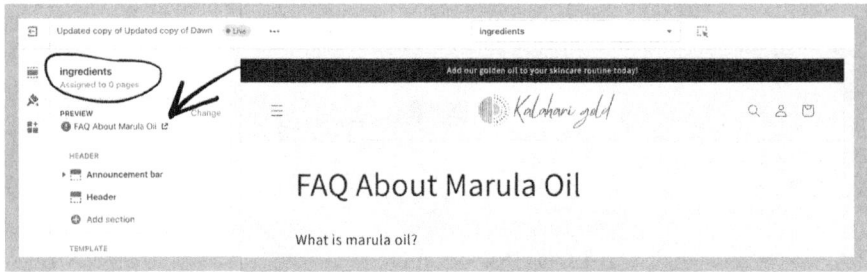

[2.13.11]

Click on the square with the arrow, which will take you to the 'Page' setting. In the 'Page' setting, assign the newly created theme template to the relevant page.

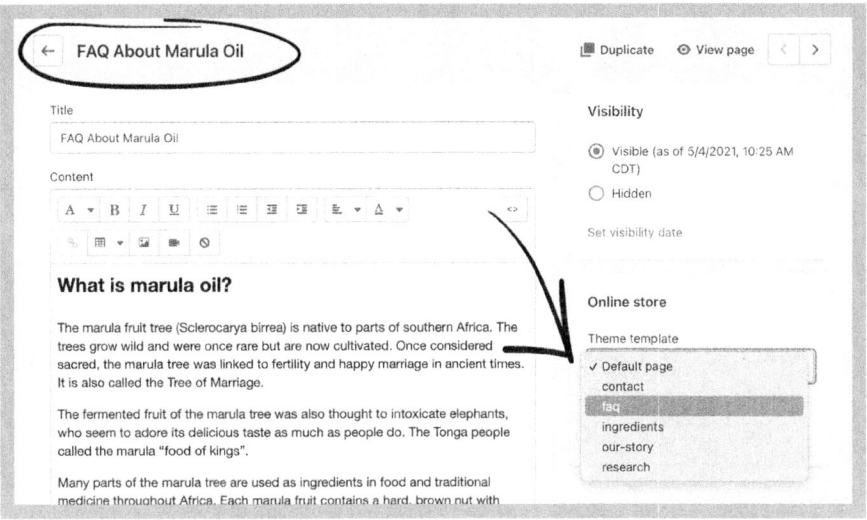

[2.13.12]

Step 6. Add more sections and blocks to the page

In the 'Customize' setting, you can add images, videos, and text to any of your pages, depending on your Shopify theme. As seen in the following image, when you add a page to the 'Customize' editor, the title of the page will be at the top of the page.

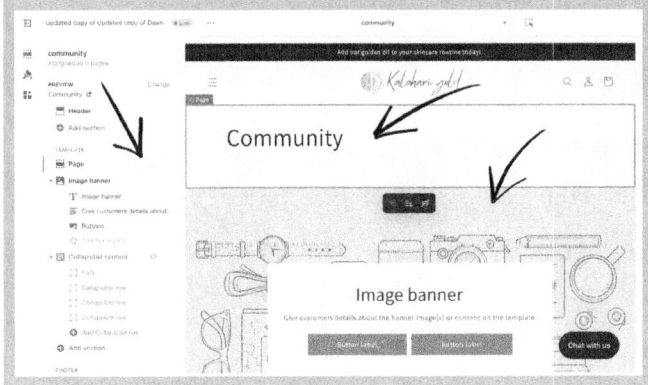

[2.13.13]

> Pro Tip: Make sure the title is improved for the page. For instance, do not just add 'Community' as the page, but rather expand it to 'WE GIVE BACK TO THE COMMUNITY' or something similar that enhances the message of the page.

> Pro Tip: If you do not want the title to show on the page, here is a workaround. Do not add any content to the page. Hide the page when viewed in the 'Customize' editor. Now you can add your sections and blocks to the page.

> Pro Tip: You do not have to use all the options. Use what makes sense instead of too much clutter. It is still important for your products to be the page's main focus.

Here are more ideas to add to your pages:

- A newsletter sign-up anywhere on the page should be on most pages. Don't miss an opportunity to attract visitors to your mailing list.
- Feature products or collections on any page.
- Banner and text to a page with one of the brand messages.
- Different banners for each page.
- Different links or collections to every page, especially if you have a promotion running.

CREATING YOUR PAGES FOR YOUR STORE

Company Information Pages

Where to find this in Shopify? Online store > Pages

Company information pages range from Contact, Reviews, Community, Blogs, About Us, and anything about your company and business. Every page is created individually except for the contact page. Shopify has created a contact form for you in 'Pages', and you can add more information to the page. Let's start creating information or content that will let your customers love you.

CONTACT Page

In Shopify, your contact page is automatically created. This is the form your customer fills in if they want to contact you, and this form will be sent to the email address in your Shopify business information.

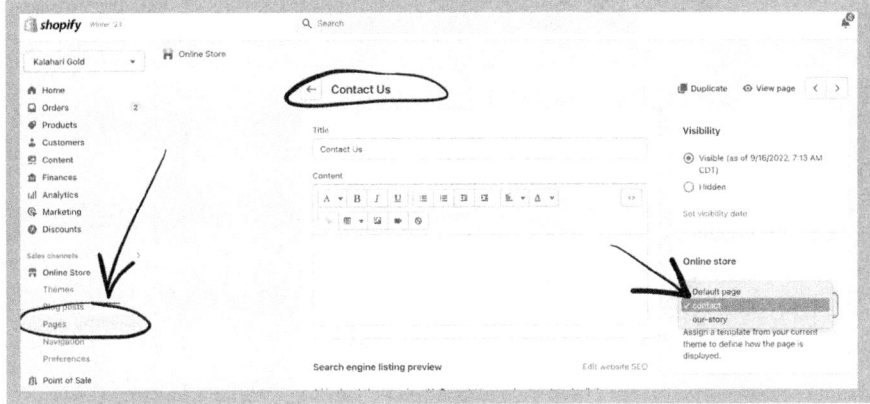

[2.7.13]

You can add more information to your contact page, which will be added to the contact form. It is a great idea to encourage your customer to connect with you and when you will contact them back. Make sure you contact them in time.

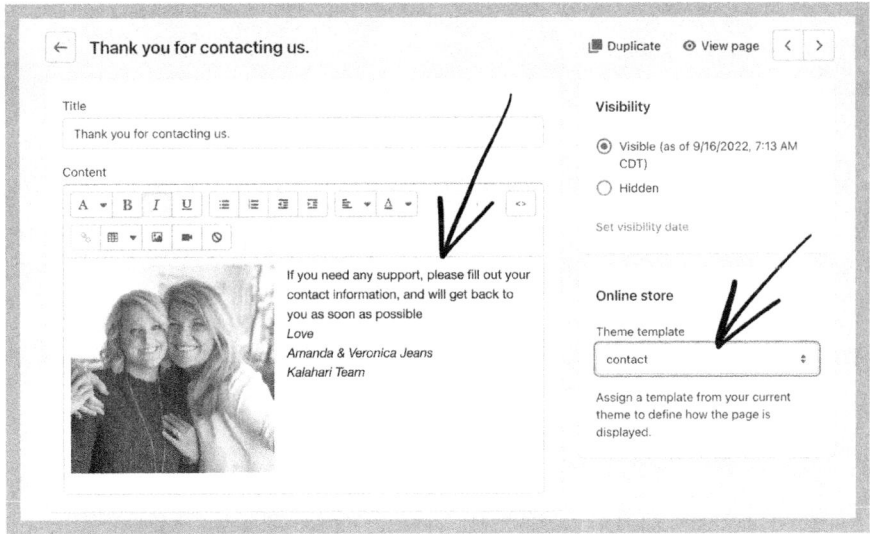

[2.7.214]

The contact form is automatically added to the page.

I have added a message and an image to my contact page in the following image. You can create this in the 'Pages' or the 'Customize' setting. In the following image, I added a theme section, 'Image with text'.

[2.7.34]

> Pro Tip: Adding your phone number, business address, and email to the page is optional. This is part of the trust factor in your online store but unnecessary if you have this information in your footer area.

A map is a great idea if you have a physical business address if you have a retail outlet.

Do not use your home address in a website.

REVIEW Page

In eCommerce, you normally have your reviews on your product page, where they have the most impact. Create a dedicated review page on your website where customers can browse and read reviews for all of your products. Then you can add this page to other sections in your store.

STORE INFORMATION PAGES

[2.7.15]

This can be a great way to build trust and credibility with potential customers.

The following image shows that the testimonials were added in the 'Customize' editor with the 'Testimonial' section. Not every theme has this option.

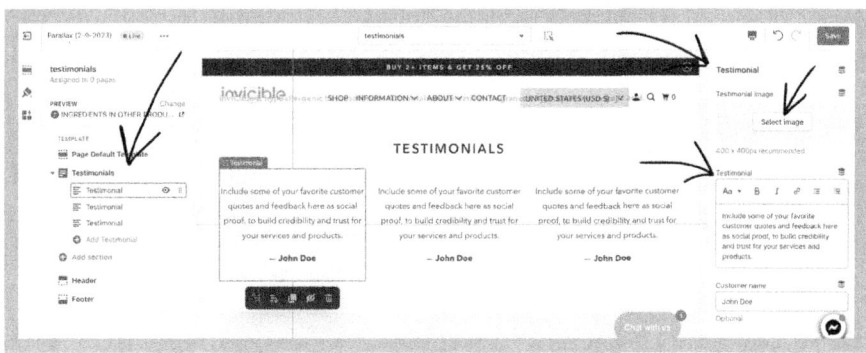

[2.7.35]

And if you add your testimonials in the 'Page' editor, images can be added very easily. Upload your image to the page. Choose a size for the image and confirm the upload.

[2.7.29]

Once that is done, click on the image and edit the position on the page in the 'Image' editor, as seen in the following image. Add a few pixels to the right or left of the image, depending on whether the image floats to the right or left. This will add some space between the image and the text. Then check the box 'Wrap the text around the image', and the text will float around the image.

See where all the options are in the following image.

[2.7.30]

Reviews will sell you more products than anything else. Adding your customer reviews or testimonials to more pages will also benefit your store for social proof.

Here are some more content ideas:

- Add a photo with the review, which makes it more personal.
- Included a video review about your products.
- Grab your reviews from social media pages and Amazon. Don't forget to add the link to the social or marketplace.

In the 'Customize' editor, I have added my blogs and the newsletter sections, which add more information for the customer. Or a great idea is to add your products at the bottom of the page.

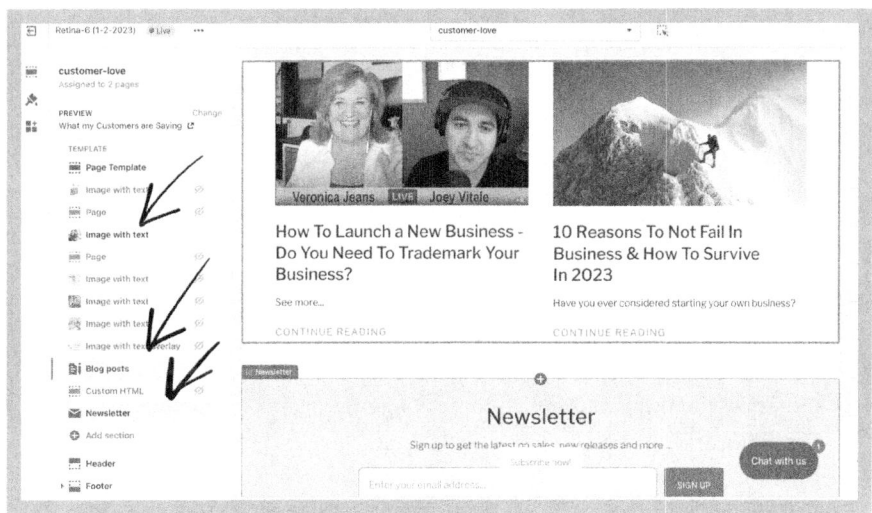

[2.7.31]

COMMUNITY Page

A Community page on your online store is a great way to connect with customers and build trust by sharing information about the company's values and impact on the community. Some examples of information that could be included on a Community page include:

- How the company passes savings on to customers.
- How the company donates a certain percentage of profits to charity.
- How the company's packaging is environmentally conscious.
- How the business positively impacts the community.

By including this information, customers can see that the company is transparent and committed to making a positive impact.

Other brands successfully incorporating a Community page into their eCommerce store include Patagonia, Warby Parker, and Toms Shoes. They share information about how they positively impact the environment and the communities they serve.

To write a Community page for your eCommerce store, consider the following steps:

- Identify your company's values and mission. What impact do you want to make on the environment and local community?
- Research and gather information on how your company is making a positive impact. This could include information on environmentally friendly practices, charitable donations, or community involvement.
- Write clear and concise descriptions of the ways your company is making a positive impact. Use specific examples to support your claims.
- Include images, videos, or testimonials to help bring your message to life and make it more engaging for readers.
- Organize the information in a logical and easy-to-navigate manner. Use headings and subheadings to break up the text and make it easy to scan.
- Include a call-to-action, such as encouraging customers to learn more about your company's values or supporting a charitable cause.

Example:

Your Community page is dedicated to sharing how you strive to positively impact the environment and the local community. Here is an example of content:

"As a company, we are committed to reducing our environmental footprint by using sustainable materials in our packaging and implementing recycling programs in our warehouses. We are proud that our packaging is 100% recyclable and biodegradable.

In addition to our environmental efforts, we also believe in giving back to the community. We donate a percentage of our profits to local non-profit organizations that align with our values and actively participate in community service events and volunteer opportunities.

We are also committed to supporting local businesses and the economy by sourcing our materials and products from local vendors and artisans whenever possible.

We believe that working together can positively impact the world around us. Thank you for choosing to shop with us and for supporting our mission.

Please take a moment to learn more about our community efforts and the organizations we support.

Thank you for your support!"

ABOUT Page

 "A brand is a story that is always being told." Scott Bedbury (Nike & Starbucks)

In most cases, whatever you are selling, is being sold elsewhere. So, you must consider a way to differentiate yourself from your competition.

As a small business, you can distinguish yourself by personalizing your business. Your **story** is one of the most critical aspects of your store.

One of the most effective ways to do this is to be personal and share your motivations and passions. People love stories, and by sharing your own story, you can create a connection that your customers can relate to.

Your customers need to feel that they know you and identify with you!

Many people ignore or create a flawed 'About' page. Your 'About' page is a valuable asset and is often underutilized.

"People buy from people they know and trust."

When you're starting your store, it may seem like there's not much to say. If you know what you do for your customers and why you do it, you have a great starting point. You can always add more as you gain insight into new business accomplishments and expand your business journey.

As an entrepreneur, your business and your products are an extension of yourself and a part of your life's story.

The bottom line is that your customers will identify with you and your story and feel they know and trust you enough to buy from you.

When creating your "About Us" page, consider including information about:

- Why you started your business: Share your motivations and goals and explain what inspired you to start your eCommerce store.
- Your passions: Share information about your hobbies, interests, and other passions your customers might identify.
- Your lifestyle: Share information about your lifestyle and how it relates to your business. For example, if you are an avid traveler, you could share information about how your travels have influenced your business and products.
- Your achievements: Share your business achievements, such as awards, milestones, or special recognition you've received.
- Your team: Introduce your team and provide information about their roles, experience, and background.
- Write about what problem caused you to respond to that need. How did you find a solution (starting your business), and what were your struggles along the way?

By providing this personal information, you can create a deeper connection with your customers and help them better understand your business and products. This can ultimately lead to increased sales and customer loyalty.

It's important to remember that your "About Us" page is a living document, it should be updated regularly to reflect any changes, achievements or new information about your business and team.

Here are some more ideas:

- The magic is - Tell mini-stories!
- What Are Your Values and Goals?
- What is your experience in the industry.
- Outline your journey
- What was your 'AHA' moment?
- Who Are You and Your Team
- Who made the product
- What inspired the creation of the product

- How was the product tested
- What obstacles did you overcome to develop the products
- Why are you in business
- Why should somebody buy from you
- What makes your business different from anybody else
- What do you add extra that your competition might not

You can also add:

- Any patents, copyrights, and other proprietary intellectual property of yours.
- Certifications and associations in the industry.
- Awards your company received
- Partners or collaborators that enhance your store and product

> Pro Tip: The best way to write your story is to just start writing with the ideas I have mentioned. Write from the heart and get all the ideas out on paper. Once you have done that, we can get to the next step.

Now that you have some basic content, we will start shaping your pages.

Your about page is a bit different from your other pages in that more personal and business information and content is shared than the other pages.

Step 1. Create a Tagline

Your tagline should be right at the top of the page, preferably on a banner image, to give it more impact.

Step 2. Create the body of your story

This is where you will expand your story. Share your business, what inspired you to start it, and what differentiates you from your competitors. This will help establish your brand and connect with your customers.

> Pro Tip: Write it in the first person, using "I" and "We," to build a personal connection.

Step 3. Add Big Wins

Tell your customers about your big wins and how your business is pursuing its mission.

You work hard to get a pat on the back for your accomplishments. You are allowed to brag a bit. Okay, well, more than a bit.

Shout it out there and add everything to your page.

For example, if you are in or contributing to blogs, mentioned in magazines, and all the other bits and pieces like accolades, associations, and groups you belong to – they all belong here.

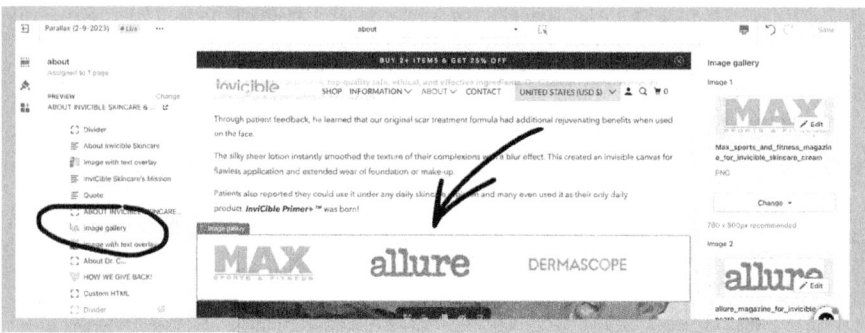

[2.7.34-1]

> 💡 Pro Tip: Add links to your associations, articles, or accomplishments with any mentions on the page.

Step 4. Add testimonials

Include customer testimonials: Testimonials from satisfied customers can be a powerful tool for building trust and credibility. Use quotes and images to highlight positive feedback from your customers.

[2.7.15]

Step 5. Add a 'Call to Action'

Add a clear and persuasive call to action: Encourage your visitors to make a purchase, sign up for your newsletter, or follow you on social media with a clear and persuasive call to action.

Ask yourself the question - what do you want your customer to do next?

Here are some ideas:

- Join our newsletter
- How to get started
- How to contribute
- How to 'Like' your Facebook page
- How to 'Share' your story
- How to buy the 'Best Selling' product

Make sure to add links to different areas of your store if you are discussing your products.

Step 6. Visual branding

We are in the social visual age....it is all about images and videos! Your eCommerce store's visual branding must reflect your products and your customer.

The story is just the start. The 'About Us' page shouldn't just tell the story, and that's it. **Your page should show your story.**

Add some great photos and videos of you with family or friends, or your team. Again, this is part of connecting visually with your customers.

People do business with people, not brands; what better way to show that real people are behind your business than to put your team's picture on your store's 'About Us' page?

Here are some ideas:

- Think of your environment - where you work and what it looks like.
- Videos are excellent options.
- Add some Behind the Scenes images or videos.
- People love to see where you create your products
- Where you are packaging your products to be sent out.

I am sure you can come up with some great ideas.

> Pro Tip: You can create a video quickly. Maybe add a bunch of photos together to make a great video. It does not have to be complicated.

BLOG

**Where to find this in Shopify? Online store > Blogs

The only page not in 'Pages' is your blogs or, as I call them, your news articles. An eCommerce blog should be an essential part of an eCommerce strategy.

Here are just a few reasons why your eCommerce store needs a blog:

- Establishes authority - a blog is a great way to establish yourself as an authority in your industry by providing valuable and informative content.
- Builds relationships - You build trust and loyalty by providing valuable and informative content to your customers.
- Showcases your products - a blog is a great platform to showcase your product, explain the features and benefits, and provide information on new arrivals and how you stack up against the industry.
- Keep up with the competition - in today's eCommerce market, having a blog is no longer an option but a necessity. If you don't have one, you miss out on many opportunities.

As unimaginable as it seems but the benefits of a blog in an ecommerce store is amazing. Donna, the owner of TheMissingPiecePuzzle.com writes about puzzles. She researched puzzle groups on Facebook to see what questions people were asking and then wrote an article it. This is one of her top-performing blogs in her store; her traffic increased by 35%. She now writes blogs regularly.

Blogs should be part of your Content and SEO (Search Engine Optimization) strategy. Creating informative content will attract visitors, and you can convert those visitors to customers.

Not everybody is ready to buy your products immediately, but you can stay in front of your audience with valuable content.

The main blog page and the blog post page can be customized.

In the free Shopify theme, the blog templates cannot have a sidebar, as shown in my blog in the next image.

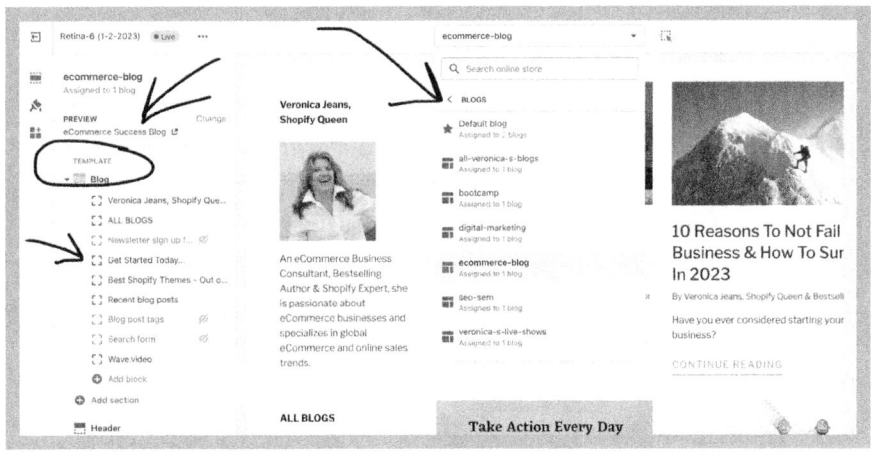

[? 7.36]

And you can also see that I have created several different blog posts for my customers. They can choose which type of blog they would like to read.

You can choose between a grid or collage desktop layout in the free Shopify theme template. In the mobile view, the blogs will flow down the page with only one blog showing in the mobile viewer.

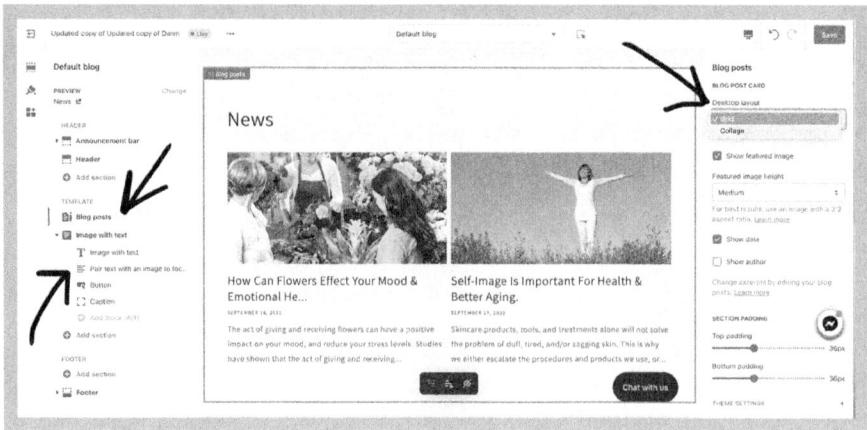

[2.7.37]

I am not going to expand on how to optimize this page, because we are still building the basic online store. There is a lot of information in my book 3 -

LEGAL PAGES

Why do you need legal policies in your eCommerce store?

This is not a choice but a necessity for your eCommerce business. You need legal documentation for your eCommerce store to protect your business because you are collecting personal data like names, email addresses, IP addresses, session activity, and payment details, to name a few.

Shopify has legal templates ready to use within the dashboard, but they will have to be edited to suit your requirements. All you need to do is update the information to your particular market.

Not every online store has the same legal issues or needs protection. It is always better to check your information with your own legal counsel.

Types of Legal Documentation

- Refund Policy
- Privacy Policy
- Terms of Service

**Where to find this in Shopify? Settings > Policies

STORE INFORMATION PAGES

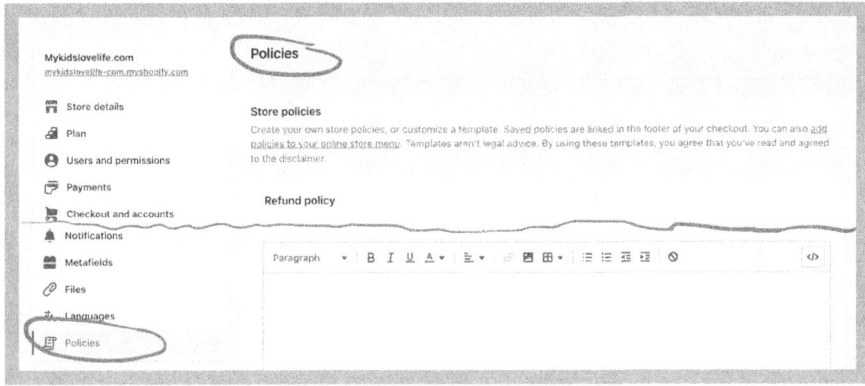

[2.7.1]

REFUND POLICY Page

The refund policy is first on your dashboard in the policy settings. The default refund template is very general and you need to add your particular information. The template gives you some ideas to use. Every single detail you can think of you need to add to this page. Do not skip this because it will and can cause problems with your customers if you do not spell out every single thing.

[2.7.2]

PRIVACY POLICY Page

The privacy policy information is a little bit different. There is no need to change anything but when Shopify has suggestions to add more information, you can either take it out or add your extra information.

[2.7.5]

As you can see in the following image, this is what it looks like when you need to delete or add your information in the privacy policy. Any text in caps is what you need to review.

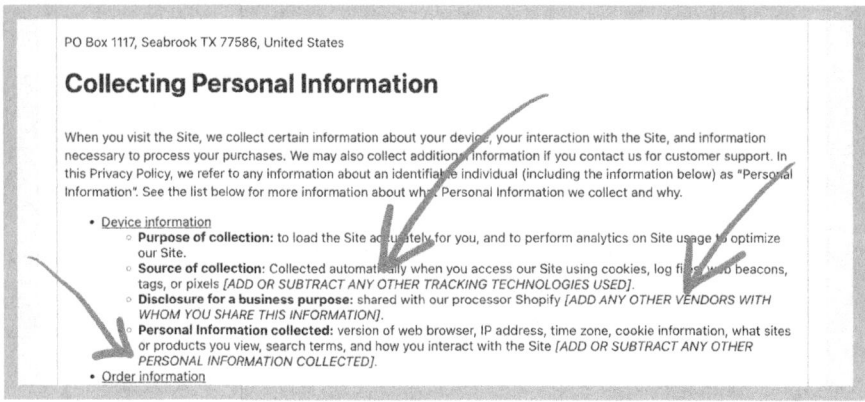

[2.7.4]

TERMS OF SERVICE POLICY Page

The terms of service policy information is about Shopify and also to the internet and website. All the information you need will be in this document. Do not take anything out but you can alway add anything you need.

STORE INFORMATION PAGES

[2.7.3]

> ⚠ Pro Tip: I have never needed to change any of this information in all the years working on online businesses. But if you do need to change, consult a business lawyer.

Your legal information pages will automatically be visible for your clients in your footer menus depending on the Shopify theme, or you add the links for the pages to your navigation.

As shown below, it depends on what theme you have.

[2.7.6]

These hyperlinks have been added to the navigation.

[2.7.7]

GENERAL INFORMATION PAGES

General information pages pertain to anything that has to do with processing your products in your store and giving your customers as much information they need to make a decision to buy your products.

You will have to create all the information in these pages. Your knowledge of your products, business and customer is the foundation for your content.

Most of the pages in this section will be created in the 'Pages' section on your main dashboard.

**Where to find this in Shopify? Online store > Pages

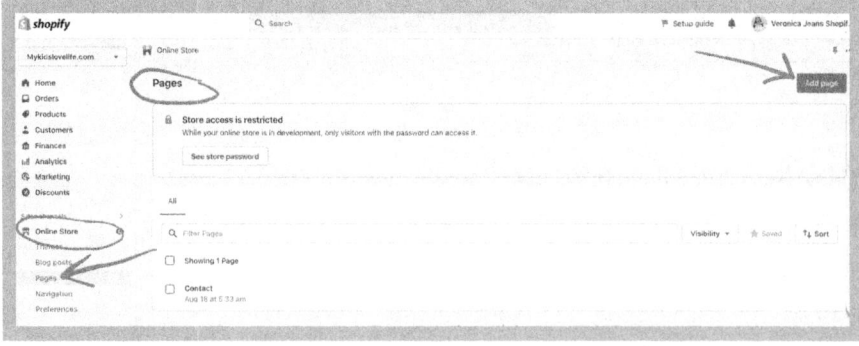

[2.7.8]

The only page that is different is the Shipping Information which will be in 'Settings' and 'Policies' on your dashboard.

**Where to find this in Shopify? Settings > Policies

If you are unsure what to add, research typical questions in your industry and competition. Check out Amazon, Google, and other brands. (DO NOT COPY).

SHIPPING INFORMATION Page

The Shipping information must be added to the Shopify policies section.

In the shipping template there is no '*Create from template*' button. You will have to create the shipping information in accordance with your shipping requirements and information.

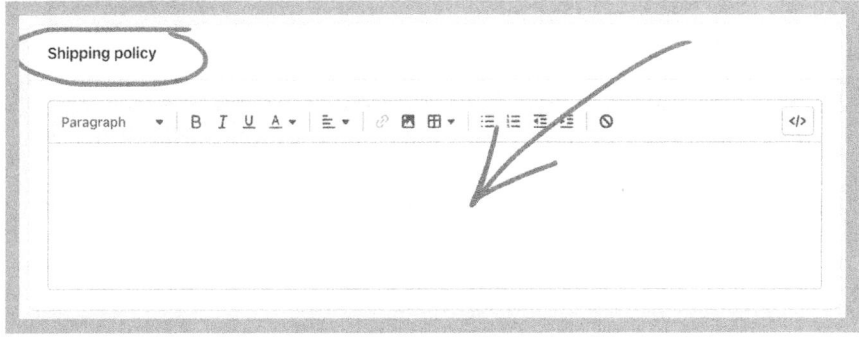

[2.7.9]

It helps to research brands and other businesses in the same niche market, because they probably have more experience with customer service and problems.

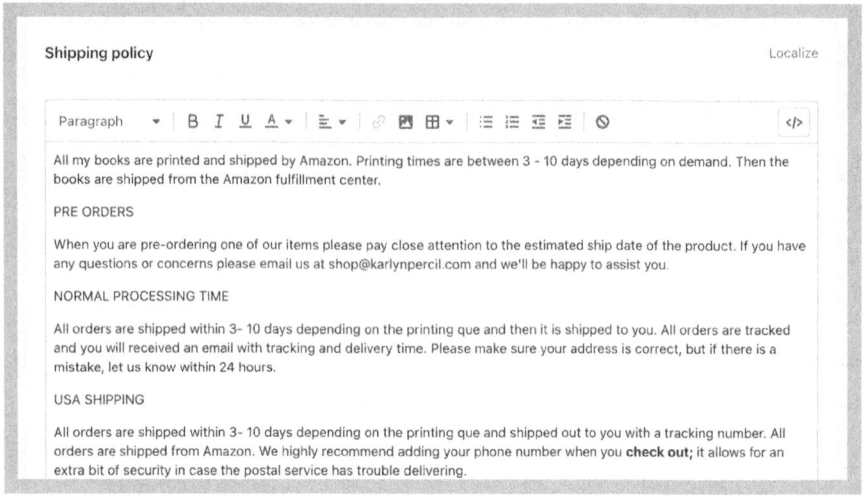

[2.7.10]

You should give your customers as much information as possible. According to your customers' questions, you might have to add more details later if you are a new store. Initially, you can add enough shipping information from your shipping carriers to satisfy your customers.

> ✓ Pro Tip: Check out your compatriots /competition and see what they have. Research larger stores and see what they have on their Shipping Information. DO NOT COPY.

Try to answer some of the shipping questions and add more information you create yourself on your page in your own words.

Remember, this is about giving your customers information so they can make an informed decision to buy from you.

For instance:

- How long your shipping time is (check with your shipping carrier) and other pertinent information your customer will need to know what will happen when that package is on the way.
- What happens if it gets damaged, or when they get their tracking code, if it goes to the wrong address, etc.

Don't forget to add your **international shipping policy information**. If you do not ship internationally, you still must let prospective buyers know your policy. For example: "*We do not ship internationally*".

RETURN POLICY/ INFORMATION Page

Your **Return Policy** should state exactly what you require for people to return your products. There is a paragraph in the default **refund policy** about the return of the items.

If you are doing personalization, obviously they cannot return their items, but you have to state that in your returns.

Your return information can be part of your Refund Policy. But it is good idea to have a separate page just for returns. State exactly what customers need to do to return an item and the required condition of the item.

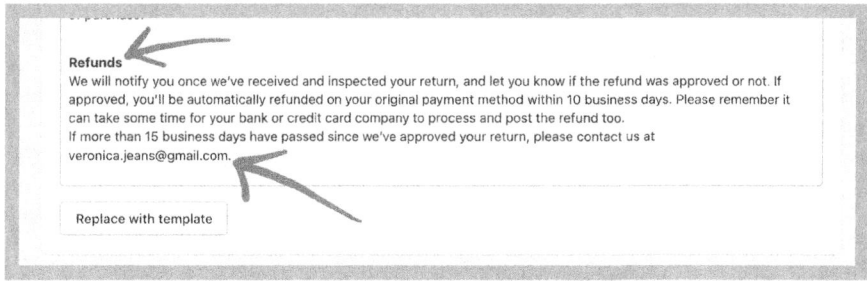

[2.7.11]

> ✓ Pro Tip: If you have insurance on shipping and your products, and you want to claim the insurance because of damage, the shipping insurance company will want photos of the damage. I suggest adding that to the return information.

We have very clear information for any claims or refunds as seen in the following image for MoyoCollections.com. This is from experience with shipping companies that do not see the 'Fragile' sticker all over the package and the items arrived damaged. The customer has to be clear what the next steps are if they want to claim shipping damages. And as a business to create a shipping claim for damages, the shipping carrier need all the information to pay the claim. It is exactly like creating an insurance claim for damages to your household goods. More information is better than less, which included photos of the damaged package and product.

> If the receiver of the shipment has a waiver with the LTL carrier for No signature required, this authorization alleviates both the company and the carrier from any responsibility.
>
> **Damaged shipments must be refused or notated on the delivery document.**
>
> **CLAIMS**
>
> The receiver must inspect the shipment prior to releasing the carrier. We are not responsible for damaged or lost product.
>
> Freight claims for lost or damaged freight must be filed with the carrier and clearly noted on Bills of Lading when receiving shipments. This is necessary for your protection.
>
> Although the responsibility is with the carrier, please notify us immediately so that we may be of some assistance.
>
> **If the item is damaged, please take photos of the inside and the outside of the package, the damaged item as proof of negligence.**
>
> Shipping and handling are nonrefundable, but we will work diligently to resolve any case.

[2.7.12]

This information is added to the Refund policy as well as the Shipping policy/information.

FAQ (Frequently Asked Questions) INFORMATION Page

It is essential for your store to have a FAQ page for your customers. If your customers have questions about your products or processes, they can quickly find them available.

How do you create a FAQ page if you don't have customers yet?

You know your products. Try to consider all the questions your customers might have when viewing your products.

You can start with your shipping and refund information - I know it is already on your policies pages, but include it on the FAQ page because you want to answer your customer's questions in every possible way so that they do not have to search for the information.

Here are some ideas of questions you might want to answer:

- How long to receive the product.
- How the processing works.
- What happens if it is not delivered.
- Information about your products.
- How to return a product.
- How to choose the right size.
- More information about ingredients.

I can go on but I hope you get the gist of more questions you can add. There can never be too many. You want to answer as many questions as you can think of.

HOW TO STYLE THE FAQS.

Your headers in the information page need to be questions - as if asked by your customer.

Your page layout should be logical - for instance:

(Question) When will I receive my product?

[Add the answer]

[Next question]

[Add the next answer]

Structure of FAQ information on the page:

- Bold the sentence of your question and leave a space between sets of Q&A.
- Make it easy for your customers to skim and read.
- Short sentences and no more than 3 sentences in one paragraph.
- Don't get too wordy or technical. Keep it simple.
- Only answer one question at a time.
- Don't just link to another page; answer the question.
- If you have yes/no questions, answer with yes/no before answering the questions.
- Make sure your FAQ page or information is easy to find.
- If you have a FAQ on a page, the questions and answers have to be about the particular topic of the page.

Create your version of typical questions, and as you get more customers, you will be able to add more information.

Also, check out Facebook groups, blogs (people asking questions), Quora, and Google for questions and answers to your FAQ.

> Pro Tip: If your FAQ gets too long, I would suggest having different pages that deal with a particular topic, and adding all the links to a main FAQ page.

SHOPPING CART PAGES

**Where to find this in Shopify? Online Store > Theme > Customize

In Shopify, your eCommerce page templates are already created for you with related sections, and you can add limited information depending on the Shopify theme or plan.

The pages for checkout, thank you, order, customer accounts, login, search results, cart, and payment are all automatically created in your shopping cart. There is normally no need to change any of these pages.

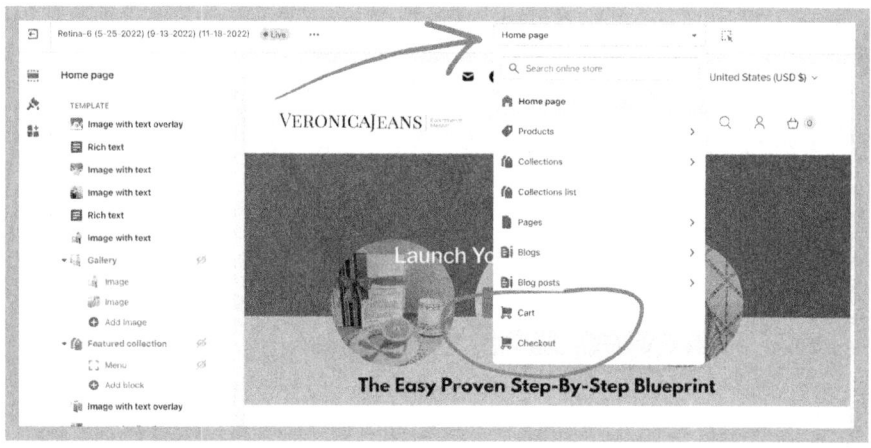

[2.7.18]

Some Ecommerce pages in your Shopify store can be improved by adding more information in 'Customize', for example, a logo to the checkout page.

The information added is either in your 'Pages' section or in the 'Customize' setting.

ADD TO CART Page

The 'Add to Cart' page has limited update sections. My recommendation is not to add too many sections to this page because you really do not want to distract your customer from buying the products.

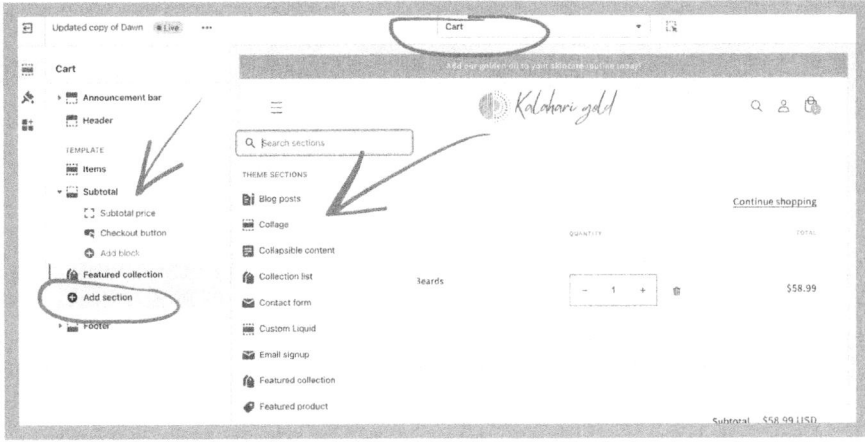

[2.7.19]

You can add a Shopify app option, as shown in the following image. I added a trust factor to the page, ensuring my customers that it is a secure website.

[2.7.20]

CHECKOUT Page

When you add the 'Checkout' page from the dropdown at the top of the 'Customize' dashboard, you will not be able to view the page.

[2.7.21]

The 'Checkout' page is only visible in the theme settings, which is indicated by the paintbrush icon on the left side of the 'Customize' dashboard.

Under the checkout setting, you can add various images, logos, fonts, and colors. These are the options:

- Banner
- Logo
- Main Content Area
- Order Summary
- Typography
- Color

Step 1. Add logo and banner

The **logo** and the **banner** are obvious choices to add to your checkout page. This will keep your branding consistent throughout the buying process.

If you do not add a logo, the name of your Shopify store will be displayed. In the following image, Amanda, the owner of ThePrettyPapier.com did not add a logo because her logo is text logo.

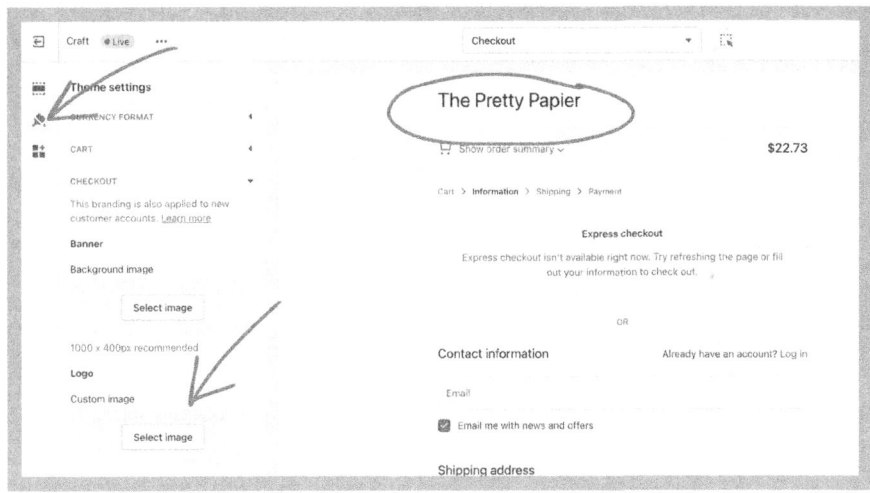

[2.7.22]

In the next image, I have added my logo to the 'Checkout' page, and the logo size is large. The way this is set up you don't want your logo to take over the page. In this instance, your logo is part of your brand but should not take over too much of the page. Your customer is ready to get their credit card out and pay for their purchases, and you do not want to distract their attention.

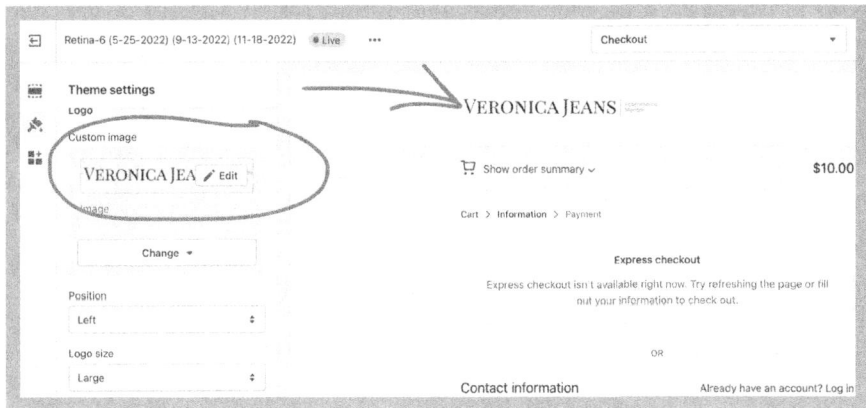

[2.7.23]

As you can see with the MoyoCollections.com 'Checkout' page, we added a banner, but the banner does not take over too much of the top of the page. As you can see, the banner image I added is huge, but when it is added to the page, it only shows the template size.

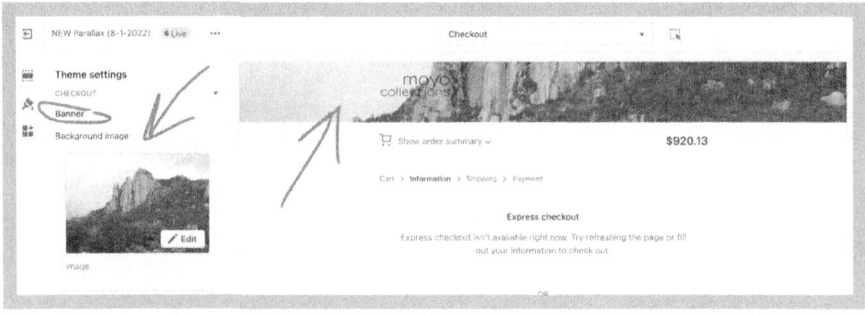

[2.7.24]

Step 2. Background image or color

You can also add an image to the main content area of your checkout page, **but I do not recommend it**. Keeping your 'Checkout' page simple and plain is the best option. We want your customer to finish the checkout with the least distractions.

The main content area covers only the left side of the checkout page.

You can also change the background of the text boxes, but I still prefer to keep everything clean and simple.

[2.7.25]

Step 3. Order summary

The order summary area is on the right side of the checkout page. I have added color so you can see the area filled with either an image or a color.

[2.7.26]

As I have said before, I recommend keeping this white and clean, but it is your choice. I have seen clients add a color, which does not detract from the checkout experience.

Step 4. Typography and colors

You can change the theme **typography** and **colors** to your brand options in this section.

[2.7.27]

Step 5. Customize more checkout settings

To change or customize more checkout settings, click on the link 'visit the admin'. This will open up the 'Settings' dashboard and the 'Checkout' options.

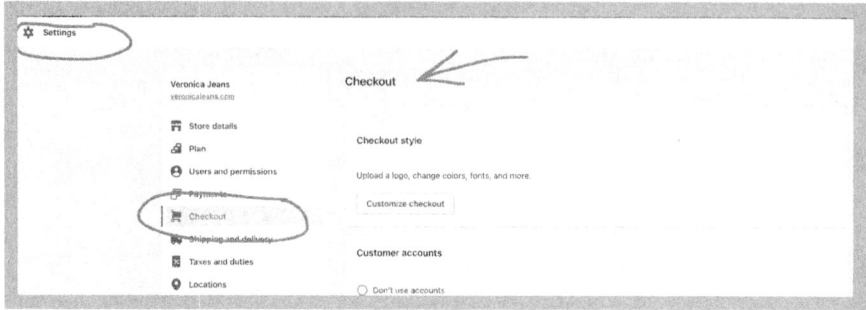

[2.7.28]

In this setting, you can add more details to your 'Checkout' page.

NOTE: *How to change and add more information is in my Shopify Made Easy Book 1 - Start Your Online Store.*

ECOMMERCE PAGES

Your homepage for your store is created in your 'Customize' editor.

The product pages and collection pages are automatically created in your Shopify store.

First, you need to add your products and collections to your store as shown in chapter 6 – Create Effective & Converting Product Pages and chapter 8 – Collections.

We will create the homepage in chapter 11 - Virtual Store Front after we have added your products and collections.

I will also show you how to optimize your pages in your 'Customize' editor.

RESOURCES:

Copy.ai

STORE INFORMATION PAGES

ChatGPT

WordTune

CHAPTER 5
STORYBOARD YOUR CUSTOMER JOURNEY

 "The customer journey doesn't start with a touchpoint. It starts with an idea." ~

CREATING a customer journey is very involved for a business, from visiting the website to customer service. For this exercise, we want to create a clear path for a visitor to become a customer in your store.

This chapter is not to be confused with creating your collections in Shopify, as shown in chapter Collections. This chapter is an exercise to create a clear picture of how and where your products will appear to your customers in your online store, leading to conversions and sales.

WHAT TO EXPECT IN THIS CHAPTER:

- What is a Storyboard?
- Why do you create a Storyboard?
- How can you optimize your customer's experience?
- Step-by-step Storyboarding

WHY DO YOU CREATE A STORYBOARD?

Wikipedia says: *"A storyboard is a graphic organizer that consists of illustrations or images displayed in sequence for pre-visualizing a motion picture, animation, motion graphic or interactive media sequence. In the form it is known today, the storyboarding process was developed at Walt Disney Productions during the early 1930s, after several years of similar processes being in use at Walt Disney and other animation studios."*

When you create a storyboard for your Shopify store, you create a customer experience that leads to sales. In essence, you make it easy for your customers to navigate your store as easily as possible. This means happy customers are spending lots of money!

Think of your customer experience as walking through a big-box department store. You have different departments, and each is separated into different sections, laid out with the customer in mind.

Once you have done a storyboard for your store, several benefits exist. You have an idea of what collections to create, what your navigation will look like, how your menus will function, what your tags are, and how to create an easy flow for adding more products.

This is how I want you to think about your online store. Two considerations for providing an excellent customer experience in your store:

1. You have a brief period to keep your prospective customer's attention.
2. Mobile shoppers are on the rise! 79% of consumers are shopping from their mobile devices, increasing yearly. Your store must be optimized for mobile shoppers.

HOW CAN YOU OPTIMIZE YOUR CUSTOMER'S EXPERIENCE?

You create the shortest path to your objective, quickly getting your customers to the right product or information.

The best practice is to get the customer from the first view to the product page as quickly as possible. Use only a maximum of 3 clicks/actions if you want customers to buy without getting frustrated.

Here is an example of a typical shopping path:

They see an ad on Facebook and land on a page in your online store. When they take action on this page, it takes them to a collection page (1st Click/Action). From the collection page, they choose a product (2nd Click/Action). Then they will add the product to the cart (3rd Click/Action).

> Pro Tip Check out at Amazon - how many actions do you need to take to get to the product? Then, please test it out to see what happens.

To enhance your customers' shopping experience, storyboarding helps you get a clear picture of your store.

When you create your central departments and different sections in Shopify, connecting your products to collections, navigation, and the homepage is accessible.

Setting up all the different aspects of your store can become confusing and frustrating if you don't do this first planning step. As a result, your customers will also be confused.

STEP-BY-STEP STORYBOARDING

Shopify identifies categories as collections. A collection is a bundle of products of the same type. Departments and sections are a **'collection'** in this exercise. It is a good idea to start thinking of your departments as 'collections' in your store as you lay out your storyboard.

Step 1. Create your storyboard

You start with a spreadsheet, document, or just a piece of paper. I like to use this next methodology - get some sticky notes in different colors and a large piece of paper. Add each department and type of product to the sticky notes. Now start brainstorming.

Step 2. Identify your products

Decide what **main and other collections** your store will have. You can have as many collections as you want, but there has to be a quick path to the product page for your customer.

I will use a kids' boutique as an example, but I will keep it simple:

1. Identify your main types of products: **Boys** and **Girls**.
2. You might have a secondary type of product: **Babies, Toddlers,** and **Tweens**.
3. In each of the **Babies, Toddlers,** and **Tweens** collections, you have different types of clothing - **Bottoms, Tops,** and **Outerwear**.

4. Breaking it down more, in the **Bottoms** section, you have **Shorts, Long Pants,** etc.

See how each collection has different levels of types of products. The following image shows you how I storyboarded the collections in a spreadsheet.

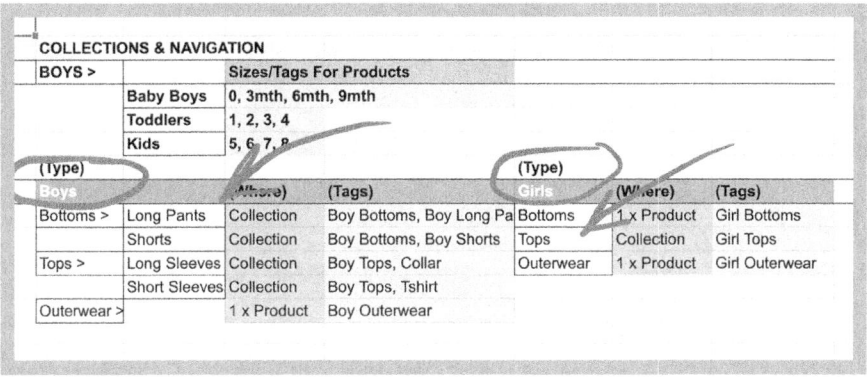

[2.1.2]

The following image is an example of a Shopify store - just the main collections in the top menu:

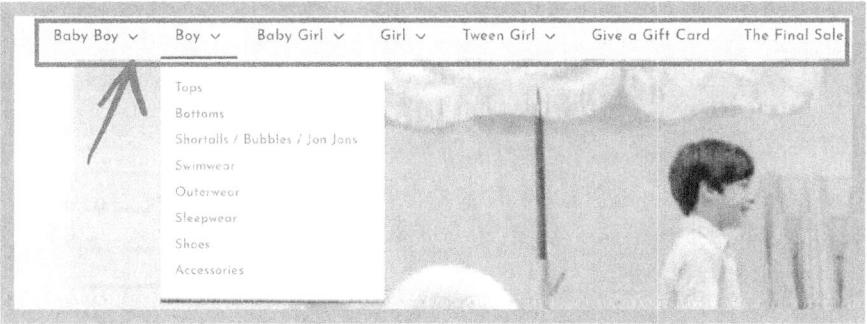

[2.1.3]

In the next image, you can see the different collections within the collection. So, you can add collections to your collections. This is part of your menu or part of your page.

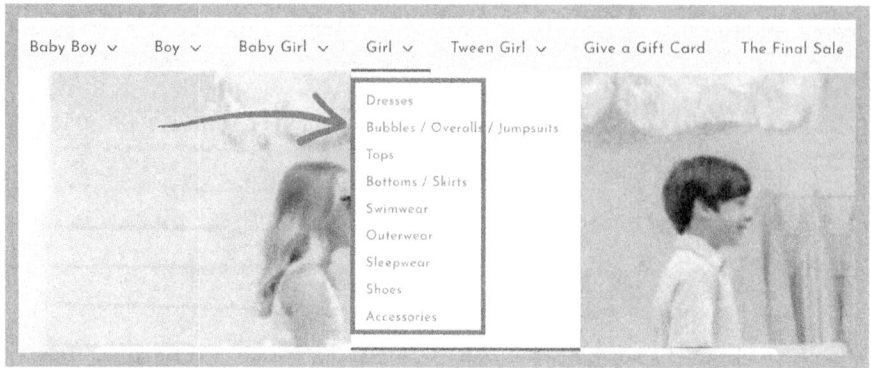

[2.1.4]

In the following image, you can see how brand collections are displayed on the homepage.

[2.1.5]

Creating your storyboard for your store this way is a great process to ensure your products end up in the correct collections.

If you do not have a lot of different products, here is an example of how to organize your primary collection, i.e., one collection as a 'Catalog'. We currently have only eight different types of products in this store. Therefore, we created a 'Catalog' collection to show all the different types of sculptures.

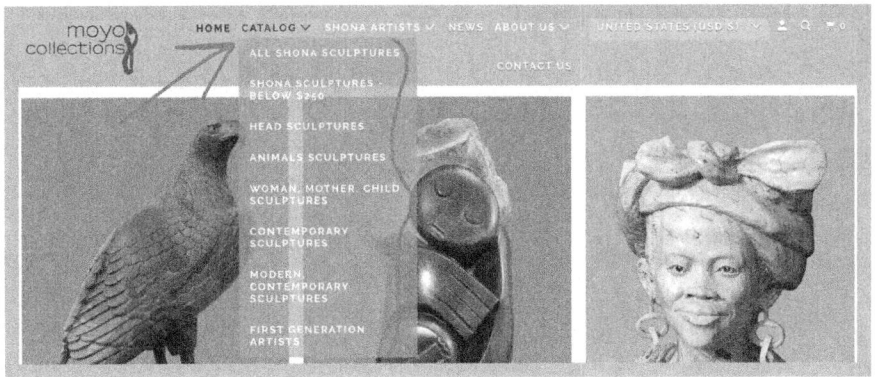

[2.1.6]

In a different example, there are only 3 products on KalahariGold.com. So it is much easier.

[2.1.7a]

Even if you only have a few products, you might plan to add more to your store. This is a great exercise to think of what you will add and when you plan to add more options in the future, how you will expand your business and add that to your goals and strategy.

Step 3. Define a main type for the products

When you create your storyboard, you can see the main type of products as 'Boys' and 'Girls'.

Decide what your main product will be your 'Type'. Then the rest of your products will be identified under the main 'Type'.

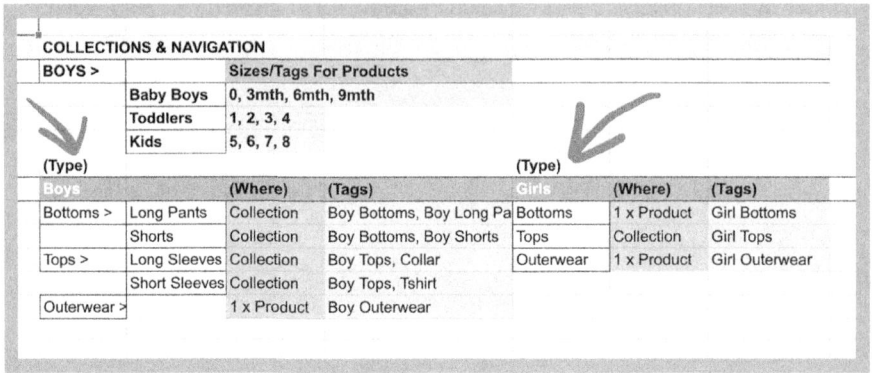

[2.1.7]

Here is another example of quite a few products in ParisianPure.com store.

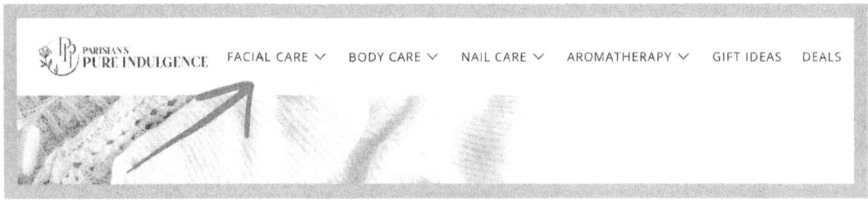

[2.1.7b]

Step 4. Add specific tags to products and collections

Tags are the secret ingredient for your store to make your life easier. Tags have different uses in your online store. They connect your products and collections, provide search capabilities in your store, and allow for keyword optimization, identifying customers and orders.

How can you use tags in your store:

- Connect products to collections automatically.

- Connect your customers to different groups in your store, i.e., Wholesale, Marketing, etc.
- Create tags in your blogs as categories.
- Add tags to your orders to filter them by a specific tag.

There are many more benefits to using tags in Shopify, but in this instance, we only want to use them to create a smooth integration.

Creating an overview of your products and adding your tags makes it much easier to identify the right product for the different collections in your store.

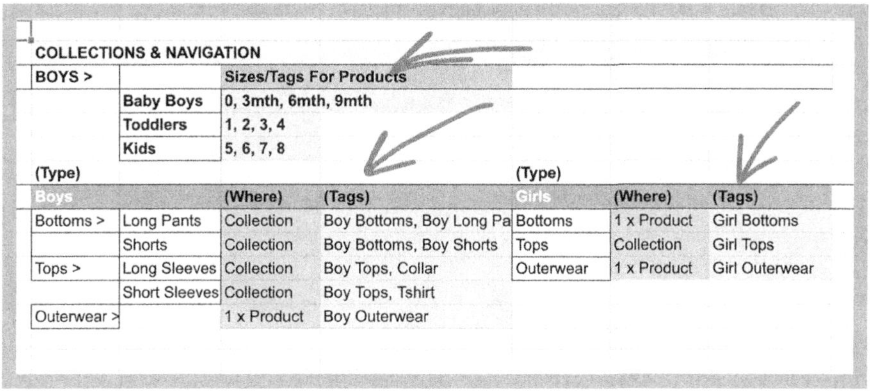

COLLECTIONS & NAVIGATION						
BOYS >		Sizes/Tags For Products				
	Baby Boys	0, 3mth, 6mth, 9mth				
	Toddlers	1, 2, 3, 4				
	Kids	5, 6, 7, 8				
(Type)				(Type)		
Boys		(Where)	(Tags)	Girls	(Where)	(Tags)
Bottoms >	Long Pants	Collection	Boy Bottoms, Boy Long Pa	Bottoms	1 x Product	Girl Bottoms
	Shorts	Collection	Boy Bottoms, Boy Shorts	Tops	Collection	Girl Tops
Tops >	Long Sleeves	Collection	Boy Tops, Collar	Outerwear	1 x Product	Girl Outerwear
	Short Sleeves	Collection	Boy Tops, Tshirt			
Outerwear >		1 x Product	Boy Outerwear			

[2.1.8]

The tag identifies the product for each collection. Therefore, if you want one product to be in different collections, your identifying tag name has to be different.

If you want the products to be added to the collection automatically, you will use the conditional collection option instead of a manual collection option on the collection page. As you can see in the following image, I added 'Boy Bottoms' as a tag in the 'Boys' collection. Now all the boy bottoms, whether long, short, or whatever material, will be added to this collection.

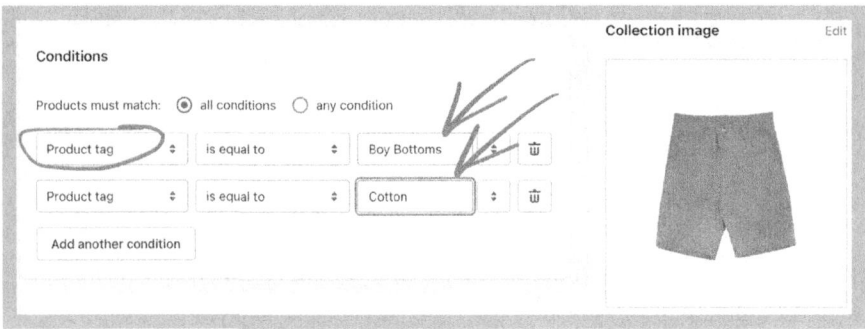

[2.1.9]

And if you want to create another collection of 'Cotton' within the 'Boy Bottoms' collection, both the tag 'Boy Bottoms' and 'Cotton' will be added to the collection condition. So now only boy bottoms made of cotton will be in this collection.

[2.1.10]

In the following image, you can see another condition in the collection to identify only 'Size 6' and 'Shoes'.

[2.1.11]

> Pro Tip Do not try to add so many tags to your product page that it becomes a mess. You can use the tags as a filter on the collection page, so the first rule is to capitalize, and the second rule is to think of how your customer will search for the product.

Step 5. Naming your collections

Think of descriptive keywords for each collection. Each of these sections will be part of your navigation in your store.

If you look at the collection 'Boys', you know your customers will want to find the different types of boys - 'Toddlers', 'Baby Boys', and 'Kids'. Then you have to identify each type of product, for instance, 'Bottoms'.

Instead of naming each collection 'Boy Bottom', Boy Baby Bottom, etc., which will look really odd in your menu, the menu will start with 'Boys', and then filter down to the types of clothing for boys.

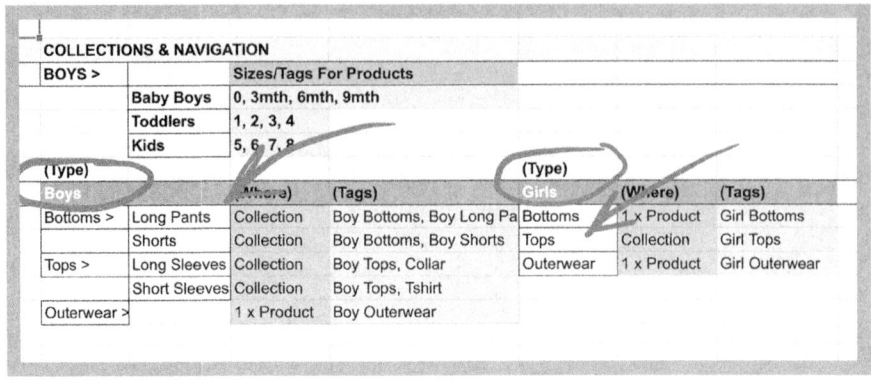

[2.1.2]

Our research started with the brand 'Gap Kids'. This is a great example of all the collections or categories under 'Boys'. Notice how short the menu titles are. Easily identifiable and to navigate.

[2.1.12]

As an example of a different product and store, in the following image, the menu at the top of the page is 'Flex Duct'.

[2.1.13]

On the collection page, it has a more descriptive title - 'Industrial Flex Duct'.

If I added 'Industrial Flex Duct' to the top menu, the menu would become very messy, take up too much space, and be hard to read.

The rule is - Keep it simple.

The title must be descriptive on the collection page to expand on the short menu title. Make it easy for customers to recognize exactly what they are looking for.

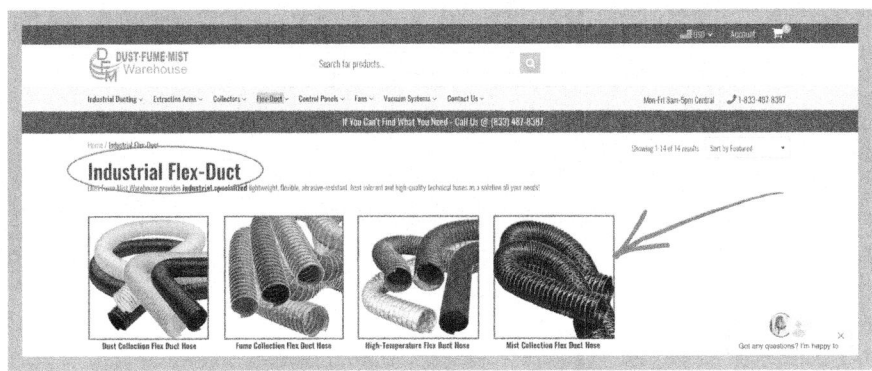

[2.1.14]

As you can see in image 2.1.14, I added a sub-collection to the collection page. We will cover the different types of collections in Chapter 4 – Collections?

> Pro Tip Search online stores that you like; they must be reasonably large or brand stores for ideas and examples. A smaller online store will not have the traffic, customers, or knowledge of what is successful.

Do not repeat the same title for another collection.

Each collection will represent a page in your Shopify store. Therefore, every page in your store must have a unique title.

Here are some quick reasons why:

1. It will confuse you when you create your navigation in your store later.
2. It will confuse your customers.
3. Google does not like pages with the same title.
4. If your customer searches, you want to ensure they will get the right page.

Step 6. Re-use your collections

When laying out your storyboard, you can add collections to different menus.

Once you have created a collection, you can re-use the collection in several different navigational areas in the menu. The reason to use the collection in different menus is that if the collection belongs to both 'Sports' and 'Equipment', you would add it to both.

It is all about your customer and getting them to the product they are looking for. For example, if your customer is specifically looking for hockey sticks in the 'Equipment' collection, they will find their product. But if they were looking for sticks in hockey or Lacrosse, they would find their product without hunting for it.

It makes sense for your visitors to find their products where they expect them.

STORYBOARD YOUR CUSTOMER JOURNEY

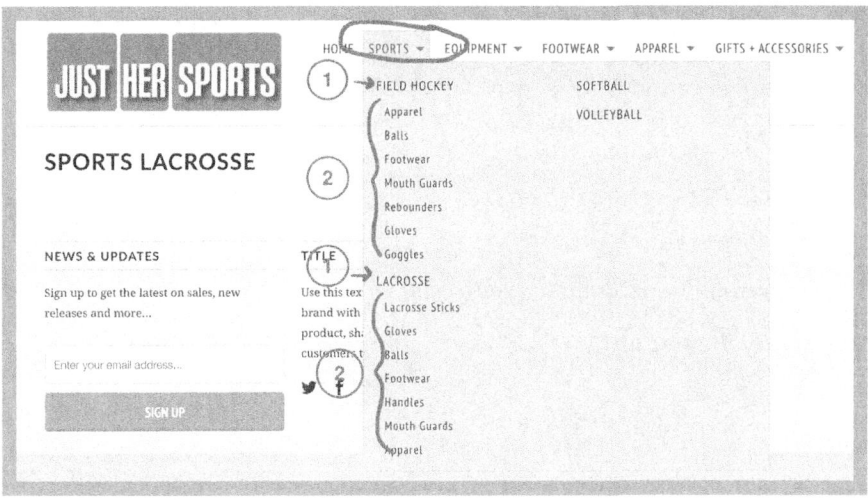

[2.1.15]

For example:

'Sports' is the primary collection.

1. Field Hockey and Lacrosse are sub-collections.
2. Within that sub-collection, for instance, you have all the Lacrosse and Hockey equipment, i.e., Lacrosse Sticks.

You can also see the Lacrosse Sticks and Gloves are added to another primary collection, 'Equipment'.

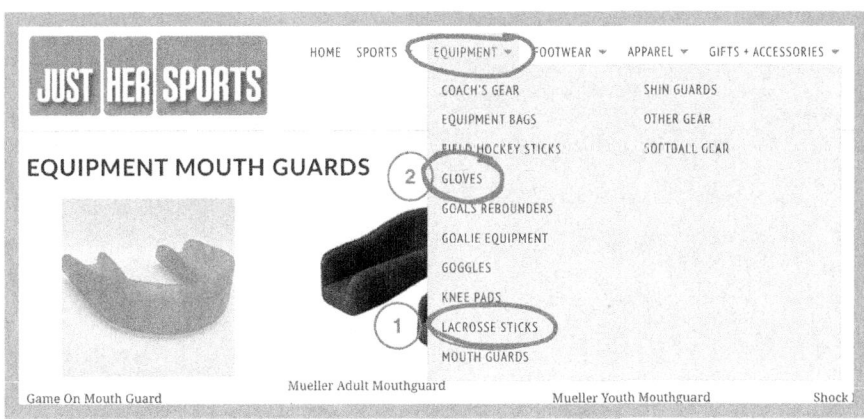

[2.1.16]

Now that you have your storyboard, you are ready to add your products and collections to your store.

RESOURCES

I have added a lot of tools for your store on my resources page on my website - www.veronicajeans.com.

https://veronicajeans.online/resources

Example of the spreadsheet that I use for storyboarding for my clients.

CHAPTER 6
CREATE EFFECTIVE & CONVERTING PRODUCT PAGES

 "Create products and offerings that sell themselves. It's not about what you know or what you sell. It's about how you position and package it." ~ Veronica Jeans

**WHERE TO FIND THIS IN SHOPIFY? PRODUCTS

MOST STORE OWNERS think the homepage is the most important part of an online store, but there is nothing more important than the **product page**. This is where your customer will make the decision to buy your products. They will actually trust and like your product enough to take out a credit card and give you all their personal information. That is a HUGE deal.

Creating products and offerings that naturally appeal to customers is truly crucial. Remember, it's not just about the knowledge you possess or the items you're selling. What truly makes a difference is the way you present and bundle your product. It's like gift wrapping - the better the presentation, the more intriguing the gift.

In this chapter, I will show you how to add all the information you need for a successful product page in your Shopify store, whether it is a physical or digital product.

This chapter will give you a more in-depth understanding of your information to help you create a great product page that can lead to better conversions.

WHAT TO EXPECT IN THIS CHAPTER:

- *9 Key Elements for an Effective Product Page:*
- *Types of Products in Shopify*
- *How to Upload Your Products to Your Shopify Store*
- *Prepare & Add Your Product Information*

The success of ANY page on your website is conversions which depend on several factors.

9 KEY ELEMENTS FOR AN EFFECTIVE PRODUCT PAGE

1. Tangible Photos or Video
2. Description & Details of Product
3. Strong 'Call to Action'
4. Social Proof
5. KLT (Know Like & Trust) Enhancers
6. Effective Persuasion
7. Product FAQ
8. Communication
9. Related products

Tangible Photos or Video

Create your photos and videos as real, vibrant, and sharp as possible.

Description & Details of Product

- Enough information for the prospective customer to make a decision to buy.
- Details of product - Specifications like height, weight, and maybe what is included when you buy the product, like batteries, a cord, etc.
- Write great content - You want to write the content as if you are speaking to your ideal customer. You want them to feel as if you are speaking to them specifically.
- Don't be salesy - try not to sell all the time but instead, have a conversation.
- Show your personality and style. Be authentic and personal. Add some personal details or behind-the-scenes information.

CREATE EFFECTIVE & CONVERTING PRODUCT PAGES

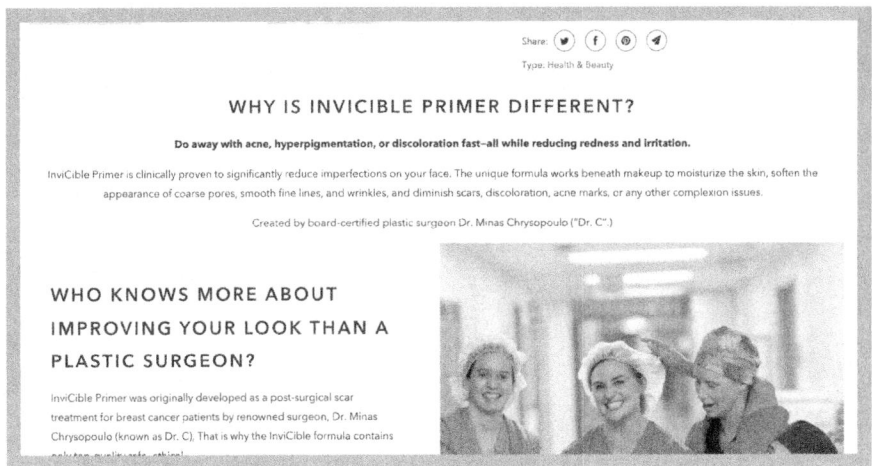

[3.5.1]

Strong 'Call to Action'

One example is the 'Add to Cart' button on your product page. The button has to be above the fold, meaning when you look at your product page in a browser, you must see the 'Add to Cart' button. Make sure the color of the button stands out.

- If you want to add more CTA (Call to Action) buttons on your product page, the buttons or icons should be below the ATC (Add to Cart) button. Don't overwhelm visitors with too many choices and CTAs on one screen.
- Examples are: Share icons, Wish List, and Learn More. You want your customers to buy on your product page without being distracted by other actions.

[3.5.14]

Social Proof

- Reviews or Customer Testimonials on the product page. Nobody wants to be the pioneer; most people want to know others have trusted you.
- Customer pictures or videos are even better.
- Experts advice
- Celebrities that use your products
- Certification

[3.5.9]

KLT (Know Like & Trust) Enhancers

- Trust icons
- Secure Shopping
- Images of credit cards your store can process are a visual signal that you use customer-trust payment choices.

CREATE EFFECTIVE & CONVERTING PRODUCT PAGES

- Amazing Guarantee and Satisfaction
- Telephone number for customer support
- Made in America (or your own country)
- SSL - Secure Sockets Layer
- Security badges like McAffee or GeoTrust.

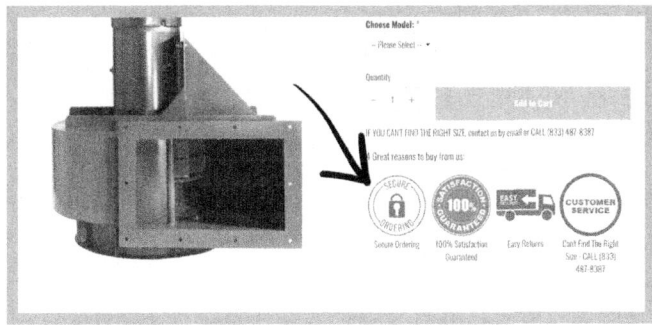

[3.5.8]

Effective Persuasion

Here are some more ideas:

- Limited inventory or time to buy
- Special Discount
- Free Shipping
- BOGO - Buy One Get One Free
- Buy 2nd item at a reduced price

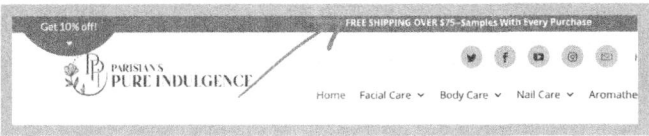

[3.5.12]

Product FAQ

Find out your customer's objections to buying your product and answer their questions.

- Customer Support availability

- Refunds
- Returns
- Shipping - How long will shipping take
- Delivery - When will they get their products
- The longevity of the product
- Treatment of the product

> **FREQUENTLY ASKED QUESTIONS**
>
> **HOW LONG WILL IT TAKE TO PROCESS AN ORDER?**
>
> Generally, orders are processed within 1-3 business days and are shipped fast. This time may vary during any Holiday or at various times during the year, such as Graduation time, etc. Mother's Day and Christmas orders usually take more time to process.
>
> **Need it fast?** We offer a RUSH OPTION on many of our products. RUSH OPTION generally will move your order up in our queue and may save a significant amount of time, especially around Holiday's. Depending on the number of orders with the rush option, your order will be placed in the front of our standard orders that were placed without the rush option. Depending on the time of year and your situation, we may be able to help expedite the order further. Please remember that this option simply moves your order up in our queue and does not impact the delivery times of shipping. It's important to choose the shipping/delivery options that best suit your needs.

[3.5.11]

Check out the FAQs here: https://themissingpiecepuzzle.com.

FAQs are a great way to get seriously good SEO (Search Engine Optimization) stars from Google because you are adding great information for your customers all in one place.

Communication

Clear communication on your product page is essential. Use a Shopify Inbox that consists of a Shopify Online Store, Facebook Page, Facebook Shop, Facebook Messenger, Apple Business Chat, and Instagram (soon to be implemented).

CREATE EFFECTIVE & CONVERTING PRODUCT PAGES

[3.5.7]

I also have a contact form at the bottom of my page, which scrolls with the page from my email provider - Omnisend. This contact form has better conversion than a signup newsletter box at the bottom.

Related products

'You will also like' products are products that compliment your main product, as shown in the following image with HerTribeAthletics.com

[3.5.16]

Let's get you ready to get your products on Shopify.

TYPES OF PRODUCTS IN SHOPIFY

Your products may be Physical Products or Digital Products.

- **Physical Products** - Physical products are merchandise, apparel, and other goods you sell and ship to customers. You'll need to add at least one shipping option to your store if you sell physical products.

- **Digital Products** - A digital product is any product that exists in an intangible format as a file. They can be streamed, downloaded, and translated into physical mediums (such as an e-book or template physical copy), but their primary point of interaction is through technology.

Getting your product details ready before you upload them will certainly make adding content to your product pages a breeze. But, it's also necessary to know how to prepare your products so you can either upload your products manually or in bulk with a spreadsheet.

HOW TO UPLOAD YOUR PRODUCTS TO YOUR SHOPIFY STORE

The quantity of products can significantly influence this decision. If you're dealing with just a handful of products, manually adding them to your store will be your best bet.

However, if you have a large number of products to upload, manually adding them may not be practical. Instead, you'll likely find it more efficient to upload your products in bulk using a spreadsheet.

So I will explain the upload methods before showing you how to prepare and add your products to Shopify.

There are 3 ways to add or upload products to Shopify:

- Upload Products Manually
- Upload Products in Bulk
- Upload Digital Products (Manually or in Bulk)

Once you pop into the 'Product' section the first time, you can add your products manually or in bulk.

CREATE EFFECTIVE & CONVERTING PRODUCT PAGES

[2.3.1a]

When you have a product in Shopify, the 'Add your product' button is on the right side of the dashboard, including an 'Import' link which is the way to upload your products in bulk.

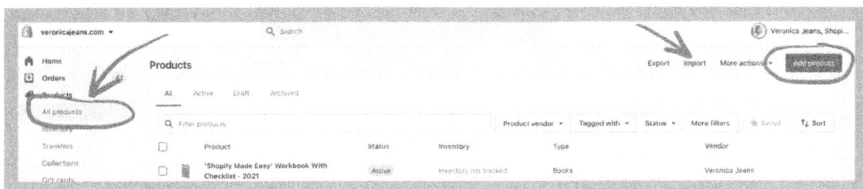

[2.3.1b]

Upload Products Manually

**Where to find this in Shopify? Products

If you have a few products, it is probably easier to manually create a product page for each product.

Upload Products in Bulk

**Where to find this in Shopify? Products or APPS (get an app)

There is a quick way to upload your products if you have a large number of products and content to add to your Shopify store.

Step 1. Get a sample import CSV file from Shopify

If you want to bulk upload your products, you need a Shopify template (spreadsheet) or one from the App - Matrixify: Bulk Import Export Update to be able to upload your products to Shopify.

Your product CSV can't exceed 15MB. If you get an error when trying to upload a new CSV file, check to make sure it doesn't exceed the size limit. I have found this is about 10,000 line items. (Your products and options/variants each count as a line item – and each should have a different SKU number).

To get a product upload spreadsheet for your products on Shopify, you need to download a Shopify Product template or your App template.

Step 2. Import your products to Shopify

Click Products on the right-hand side of your screen in your dashboard, and you will see the screen below. Now click on 'Import.'

[2.3.1c]

Step 3. Download the sample CSV template

Download the sample CSV template. This is a spreadsheet example to which you can add your information.

Once you have added all your information, start importing your CSV file to your store.

CREATE EFFECTIVE & CONVERTING PRODUCT PAGES

[2.3.1d]

> Pro Tip: I recommend using an App - Matrixify - to upload bulk imports.

I use it in all my Shopify client stores, making it so easy to upload your products, pages, blogs, collections, etc. I recommend this app for Bulk Import Export Update because Shopify only uploads 10,000 products at a time.

I have used this app for years, and it is excellent. It has really cut my time of bulk imports of products. It does so much more than just product upload as well. Great investment. And you can use it as short or as long as you like.

Support is superb!

Upload Digital Products

Adding your digital products is the same as for physical products. The exceptions from the information of the physical products are:

- No Weights.

- No Location
- No Customs information

You will also need to add an App because the files must be stored and delivered to the customer by order notification unless you have another method of delivering the digital product link to your customers.

**Where to find this in Shopify? Products or APPS (get an app)

With Shopify's free 'Digital Downloads app', you can upload digital files like videos, songs, and graphic art as products in your store. When customers purchase the digital product, they receive a link with their order email to download the file they have purchased.

PREPARE & ADD YOUR PRODUCT INFORMATION

Each product page dashboard will consist of different sections. Each section has different choices depending on what you sell and how you ship your products to your customer.

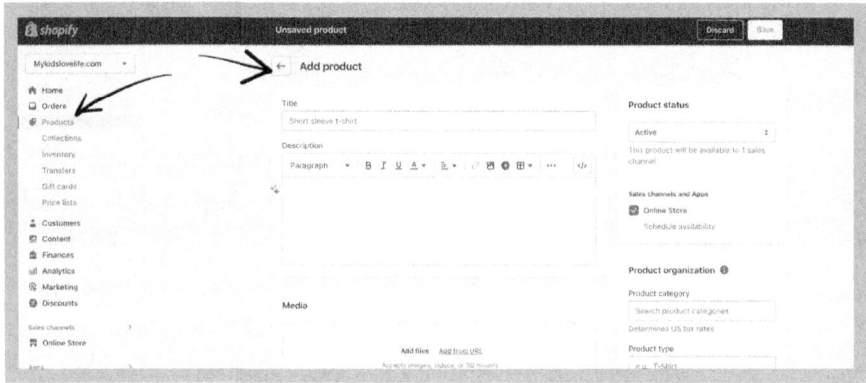

[2.3.2a]

I will show you step-by-step actions for adding information to your product page and some tips. And each section might have tools to help you.

In each section, I will also indicate if there is a difference between a physical and a digital product in each setup section.

CREATE EFFECTIVE & CONVERTING PRODUCT PAGES

If you upload the product information in bulk with a spreadsheet (CSV or Excel), you will still follow the steps to create your information but add it to the spreadsheet under the correct heading.

NOTE: *Shopify DOES NOT save your information automatically. You must hit the save button to save information to your Shopify store.*

A notice will pop up to alert you to your unsaved information.

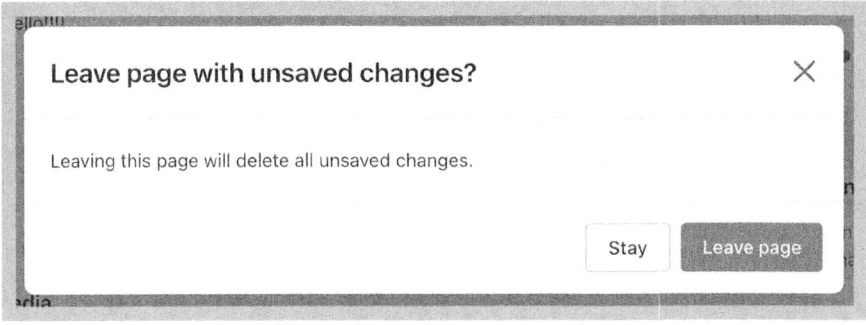

[2.3.0]

The following list shows all the sections in the 'Product' dashboard where you will be adding your product information and details:

- Product: Title & Description
- Media: Images, Videos & 3D Models
- Pricing: Prices, Compare at Price & Cost Per Item, Charge Tax
- Inventory: SKU, Barcode, Track, Quantity, Location
- Shipping: Weight & Customs
- Variants: Options
- Status
- Publishing
- Insights
- Product Organization
- Online Store: Theme Template
- Search Engine Listing

PRODUCT: TITLE & DESCRIPTION

There is one important fact about naming your product. Your title is the single most effective copy you use to reach customers.

Your title has to reflect the ONE problem the product is solving. Consider how customers search for your products! They search for products according to their needs.

How to write a good title for your products:

- Watch your title length - Short, catchy titles resonate better than long, detailed titles
- Give every product a unique title - Don't confuse the customer with the same titles.
- Use a primary keyword in your title - The keyword is how your customer will search for your product.
- Put important primary keywords first.
- Write for your customers - Don't get too fancy with your titles or nobody will find your product. Plain and simple is best.
- Don't overdo SEO (Search Engine Optimization) keywords. Do not add too many main keywords in the title because your customer needs to resonate with the product title to buy it.

Step 1. Add your product title

The product page editor's first text box is your 'Title' for the product. Use capitalized words unless your whole store text format is non-capitalized words.

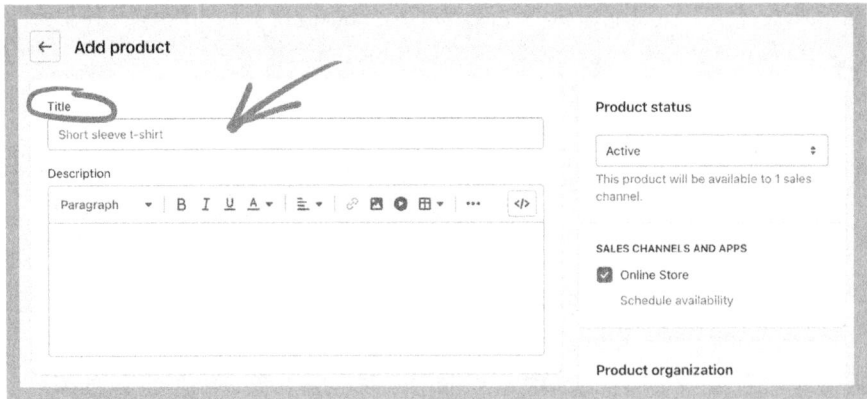

[2.3.2]

CREATE EFFECTIVE & CONVERTING PRODUCT PAGES

> 💡 Pro Tip: You cannot format the title on the product page. The only way to change the title size, color, etc., will be in the CSS code. (Cascading Style Sheet). The title will always be in an H1 format, which should never be changed.

In the next image, the title is repeated at the top of the dashboard.

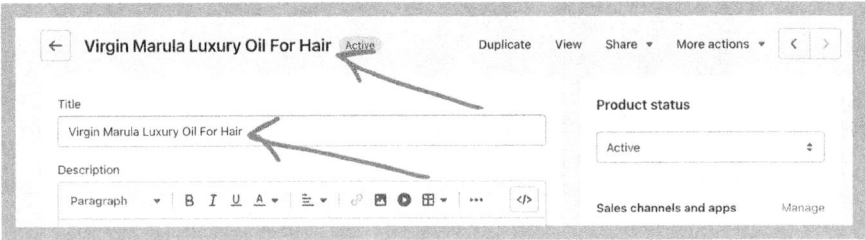

[2.3.3]

The title is shown on the product's dashboard, and each product is easily identified.

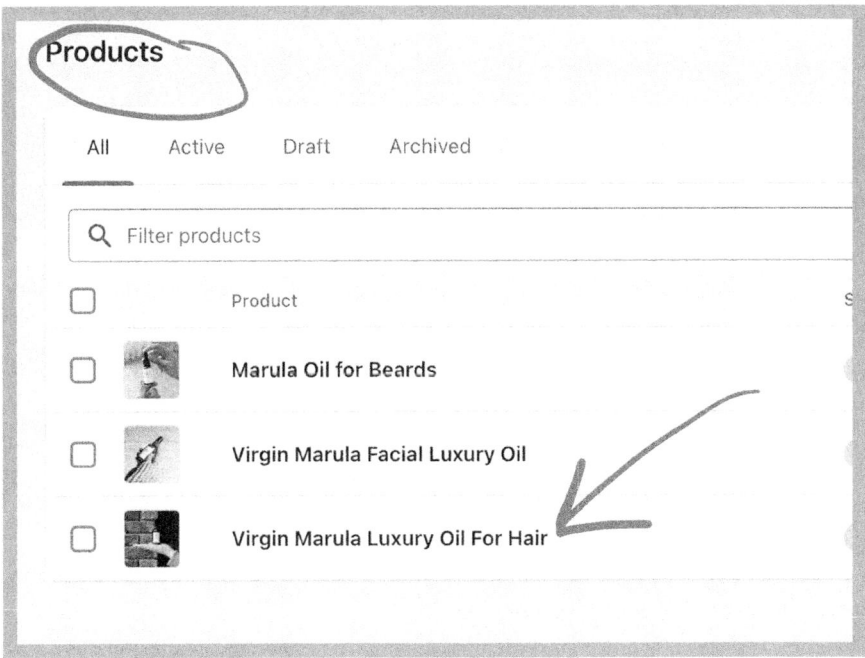

[2.3.4]

The Missing Piece Puzzle has added her keyword to her title - 'Cheap Custom Puzzle Gift' and 'Puzzle for Children'. Donna optimized all her titles with keyword phrases. She competes with big puzzle brands and still gets onto page #1 on Google.

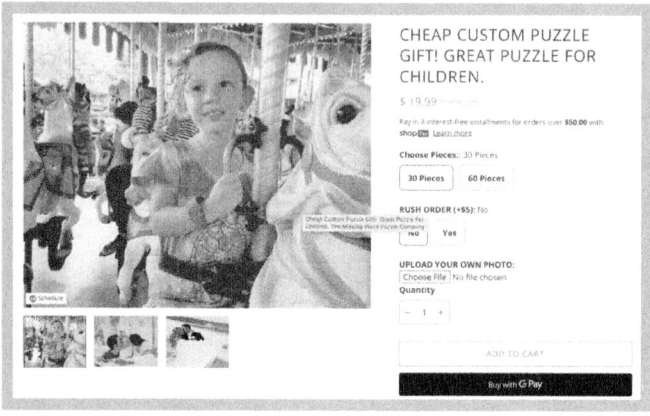

[2.3.5]

Step 2. Research your product description

Here are some ideas for writing descriptions:

- Your descriptions should promise value. You increase conversions if the descriptions reference the customer and talk 'to' the customer.
- As you know, reaching your customers deeply and emotionally is the key to successful conversions.
- The content of your product description should convince potential customers that it will improve their lives in obvious, measurable ways.
- Thousands of similar or identical products are available on the internet. If someone searches for your product, you want to appear on the search engine's search results page.
- Sell a lifestyle, not just a product! This is a very sophisticated form of marketing.
- Shopify Blogs have excellent tips on how to write descriptions that sell successfully.

7 Easy Rules to Write Product Descriptions:

1. Know Your Target Audience
2. Focus on Product Benefits
3. Tell Mini Stories
4. Use Natural Language and Tone
5. Use Power Words That Sell
6. Make It Easy to Scan
7. Optimize for Search Engines

Step 3. Outline features and benefits

Before you begin writing your product descriptions, outline the features and benefits of your product. Think about how the product either increases pleasure or reduces a pain point. Your solution solves your customer's problem.

What is the difference between **Features** and **Benefits** for your products?

Features: For every feature you list, figure out how this will directly benefit the buyer. A feature is something that your product has or is. The dimensions, specifications, ingredients, material, etc., of your product. Features work on a factual level rather than on an emotional level. Try to answer - 'what is the Product'?

Benefits: Benefits are the outcomes or results that users will (hopefully) experience by using your product or service – the very reason why a prospective customer becomes an actual customer. It is the result your customer gets! Question for the benefits of your product: As a result of owning this product, you will get/have/obtain/become/feel/be perceived/look/etc.

Remember: *Nobody wants to buy what you sell. The reality is that your buyer only wants to know WIIFM (what's in it for me).*

> Pro Tip 1: Do some research and ask your audience (friends and family if you don't have an audience yet) to see if they understand what you are selling and why they should buy your products.

> Pro Tip 2: Check to see what other brands are doing. When you are writing the benefits and features of your product, be prepared to change how you think about describing your product.

Now that you have your description of the benefits and features of your product worked out and added to your product page, you need to ensure that your description immediately impacts a potential buyer.

Step 4. Add a short description on the product page

Your product page must have a short, punchy description and a long, detailed information description. Both are necessary to reach impulse buyers and to reach your buyer who needs more information.

Where and how you place your descriptions on your product page is important.

Your short description should remind buyers of the advantages at every turn. When a potential customer is on the verge of completing a purchase from your business, they are heavily influenced by how quickly they can receive gratification for parting with their hard-earned money.

Our brains love instant gratification, and we buy faster when we're reminded that we can solve our problems quickly. When consumers know they will be rewarded immediately, they will be anxious to buy your products.

Here is a FORMULA for your short descriptions of your product.

- 1st Paragraph: Ownership benefit-focused (ALL CAPS)
- 2nd Paragraph: 1 - 2 sentences about the product benefits.

A short benefit description should be above the 'Buy' button, but not so much that it pushes the 'Add to Cart' button too far down your page when viewed in a browser.

In the following images, you can see the benefits of the product are above the fold and very noticeable by using different font formats.

CREATE EFFECTIVE & CONVERTING PRODUCT PAGES

[2.3.6]

Add the short description on the product information page. You have a few seconds to draw people's attention to your description. Once you add your description in the editor, you can add different font sizes, bold, bullet points, etc.

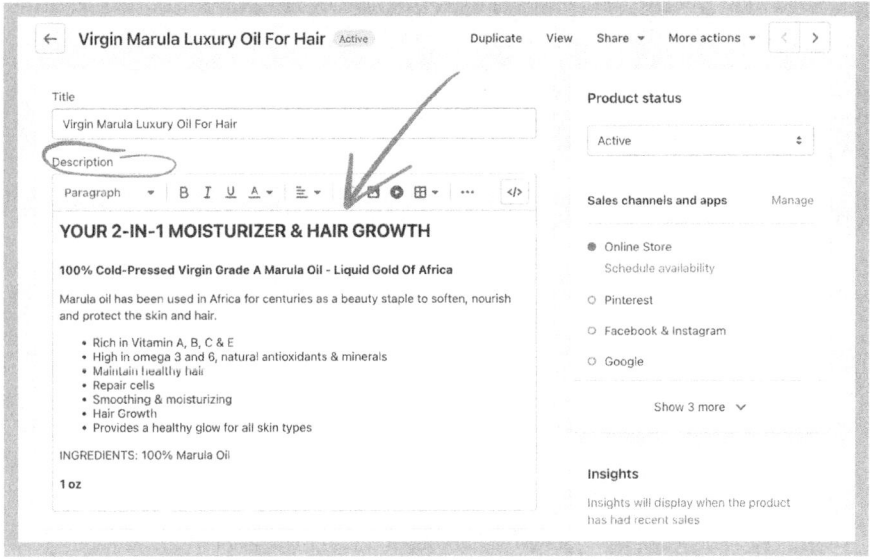

[2.3.10]

The following image shows you the view in the browser.

[2.3.11]

Step 5. Add a longer description

Every product page should be treated as a sales page. Sometimes a buyer must be persuaded to buy your product because they are not convinced whether the product will solve their problem.

The long description is below the 'Buy Button' or 'Add to Cart' button.

Go to 'Themes' in your dashboard and to 'Customize'.

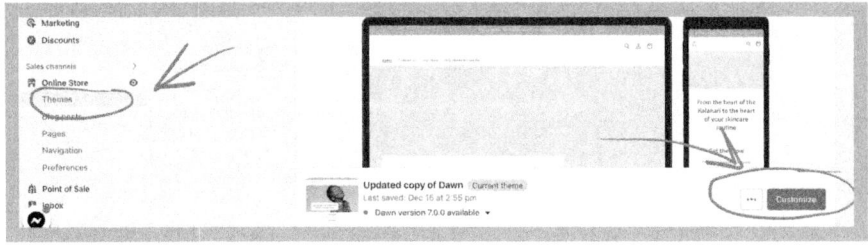

[2.3.12]

Once in the 'Customize' editor, click on the dropdown menu at the top and navigate to the default product template.

CREATE EFFECTIVE & CONVERTING PRODUCT PAGES

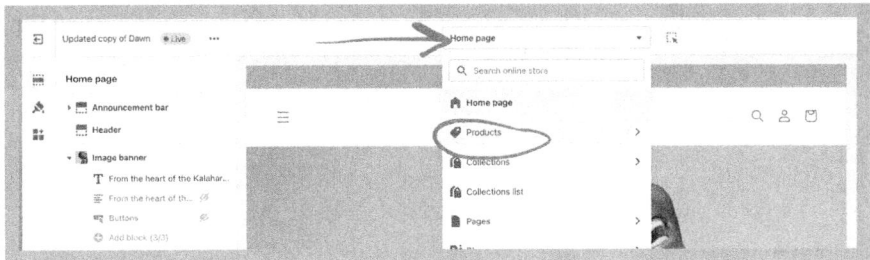

[2.3.13]

Now you can add different sections to your page with more information about your product. Type of information to add:

- Extended benefits
- Ingredients
- Why buy from us information
- Icons for specialties - Made locally, Organic, Women-owned, Natural Ingredients, Safe
- Shipping information - you can just add some information with a link to your shipping page.
- About the Artist or story of the owner

The following images show the 'Why Buy from Us' discussion, icons, and the artist. So here I added a text with an image section and the text and image on the right-side panel with a link to the product.

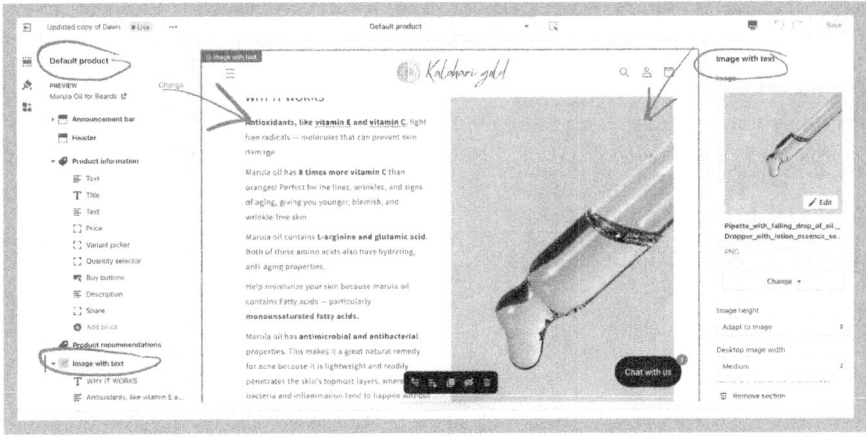

[2.3.9]

In the next image, I created a page with the image because the logo sizes in the theme are too small. Normally I would add icons with the logo section.

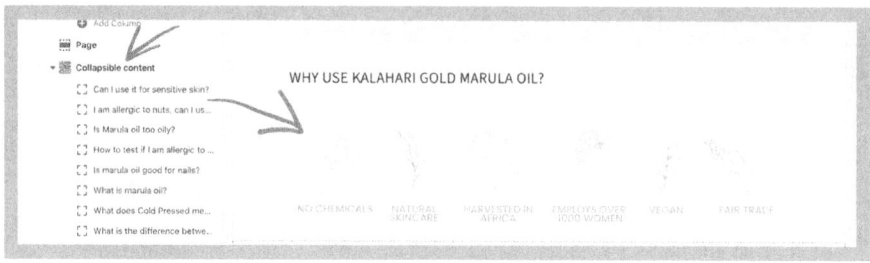

[2.3.7]

We added the icons to the Maggi Cummings Art website. If you don't have a lot of normal icons, think about how you can make them special.

[2.3.14]

And then we added the artist and her story - short, and this links to the an 'About' page. I don't ever recommend linking to another page from the product page, but it also depends on the product and customer. In this instance the product is art and the artist is highlighted. If the customer was an impulsive buyer, they would already fall in love with the product and buy it.

The information about the artist is for customers that like to do research and have as much information before they purchase their products.

So this product page caters to both types of buyers.

CREATE EFFECTIVE & CONVERTING PRODUCT PAGES

[2.3.15]

NOTE: *Do not use the vendor's or manufacturer's descriptions!*

If you are reselling products or have a manufacturer who drop ships, don't be lazy and add their descriptions. Add your own spin and voice to the descriptions. Otherwise, you have the same description as many other stores, and you will not get any benefits from customers searching for the products.

This latest advice from Google is helpful in that it clarifies Google's position, which I quickly paraphrase below:

There is no duplicate content penalty. Google rewards UNIQUENESS and the signals associated with ADDED VALUE. A good rule of thumb is; Do NOT expect to rank high in Google with content found on other, more trusted sites, and don't expect to rank at all if all you are using is automatically generated pages with no 'value add.'

Google wants to reward RICH, UNIQUE, RELEVANT, INFORMATIVE, and REMARKABLE content in its organic listings – and it has raised the quality bar over the last few years.

TOOLS:

Headline Analyzer - *This free tool will analyze your headline to determine the Emotional Marketing Value (EMV) score. Your headline will be analyzed and scored based on the total number of EMV words it has about the total number of words it contains. This will determine the EMV score of your headline. Try it out: Https://headlineanalyzer.com*

Copy.ai is an excellent extension for the content creation of your pages and information, product descriptions, titles, benefits and features, and much more. https://veronicajeans.online/copy-ai

Grammarly, which you can add as an extension of Chrome. Grammarly will help you with grammar and spelling mistakes.

https://grammarly.com

Wordtune - Chrome extension is a great tool to use to improve your sentences and change your content from your vendors and manufacturers. https://www.wordtune.com/

MEDIA: IMAGES, VIDEOS & 3D MODELS

You can add images, videos, and 3D models for your product media.

Your images and videos sell the product. But also crucial, the image has to be relevant to the product.

Your customers cannot smell, taste, or feel your product - make your product images visually appealing.

You need to give your customer enough visual information to persuade them to buy it.

Important ideas for your product media:

- Show off the product - center your product in the middle of the image.
- Demonstrate ownership benefit.
- Load FAST (image optimized) - make sure the resolution is low.
- Have at least 6 - 8 'looks', which means different types of images, as mentioned before.
- Build a desire for the products - create lifestyle photos.
- Showcase product videos/gifs to show the use of the product or how the product is made.

For instance, here are two types of products and the relevant images you can create for each type:

Examples of images for a purse or handbag:

- Front of the purse
- Back of the purse
- Bottom of the purse
- Inside view of the purse
- Show a variety of items you can fit in the purse.
- And a close-up of special tags or stitching.
- Lifestyle image of somebody wearing the purse.

Here are some images to show you some ideas:

[2.3.16]

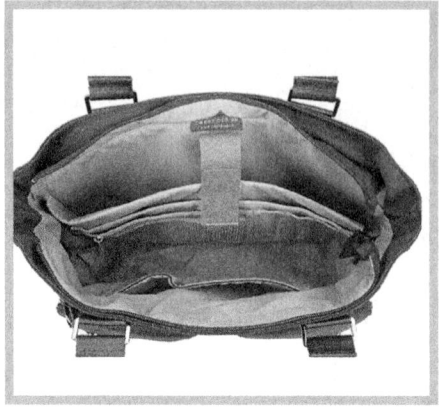

[2.3.17]

Now for a skincare product, you can show a variety of images as well:

- The container, whether it is a tube, bottle, or tub.
- The products' texture: the lipstick's glitter, the powder's finest texture, and the cream's glossy surface.
- Front shot with a lid next to the package
- Lifestyle image with featured ingredients.
- Lifestyle image with a hand holding the product.

Here are some images to show image ideas:

[2.3.18]

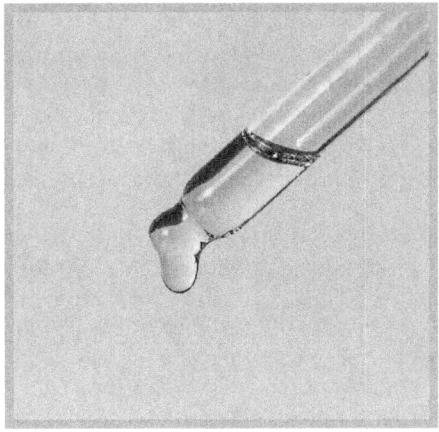

[2.3.19]

Ideas for videos for your product page:

Do you know that a video on your product page will seriously boost the possibility of selling your product by 85%?

- What type of videos?
- Unboxing videos[
- Product tour videos
- "How to" videos
- Lifestyle videos
- Production line videos
- Customer testimonial videos

Image file requirements:

Your image files reside (are hosted) on Shopify servers. There is a limit to the hosting of videos and 3D models on Shopify,

Basic Shopify	Shopify	Advanced Shopify	Shopify Plus
250	1000	5000	Contact Shopify Plus Support

[2.3.33]

Image size up to 4472 x 4472 px, or 20 MB. Shopify recommends 2048 x 2048 px for product images, but you always have to consider how large files can impede your website's download speed for customers.

I use an image size of 1000 x 1000 pixels so that the images are also ready to upload to Amazon. It is a required size for Amazon images.

Keep your DPI (Dots Per Inch) as small as possible. As shown, instead, have your images low in KB (kilobits) and not high in MB (Megabits).

In the following image, you can see the image has a low resolution (144), and the KB is only 60. This is great for a website.

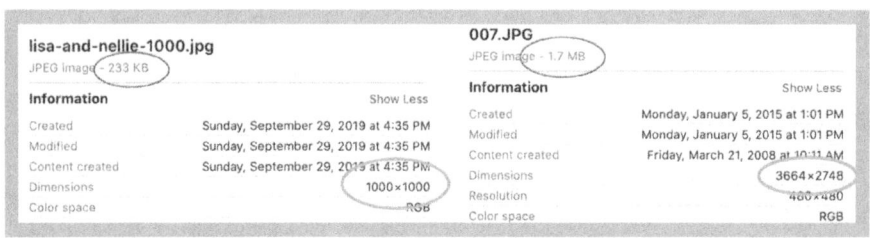

[2.3.31]

Video file requirements:

Video length: Up to 10 minutes

Video size: Up to 1 GB

Video resolution: Up to 4K (4096 x 2160 px)

Video file type: .mp4 or .mov

Video files can be uploaded to the product page, but if they are over the limit, store them on YouTube or Vimeo, then you can embed the code in your product page. I will show you how to do this in the following steps.

3D models file requirements:

File size: Up to 500 MB

File type: GLB, USDZ

But if you upload a 3D model file and it is larger than 15MB, then Shopify will optimize the file. Which means the file will be reduced in size. This can change the output of the file.

CREATE EFFECTIVE & CONVERTING PRODUCT PAGES

> Pro Tip: It is a good habit not to upload any type of media that is too large. Keep to 1 x 3D model or video on your product page.

NOTE: *I will show you how to upload each type of media in separate options in each step.*

> Pro Tip: Make sure your theme supports 3D models and videos. If you're using one of these themes and your 3D models and videos don't display, you may need to update to a newer version.

Step 1. Turn your photos into images

What is the difference between Photos and Images?

There are a lot of interpretations, but for our purposes - Photos are what you create with a camera or mobile phone and images that are optimized photos for your store.

Optimized images will download from your website quickly and are marvelous for your online store speed. Customers will love you for it. If the image resolution is too high

Shopify will not optimize your photos except resizes, crop, or rotate. You will have to use a tool to change your photos to images.

Let me show you how to do that.

Canva.com is a great tool to use for this, and there are a few other ones as well.

Create a custom size for your images (1000 px X1000 px for square), but you can also use rectangular image size. Keep the sizes the same for all your product images.

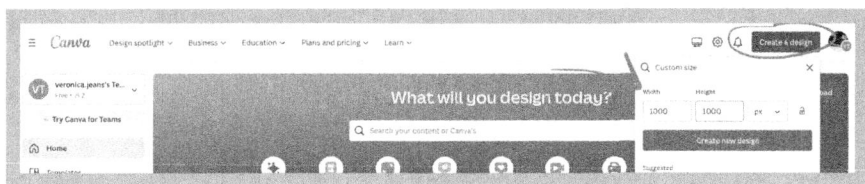

[2.3.20]

Upload your photo to your project, and you can add more images, take out the background, lighten or darken, add a background color, etc.

In the following image, you can see I create a 667px X 1000px product image, and all the products have a background color.

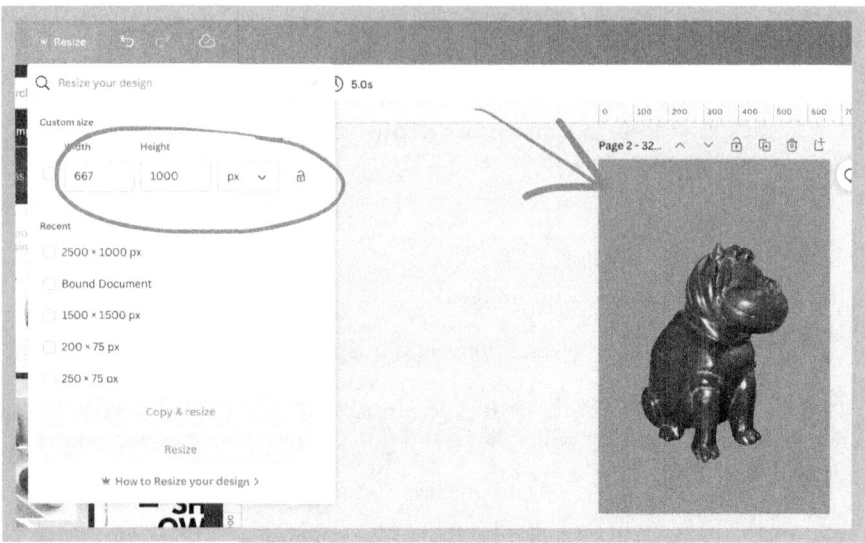

[2.3.21]

See the products on Moyocollections.com. Then download as a JPEG or PNG, compress your files (images), and download to your computer.

CREATE EFFECTIVE & CONVERTING PRODUCT PAGES

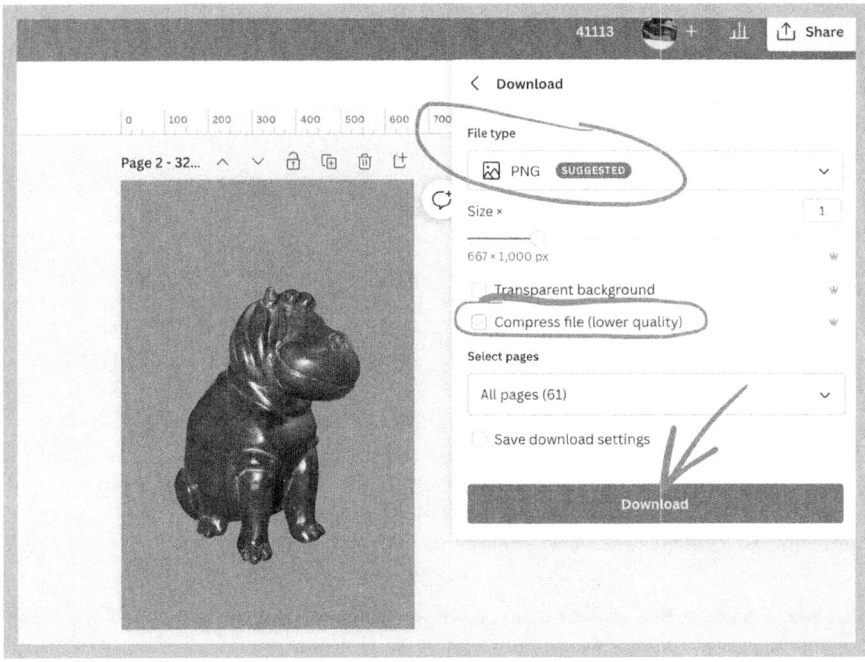

[2.3.22]

You can change all your photos for all your products in one fell swoop.

> ⚡ Pro Tip: Please do not upload your photos straight from your camera or phone to your website. Photos tend to be huge files; if it is over 2 megabytes of pixels, Shopify will not upload the image. But imagine all these big files or photos on your store and how long it will take to view your store by visitors. Visitors don't tend to hang around if they have to wait for images to download.

Step 2. Add media to your product page

The first media item for each product is known as the featured or main media item. The main media item is shown on the collection page, the cart page, the checkout page, and your home page.

Step 3. Upload Images & Videos

Drag and drop your images and videos or upload them from your computer to your product page.

[2.3.23]

Or you can also add your images and videos from a URL (website address). The image URL address will be changed to your Shopify file.

You must park videos on YouTube or Vimeo, and then copy the URL address to your Shopify store.

[2.3.25]

Put your cursor on the six dots, wait for your cursor to change to a hand, and hold your mouse button down to drag the images and sort them to different positions while on your product information page. The larger image on the left is the first image you will see on your product page.

CREATE EFFECTIVE & CONVERTING PRODUCT PAGES

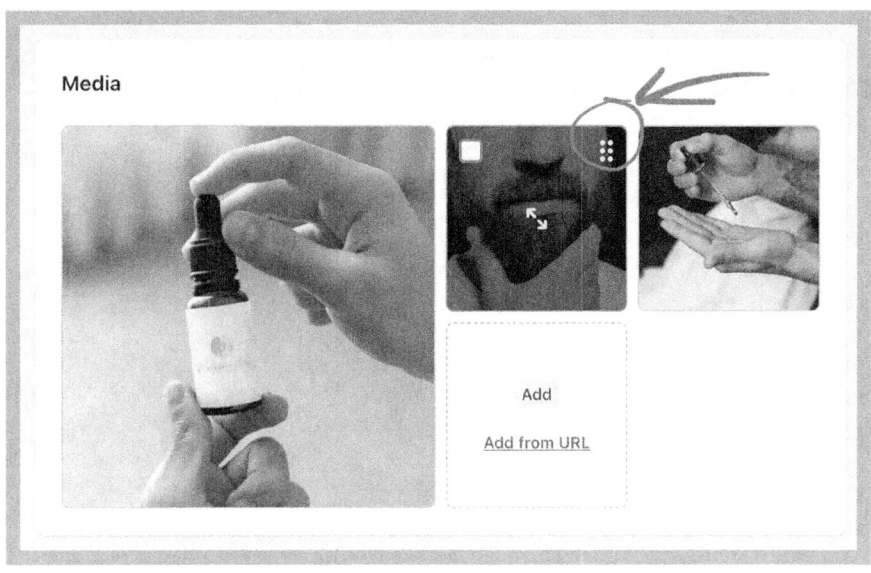

[2.3.24]

Step 4. Edit Images

You can edit your images in Shopify - it is a bit limited to resizing or changing the shape (crop) and rotation, but it is a fast way to improve your images if you have not done so before you upload them to Shopify. Click on the image, and your image editor will pop up. Now you can edit your image - see icons at the bottom left of the screen. Resize your images - if your images are too large, this is a great way to size them smaller, for instance, from 2500px to 1000px.

[2.3.28]

Draw on your images. Different colors are available.

[2.3.27]

Change the size of your images- crop or rotate.

CREATE EFFECTIVE & CONVERTING PRODUCT PAGES

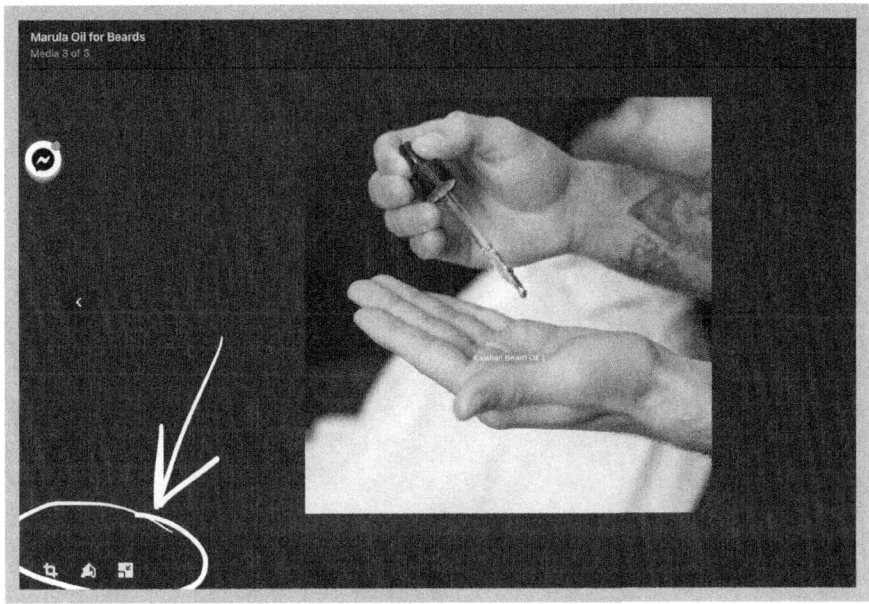

[2.3.30]

> 💡 Pro Tip: Don't try to make your image a larger size from a small image. The quality of your image will degenerate and look pixelated or unclear. If you only have one image and it is smaller than recommended, you may be able to have it professionally enlarged with photo software.

Step 5 - Delete Images

Check the image you want to delete and click on the 'Delete file' link.

[2.3.29]

Step 6. Edit Videos

You can change the thumbnail image for your video in the image editor. There are no other editing options for videos.

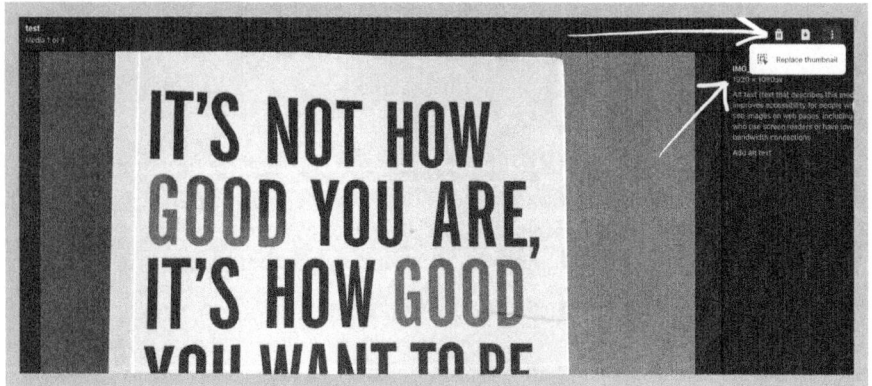

[2.3.34]

Upload a 1920px X 1080px size thumbnail image for your video so it fits in the video screen.

Step 7. Add alt text for your images

Known also as alt tags and alt descriptions, alt text appears on a webpage in place of an image if the image fails to load. By including a description for your image, screen-reading tools can describe images to visually impaired readers, and search engines can better crawl and rank your website.

Here is a great way to add a keyword to your page. Do not keyword stuff.

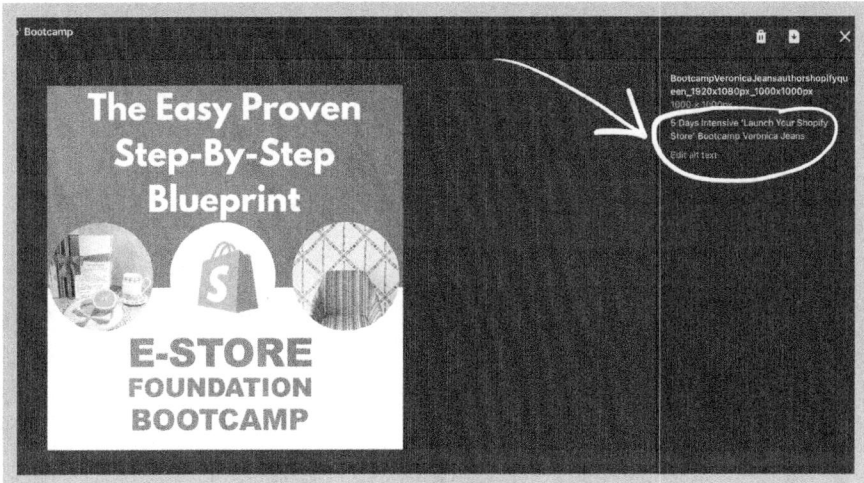

[2.3.26]

Step 8. Protect Your Images - Watermark

If you want to protect your images, you can use a Shopify App to add a watermark or add it manually. This protects you to a certain extent from image piracy.

Step 9. Add more media to the product page

As I have mentioned before, adding more information to your product page can increase conversions. Go to 'Themes' in your dashboard and to 'Customize'.

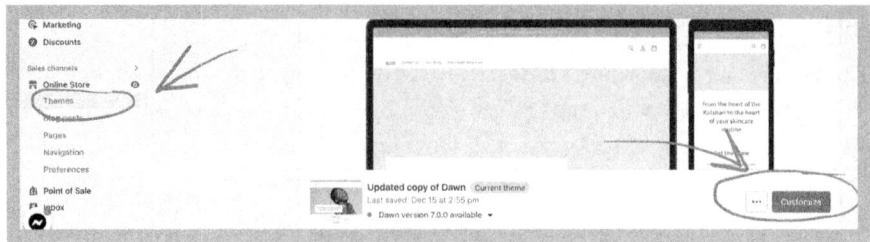

[2.3.12]

Once in the 'Customize' editor, click on the dropdown menu at the top and navigate to the default product template.

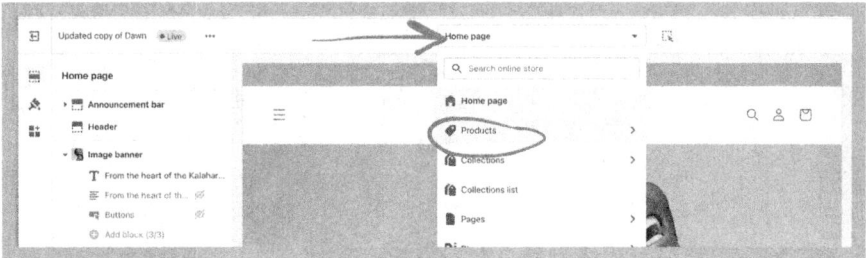

[2.3.13]

On the right sidebar, add a video section. On the left sidebar, add the URL of the video on YouTube, Vimeo, Wave. video, or any other video hosting platform.

[2.3.32]

CREATE EFFECTIVE & CONVERTING PRODUCT PAGES

Don't forget to add your video thumbnail.

TOOLS:

Image & video editors:

- Canva.com
- Wave.video
- Lumen5.com

PRICING: PRICES, COMPARE AT PRICES & COST PER ITEM, CHARGE TAX

This is probably the most important part of your business. If you don't price your products correctly, you could lose money without even realizing it.

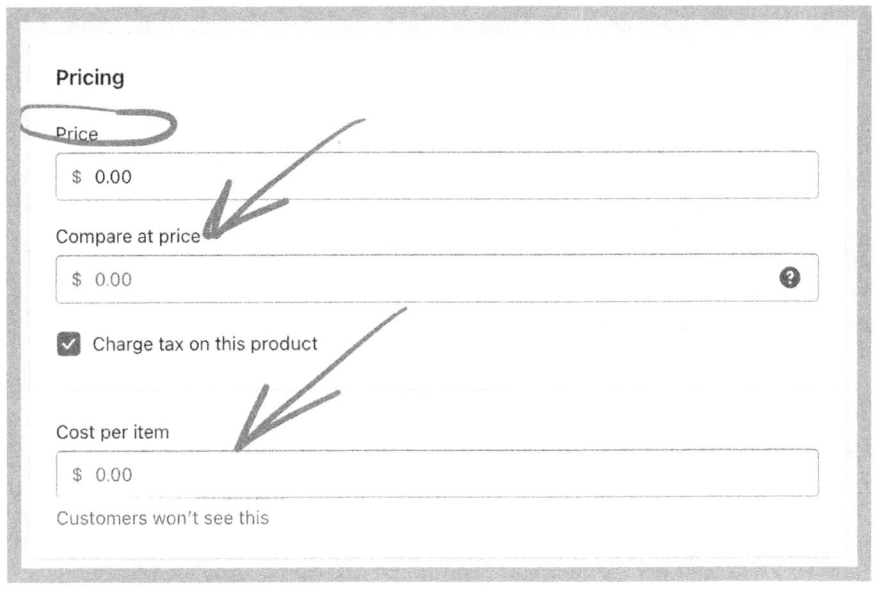

[2.3.36]

Step 1. Add the price of your product

Price: Add your product price.

Compare at price: If you want to offer products on sale, add your original price in this section and the sales price in the 'Price' section.

Step 2. Add the cost price of your product

Cost per item: Your costs must include all your fixed costs (monthly costs) and variable cost (cost per product). This is a great tool to see your profit margins in 'Analytics' and 'Reports'.

Step 3. Charge tax on this product

Charge tax on this product: Check this box if you are charging tax on the product.

You can collect the most accurate sales tax rates in Shopify with precise, address-based calculations and product categorization.

The city, state, region, and country tax codes are automatically added to your store 'Settings' in 'Taxes and duties' when you add your business address.

Not every state or country charges sales tax on all products or even the same tax on different products.

Some products are taxed differently, so you might have to separate your products for tax purposes which can be correctly allocated in 'Settings' and 'Taxes and duties'.

Some products might be taxed differently by state or country.

What types of products are taxed? It depends if the product is physical or digital and the laws in the state in the USA or your country.

For instance, the information for digital products on the Comptroller.texas.gov website: *"**Texas law applies sales tax to digital goods if the items would be taxable if delivered in physical form.** Digital products, such as photographs and music are tangible personal property as defined in Section 151.009 of the Texas Tax Code."*

If you are shipping from a different location than where your business is registered, you have to register taxes in both states. For example, the business is located in Texas, and the shipping location is in Missouri.

> **Pro Tip:** Check if you must pay taxes on digital products in your state or country. You will find this on the state or country's tax website. Research any tax implications for your products if you do not know what it is. Work with your tax professional to figure out the best category.

Quick Lesson about Prices, Costs, and Profits

Here is a quick example of what you should be thinking about:

- **Fixed Costs:** These are expenditures you have every month, e.g., Shopify store, hosting, rent, electricity, equipment rentals, software, marketing, etc.
- **Variable Costs:** Costs for each product which is different for each product you sell. These might include shipping, labor, materials, packaging, etc. The following fees are also part of your Variable Costs for your products.
- Merchant Cost: The merchant fees you pay for selling your products.
- Affiliate Cost: The people who help you sell your products.

A little BONUS - I have added a link to a Breakeven Analysis (BEA) spreadsheet for you to determine your product prices and costs.

There is also a price widget on my website once you sign up for in my resources page.

How to Use the Break-Even Analysis

Add all your costs/numbers to the yellow and orange cells. Add the price of your product to the bright green cell.

In the top row are your Variable costs per product, your Profit margin, and how many units you must sell to break even.

Fixed Costs	Average Price	Variable Costs	Profit Margin	Break-Even Units	
$72.28	$39.99	$18.71	$21.28	3.40	
	(Price of Product)	12		(How Many Items)	
Fixed Costs	Amount/Monthly	Add Yearly Cost	Variable Costs	Per Unit Amount	
Storage	$0.00		Base Price of Item	$12.75	Merchant %
Insurance (mthly)	$0.00		Merchant Cost	$1.46	2.90%
Accountant/Bookkeeper	$0.00	$0.00	Transaction Cost		$0.30
Merchants	$0.00		Marketing Materials	$0.20	
Hosting - web & blog	$0.60	$19.99			
Online Software	$30.48				
			Shipping Paperwork	$0.50	
			(Label & Invoice)		
Ink & Paper for Printer			Shipping Materials	$0.50	
Bank Costs	$15.00		(Box, tishue, etc)		
Shipping Software	$0.00		Labor - fixed /hr		
Marketing Budget	$25.00				Affiliate %
Staff/etc	$0.00		Affiliate Comission		10.00%
Cost of Company	$0.60	$20.00			
(registration/etc)					
Domains	$0.60	$20.00	VAT/GST	$3.30	8%
Total	$72.28		Total	$18.71	

[2.3.37]

INVENTORY: SKU, BARCODE, TRACK & QUANTITY, LOCATION

This is the section that handles your inventory and shipping.

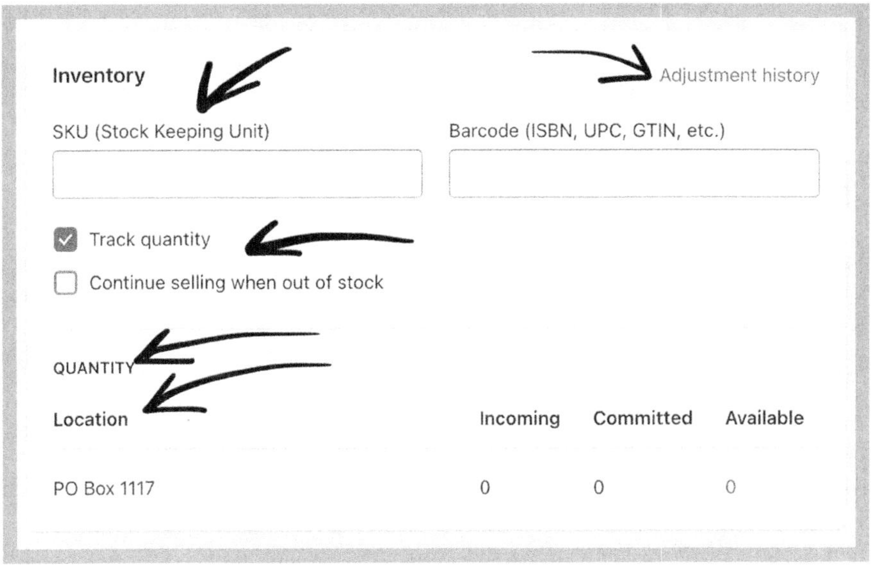

CREATE EFFECTIVE & CONVERTING PRODUCT PAGES

[2.3.38]

Step 1. SKU = Stock Keeping Unit

This is **your** product tracking number for your inventory.

It is good practice to create your own internal SKU numbers for the identification of your products in your orders.

In the following image, Moyo Collections identifies all their sculptures by a unique number. So that is why we added them as a SKU.

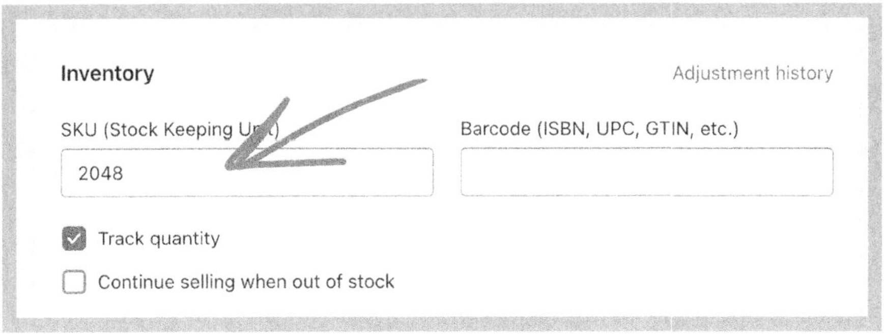

[2.3.39]

In my Shopify store, I have added my ASIN number for Amazon, and my ISBN for any other stores where I sell my books. My Amazon orders are processed and printed by Amazon, so I do not have to use the ASIN number in my orders in Shopify. But when I get an order on my website, I sometimes process the order manually with Amazon, and I need to know my ASIN number for my own tracking.

Inventory

Inventory will be stocked at

Multiple locations	⇕

SKU (Stock Keeping Unit)	Barcode (ISBN, UPC, GTIN, etc.)
0B095G5K2QW-1	978-1-7377760-2-4

☐ Track quantity

QUANTITY Edit locations

Location Available

1900 SHIPYARD DR Not tracked

[2.3.40]

Step 2. Barcode (ISBN, UPC, etc.)

A barcode is an identification number for your manufacturer or vendor.

If you are drop-shipping your products from a manufacturer or vendor, it will be easier to use their product identification number to identify their products in the orders.

This is also the place to add your product identifier number for Amazon if you connect your Shopify store to Amazon.

If you sell your products on Amazon, you will need a product identifier number.

CREATE EFFECTIVE & CONVERTING PRODUCT PAGES

AMAZON says: *"For most categories, you are required to use a product identifier to create new product pages and listings. The specific GTIN (Global Trade Item Number) required for product page creation and matching varies by category. The following are the most commonly used GTINs in the Amazon catalog:*

Universal Product Code (UPC)

International Standard Book Number (ISBN)

European Article Number (EAN)

Japanese Article Number (JAN)

The requirements of each category, including exceptions and exemptions where available, are summarized in the table on the Overview of category UPC requirements page."

Once you create an Amazon Seller account, you will get all the information you need to create your product identifier number.

In - Shopify Made Easy - Grow Your Shopify Store Book 3 - I do an in-depth chapter about the Amazon sales channel. (https://veronicajeans.online/book3)

Step 3. Track Quantity

If you have any products, you can track your quantities. Most of the time, there is no tracking for digital products because it is not necessary to keep an inventory.

Although my books are physical, I don't track them because I do not keep inventory - they are printed on demand. I can track how many books I have sold with my reports in my Shopify store.

Inventory	
Inventory will be stocked at	
Multiple locations	
SKU (Stock Keeping Unit)	Barcode (ISBN, UPC, GTIN, etc.)
0B095G5K2QW-1	978-1-7377760-2-4

☐ Track quantity

QUANTITY	Edit locations
Location	Available
1900 SHIPYARD DR	Not tracked

[2.3.40]

If you are selling hand-crafted products, you might not need to track your quantities unless you created an inventory to sell. It is a good idea to track your quantities to determine when you need more ingredients.

Once you check the 'Track Quantity' box, another option will appear - the 'Continue selling when out of stock' check box.

You can then choose to 'Continue selling when out of stock' - so your customers can still buy even if your inventory is at '0'. Which means that the 'Buy' or 'Add to Cart' button is still visible even if you do not have any inventory.

Here are two examples of when you will utilize this option:

- If you only want to create products that are out of stock only when you get an order.
- If you sell one-of-a-kind items and you want to give your customers an option to order a similar item.

If you want to track your inventory, check the box in this section!

CREATE EFFECTIVE & CONVERTING PRODUCT PAGES

There is an alternative. If you have a paid Shopify theme, for example, Out of The Sandbox, then instead of 'Sold Out' on your product page if you don't have the 'Continue selling when out of stock' checked. it allows your buyer to be notified when the product is available.

This is a good option if you are hand-making your product and the products will not be available immediately.

Activate this option in 'Themes' and 'Customize'. At the top of the page, go to the dropdown and navigate to the 'Product default' template. You will see the 'Back in stock request form' on the right sidebar in the 'Theme settings' - 'Product Grid'.

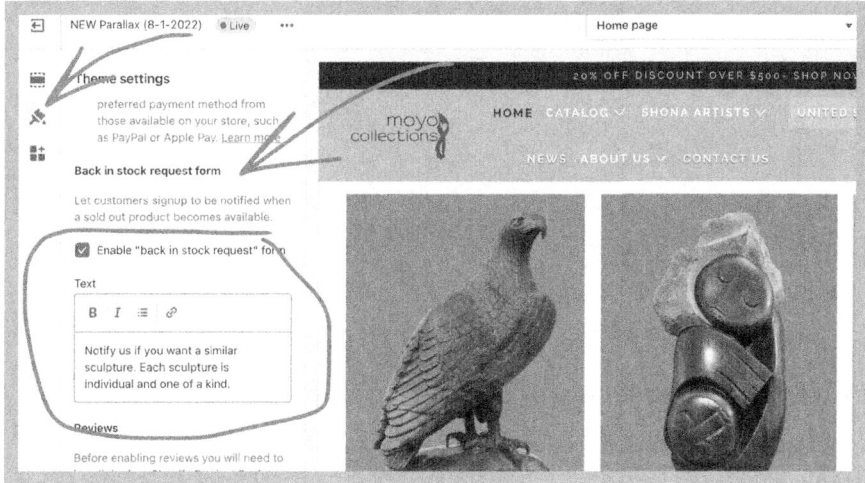

[2.3.41]

This is what it looks like on the page. The customer gives their email to send them a notification. In the following product page, we gave customers an option to order a similar sculpture from the artist.

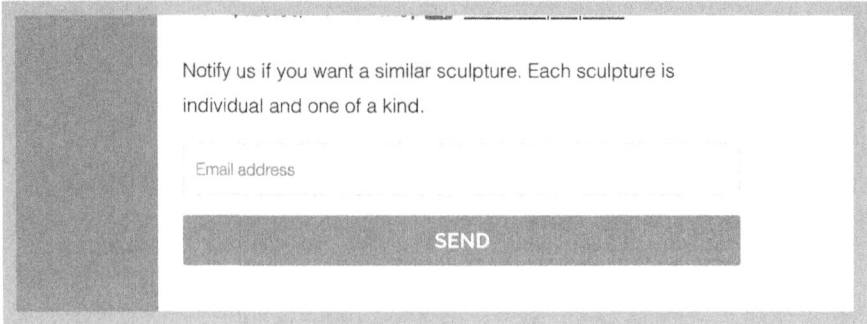

[2.3.42]

For the form to appear, your product must meet these requirements under the "Inventory" section of the product management page:

1. The product must be active and available in the online store sales channel.
2. Have the "Shopify tracks this product's inventory" inventory policy selected.
3. Have a stock level of 0 or lower. This means products have been purchased, and the inventory goes below 0.

Step 4. Quantity & Location

This section is only available if you have physical products to ship.

Now you can add your available quantities of products for each product per location.

If you have different locations, you can choose which location the product will ship from and see how much inventory is available from that location.

CREATE EFFECTIVE & CONVERTING PRODUCT PAGES

Inventory

Inventory will be stocked at

| Multiple locations | ⇕ |

SKU (Stock Keeping Unit)

`0B095G5K2QW-1`

Barcode (ISBN, UPC, GTIN, etc.)

`978-1-7377760-2-4`

☐ Track quantity

QUANTITY

Location   Edit locations

                 Available

1900 SHIPYARD DR   Not tracked

[2.3.40a]

You can add a different location and change the quantities from the 'location'. In this example, the business is located in Texas, and the shipping location is in Missouri.

QUANTITY

Location	Incoming	Committed	Available
Katie	0	0	1,785

[2.3.43]

If you have a second location added in 'Settings' - 'Locations', then you can actually change the locations where the products are shipped from in the product information page.

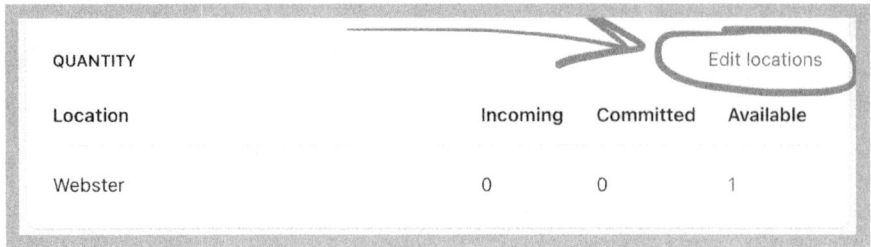

[2.3.44]

Once you click on 'Edit locations', another window opens, and you can change the locations. Check the box of the new location and save.

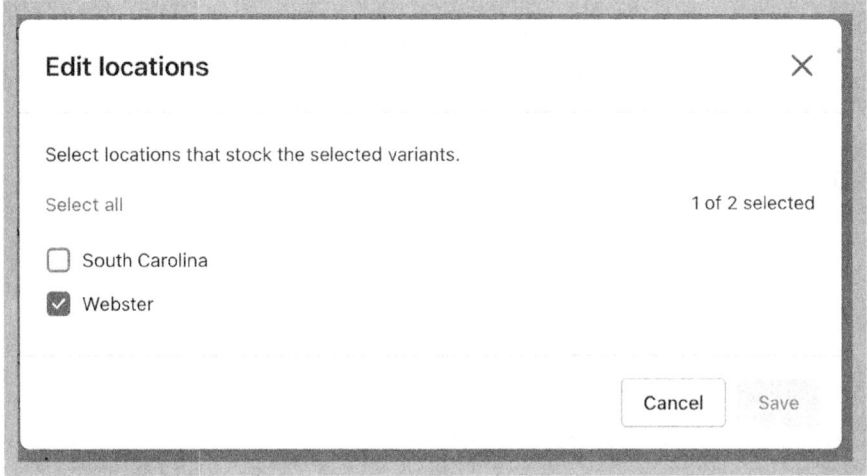

[2.3.45]

SHIPPING: WEIGHT & CUSTOMS

If you are drop shipping, your manufacturer or vendor will provide you with the correct weight information.

If they are integrated with Shopify, the data is automatically added to the products.

If you make your own products, buy a kitchen scale, and weigh your own products. If your products are large, use a fish scale—one of those hook scales.

CREATE EFFECTIVE & CONVERTING PRODUCT PAGES

The reason not to use your personal weight scale is that you need to have a very accurate weight to charge your customer the correct shipping cost.

> Pro Tip: Do not include the weight of your packaging in the product weight. Only add the weight of the product. The weight of your product and the package weight and dimensions will be automatically added together to calculate the shipping costs.

The main reason to be accurate with your product weight is your fierce pricing competition. You don't want to lose your customers because your shipping costs are too high. **This is one of the main reasons for 'abandoned cart' actions!**

I covered free shipping and how to set up free shipping in my first book in the **Shopify Made Easy - Start Your Online Store - Book 1. (https://veronicajeans.online/book1)**

Step 1. Determine what type of product: Physical or Digital products

A **physical product** is a default option. Check the box 'Digital product or service' if you sell **digital products.**

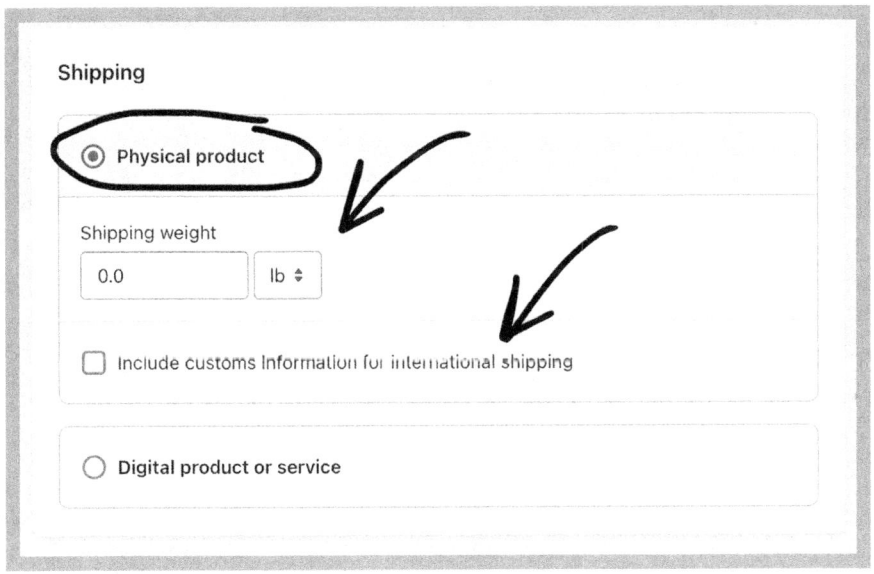

[2.3.46]

If you check the box '**Digital product**' option, the weight information will disappear. You only need to add weights for physical products.

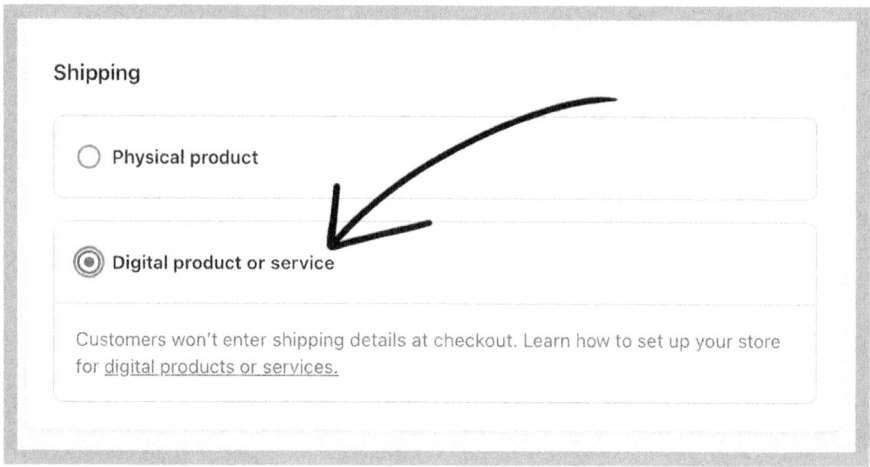

[2.3.46a]

Step 2. Weight of product

Add the physical product's weight in the either imperial or metric depending on your country.

If you want your automatic shipping functionality to work, you need to add the weight of your products on the product page.

[2.3.47]

Step 3. Origin of product

Check the box **'Include customs information for international shipping'** if you are selling to international customers. Customs authorities use this information to calculate shipping duties internationally as shown on printed customs forms.

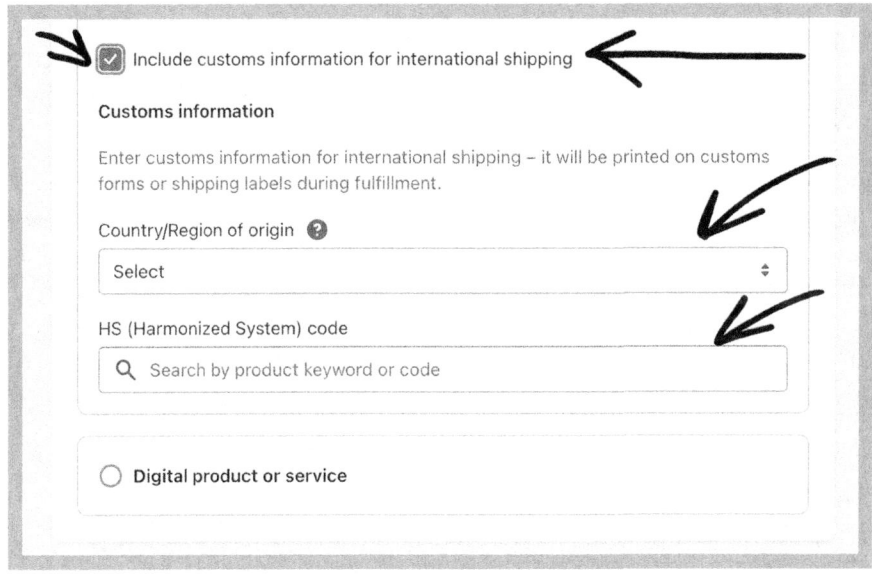

[2.3.48]

If your business is in the USA, and you are shipping to your international customers, customs fees, duties, and taxes will be calculated depending on the rules and regulations for the country the products are shipped to.

To improve accuracy, you should include the country or region of origin and HS code in your product details. Calculations are based on the description and category of the product if there is no HS code. When a product does not have an HS code, description, or category, duties and import taxes are not calculated, even if you have set a country or region to collect duties and import taxes.

It is the country or region of origin, or COO, where a product is created or assembled, and where it receives its HS code classification. You sell a table, for instance - The table is made from Canadian wood, Mexican glue, and Chinese screws. Since the tables is assembled in the United States, the country or region of origin is the United States.

'Harmonized Item Description and Coding System' codes, or HS codes, are used in international trade to identify products. A HS code typically consists of six digits. The World Customs Organization has more information about HS codes.

Here is the link to the World Customs Organization:

http://www.wcoomd.org/en/topics/nomenclature/overview/what-is-the-harmonized-system.aspx

Add this code to your product page, including the country from which you are shipping your product. You can either pay the fees, duties, and taxes, OR your international customer can pay them depending on the rules, regulations, and the threshold of taxes for each different country. Most people know that they will pay duties and taxes if they buy something internationally. Of course, not all products are taxed.

It is a great idea to have this information in your Shipping FAQ to inform your international customers.

There are a few problems if you are responsible for customs duties and taxes:

- Duties and taxes are only assessed after customs have cleared the product.
- Every country will have different regulations and taxes.
- Custom and tax regulations change all the time in all the different countries.
- There is no way to know the cost or charges until the particular country's customs officials clear the product.
- You are not likely to get the money back you paid for customs and taxes if the product is returned.

If you want your customer to be responsible for paying the import taxes and duties, you must make it **VERY clear** in your shipping information and disclose the customer's responsibilities.

CREATE EFFECTIVE & CONVERTING PRODUCT PAGES

Shopify says: *"Duties are costs associated with buying a product that's shipped from a different country. When international customers buy a product in your store, their country can charge them duties on the shipment.*

Some shipping carriers offer you the option to pay duties so that your customers don't have to pay anything at delivery. If you pay duties, you can plan for that cost as a part of your product pricing or collect the fees at checkout.

Duties can be paid by customers on delivery. If your customers might have to pay any duties, then make sure that you tell them ahead of time. Otherwise, customers might refuse to pay the unexpected costs, and your shipments might be returned."

VARIANTS: OPTIONS

Options are available when you need to add different styles to your product.

In Shopify, the different nomenclature is:

Variant: You add variants to a product that comes more in more than one options, such as size or color.

Options: Each option has a name and a value. For instance, the 'Option name' is **Size** and the 'Option values' are the different sizes, i.e., Large, Medium, Small. Another 'Option name' can be **Colors** and the 'Option values' are Blue and Green.

So, the variant will be a Large Blue Shirt. Each variant will count as 1 product in your store.

In this example you will have 6 different products.

Now let's start adding your variants.

Step 1. Add option name

Check the box to add your 'Options'.

Options

This product has options, like size or color

Option name
Size

Option values
Medium

Done

+ Add another option

[2.3.50]

Once you have checked the box, you can now add your different options names. Add your title for your 'Option 1', e.g., size, color, scent, type, etc.

Step 2. Add option values

Add each of the option values in separate field areas in the text box.

Option name
Color

Option values
BLACK
WHITE
Add another value

Done

[2.3.51]

Click 'Done' and your options will be added to the product information page.

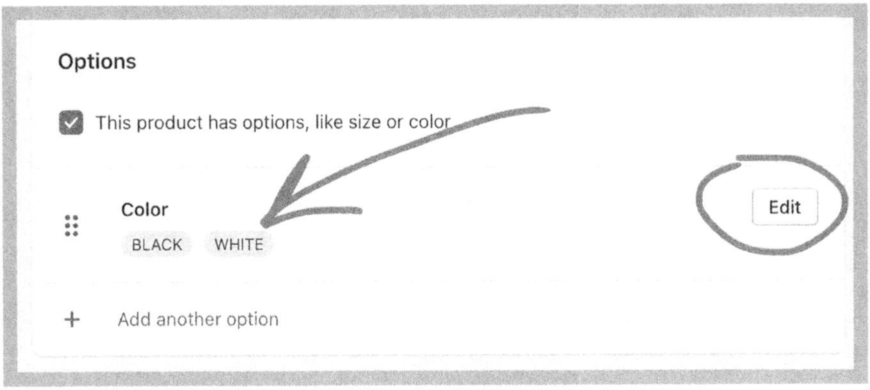

[2.3.52]

Step 3. Add more options

Continue with **'Option 2'** and add your values.

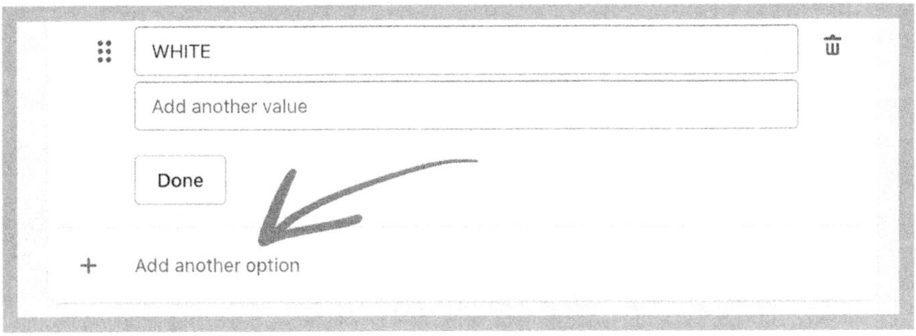

[2.3.53]

You can add all your options at the same time or not. When you add your options one at a time, the variants are shown as 'new', as shown in the following image.

[2.3.54]

> ✏ Pro Tip: When you add a different option name to Shopify's suggestions, make sure your cursor is NOT in the text box when you hit return to confirm the name.

> ✏ Pro Tip: Apps I have used are Bold Options and Advanced Product Option (APO). I prefer APO because of the look on the product page. Most Apps come with a trial period. Test them out to see if you like the look on your product page.

Step 4. Add information to variants

In Shopify, each combination of option values for a product is a variant of that product.

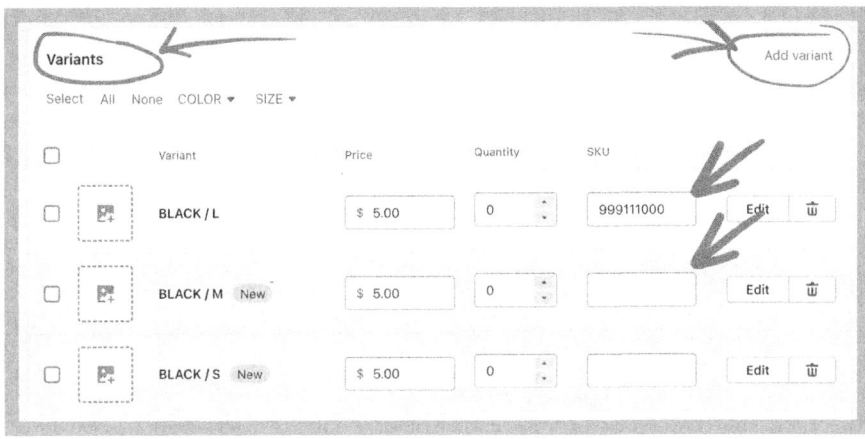

[2.3.55]

NOTE: *I expanded the screenshot to show all the values. You need to expand your view with the slider in Shopify.*

The product information previously added is automatically included in your variants.

A consecutive number will be automatically added at the end of the first product SKU, as shown in image 2.3.55 previously.

For example, SKU# - 999111000, 999111001, etc.

NOTE: *There is a limit to how many options and values you can add. You can add up to 100 options and option values collectively. Each variant is a line item or product; you can only add 100 line items/products. If you have more, you will need to add an Options App.*

There are various ways to add more information to your variants:

You can add or edit the information if the prices, weight, SKUs, or bar codes differ for each product variant. For example, a king-sized sheet set will weigh more than a twin bed sheet set.

Information can be changed or added for one type of option or all option variants in bulk.

Add or change directly - Add or change information directly on the product information page in the variant section. If you only have **one option** to add to your products and want to add or change your information, navigate to 'Edit', and a dropdown will show you various edits.

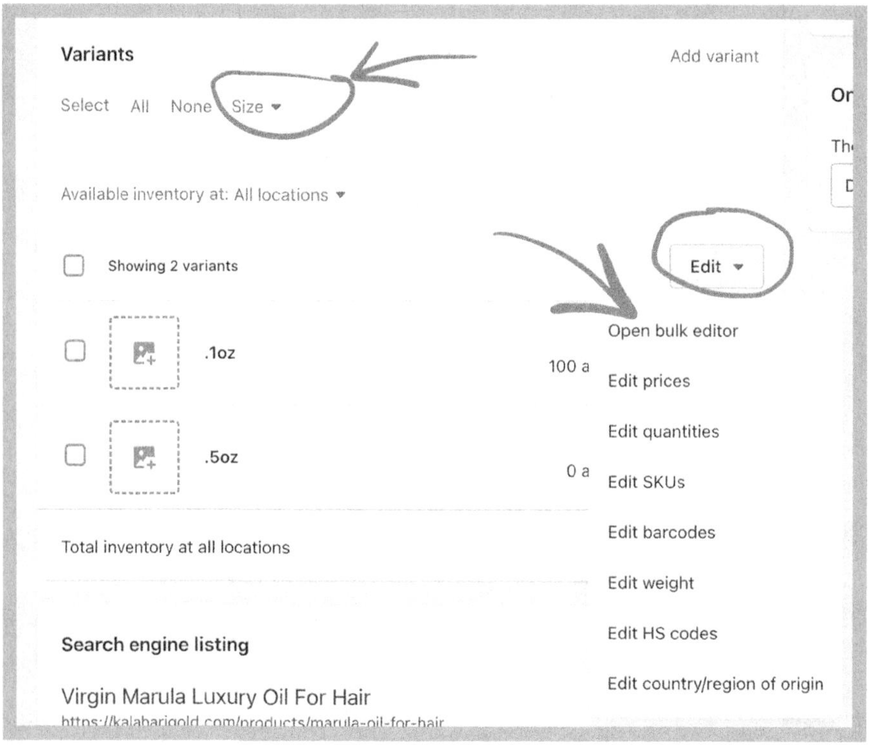

[2.3.64]

It will open up each variant section you can edit individually.

[2.3.65]

If you have **more than one option** added to your products, your variants are on a slider, and you can edit the variants' text boxes individually.

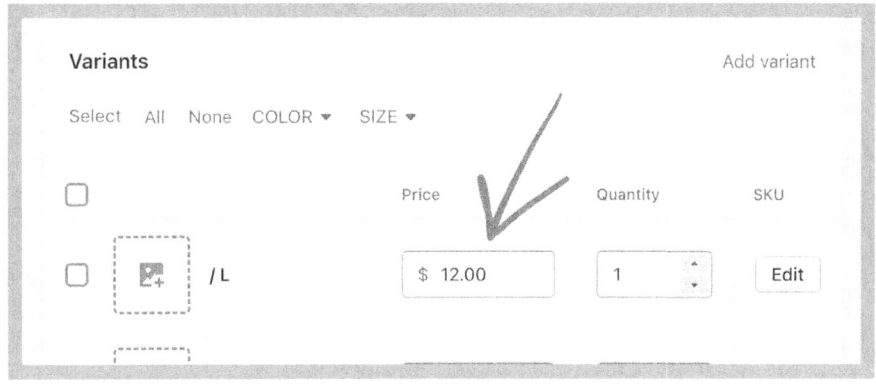

[2.3.61]

Bulk edit - At the top of the 'Variant' section, select 'All' or per option, i.e., COLOR or SIZE, and the dropdown gives you a choice of the colors you want to edit. For any choice, the number of variants that can be edited is checked, as shown in the following image.

[2.3.56]

An editing option will pop up at the bottom of the page. Now you can either bulk edit or individually change information. The 'Open bulk editor' will open the 'Bulk editor', which shows all the information and spaces to add more information.

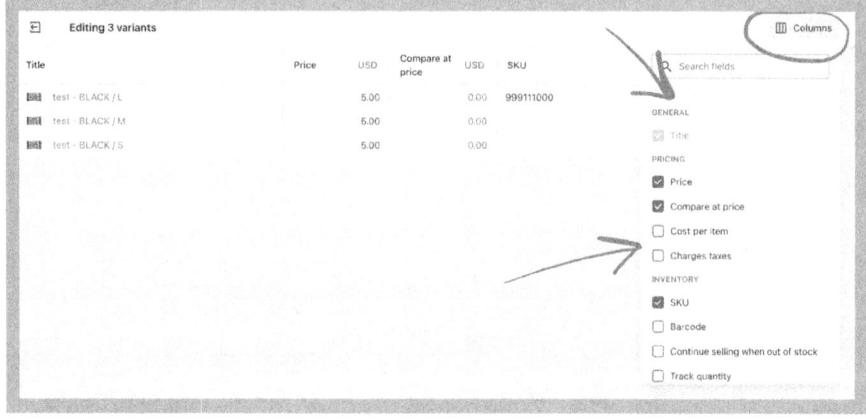

[2.3.57]

On the top-right corner, the link 'Columns' will open a choice of additional spaces to add to your window. Now you can add all the information you need for your variants. Make sure to wait until the Shopify notice pops up when you save the information. It takes a little time for the new information to be added.

Change or add individual information per option - Choose your option variant to change as in a bulk edit and click on the three (3) dots at the bottom of the page.

CREATE EFFECTIVE & CONVERTING PRODUCT PAGES

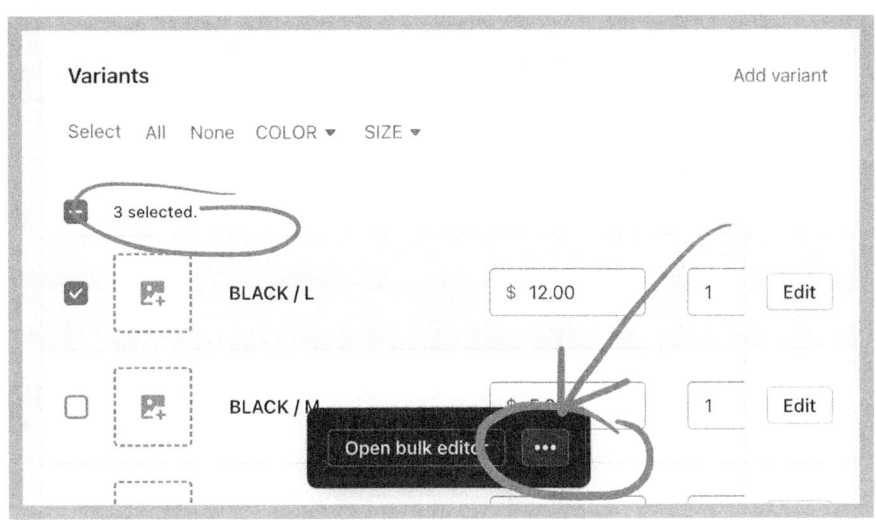

[2.3.58]

A long list of choices will pop up:

- Edit prices
- Edit quantities
- Edit SKUs
- Edit barcodes
- Edit weight
- Edit HS codes
- Edit country / region of origin
- Edit images
- Remove images
- Delete variants
- Continue selling when out of stock

[2.3.59]

The choice will appear in a pop-up, and you can add or change the information and apply it to all and save.

CREATE EFFECTIVE & CONVERTING PRODUCT PAGES

[2.3.60]

NOTE: You cannot add or change tracking, charge tax, or location in this area. You can only do it in the 'Bulk editor' or if you 'Edit' each variant individually.

Step 5. Add another variant

If you need to add one special option with only one value, this is a great way to add it to your product.

I added the color 'Purple' but only in XL. So on the product page, the choice for the customer for any of the other options will show as 'unavailable'. This product will only be available as Purple and XL.

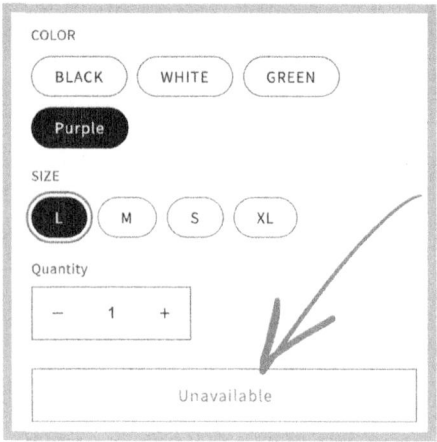

[2.3.62]

To add another variant, click on 'Add Variant'.

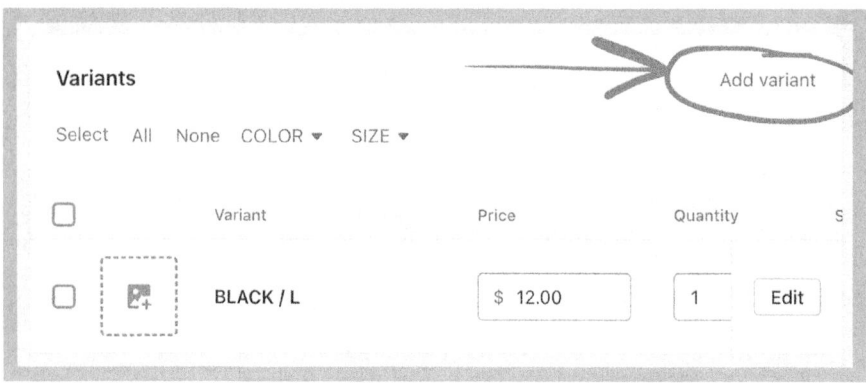

[2.3.63]

A complete window will open with all the same choices for the product information page. Add the information you need.

Step 6. Add images to your variants

When you add an image to your variant, a customer will see that variant and the image for that product will appear. See the following image of what that looks like. To add an image to each individual variant, click on the image next to the appropriate variant.

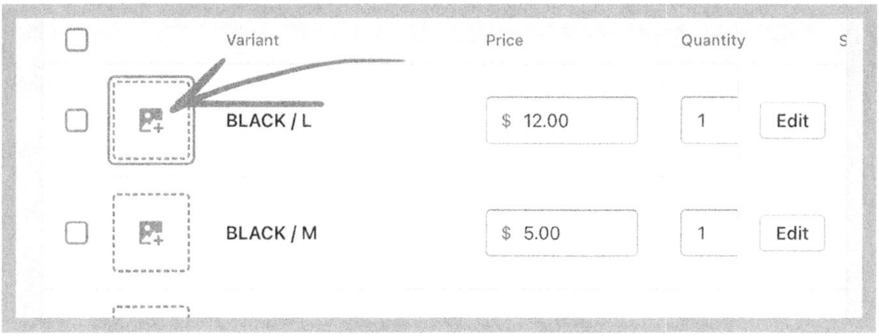

[2.3.66]

If you have no images uploaded for any product or in your store, you can upload your variant image from your computer.

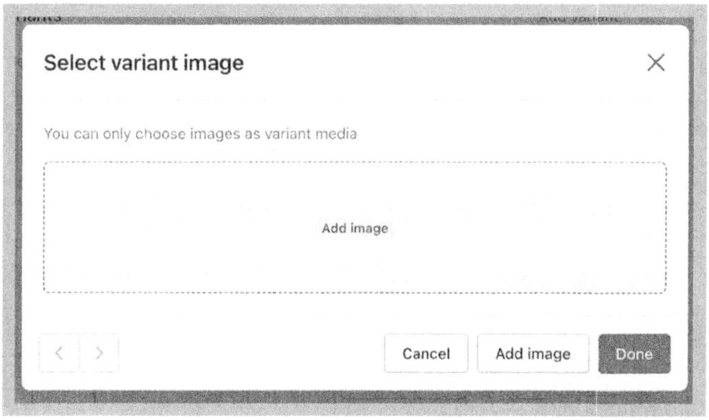

[2.3.67]

Otherwise, choose the images you have uploaded previously or upload a new image.

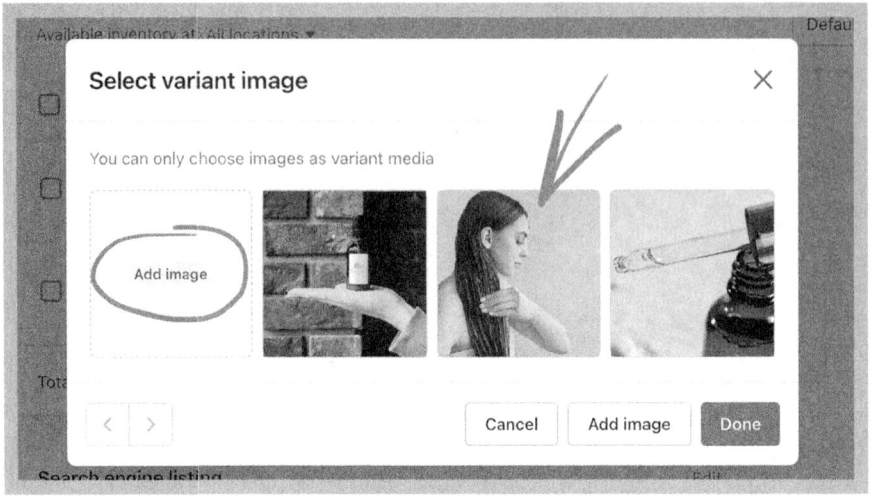

[2.3.68]

This is a great way to add different color styles to your products, as you can see here with Hugpatrol.net. These are called color swatches.

[2.3.69]

Depending on your template, the colors named in the option values will show on the product page variants, i.e., black = black color swatch, green = green color swatch. But if you have a color value that is not a recognized browser color, the store template will not show the correct color.

All modern browsers support 140 color names. Here is a link to the colors: https://www.w3schools.com/colors/colors_names.asp

> 💡 Pro Tip: Again, it depends on your template. You can add color swatches as images to your assets. This advanced technique will be covered in my book 3 - Grow Your Shopify Store.

STATUS

Your products can be either in a draft or active status, which means the '**Active**' status shows the product online, and the '**Draft**' status is hidden from the online store.

If you want to discontinue a product for a season, you can allocate the draft choice to the product. If you want to launch the product at a future date, it will stay in draft until the allocated date.

Step 1. Active or Draft

Choose either 'Active' or 'Draft' for your product status.

[2.3.70]

Step 2. Publishing

Physical products can be sold on all sales channels. But you might not want to sell every product on all sales channels.

For instance, TheMissingPiecePuzzle.com has 2 products - one for her store and one for Facebook. Facebook will always show your most expensive product option price, not how you sort it on your product page. So, it is a bit misleading on Facebook. The workaround is to sell the individual product with no different price options that can connect to Facebook.

Digital products cannot be sold on Facebook, Instagram, or Google. If you checked those boxes to add them to the sales channel, you will get a review error in the sales channel app.

Depending on what sales channels you add to your store, your products can be selected to show on different sales channels.

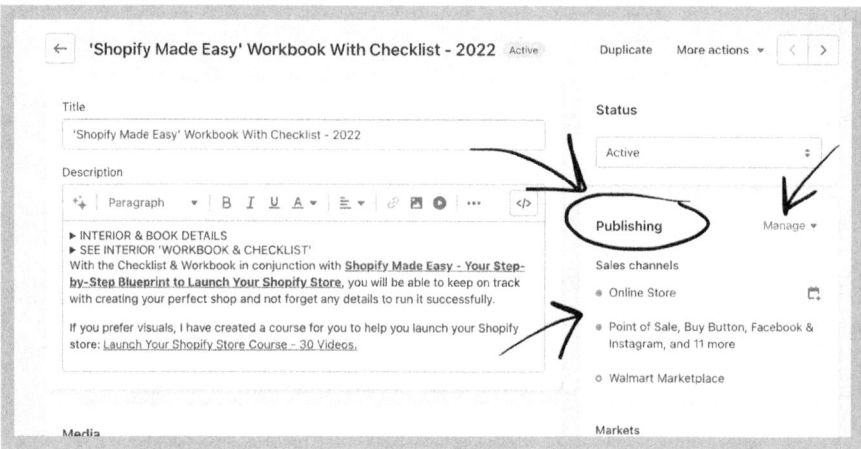

[2.3.71]

Availability on sales channels when you start will be '**Online Store**'. Your product must be online to show anywhere on your store or the internet. You will not be able to add it to your navigation or the 'Buy Button' app.

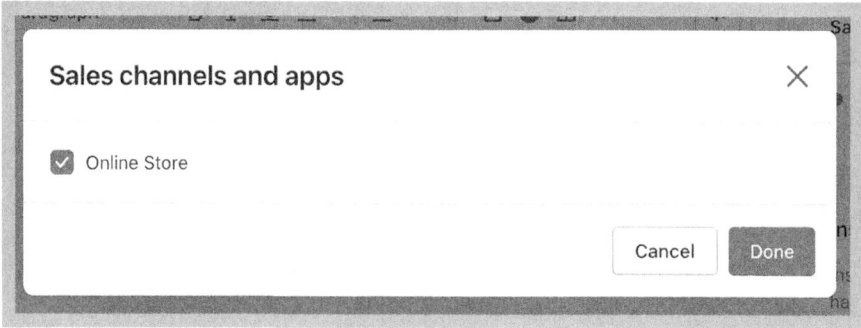

[2.3.72]

CREATE EFFECTIVE & CONVERTING PRODUCT PAGES

As you can see on the following Sales channels, I have my course up on only some of the sales channels because it is a digital product.

[2.3.73]

Any of your products can be scheduled to go active for any sales channel. This is a great tool to use for promotions or special launches.

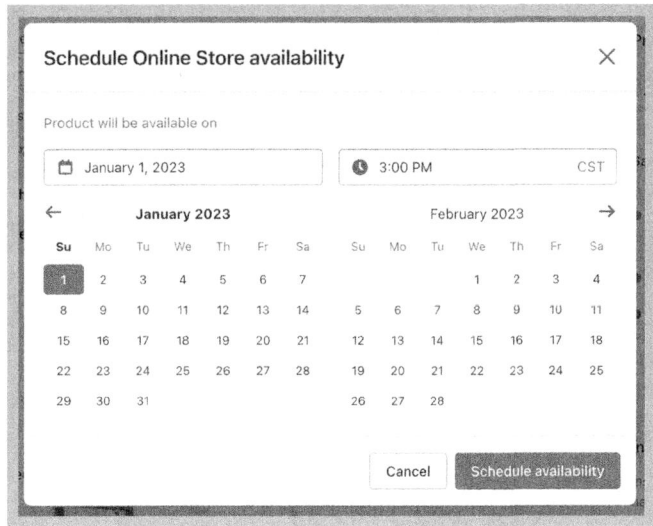

[2.3.74]

My next book Grow Your Shopify Store – Book 3 shows you how to add all the sales channels to your store and how to integrate all the services and products.

INSIGHTS

The '**Insights**' section will appear when you have saved your product information.

'Insights' will display when the product has had recent sales and show you all the sales details. i.e., net sales over time, which sales channel or traffic source, how many first-time or returning customers.

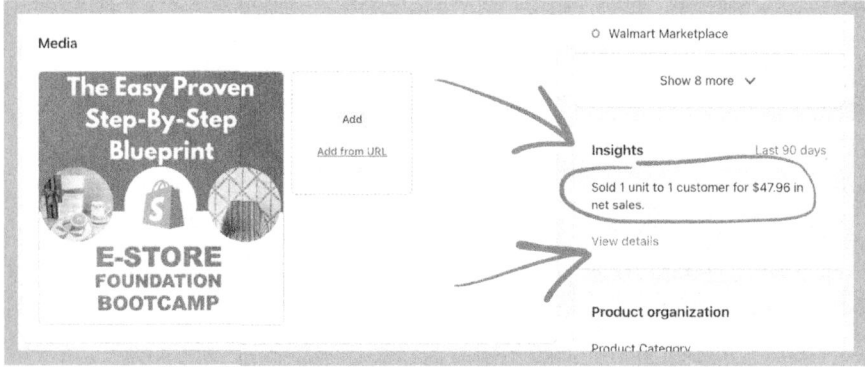

[2.3.75]

PRODUCT ORGANIZATION

The product organization section is about identifying where your product will appear in your online store and, more importantly, what your customers will be charged. In this section are different organizational identification for your products

1. Product Category
2. Product Type
3. Vendor
4. Collections
5. Tags

CREATE EFFECTIVE & CONVERTING PRODUCT PAGES

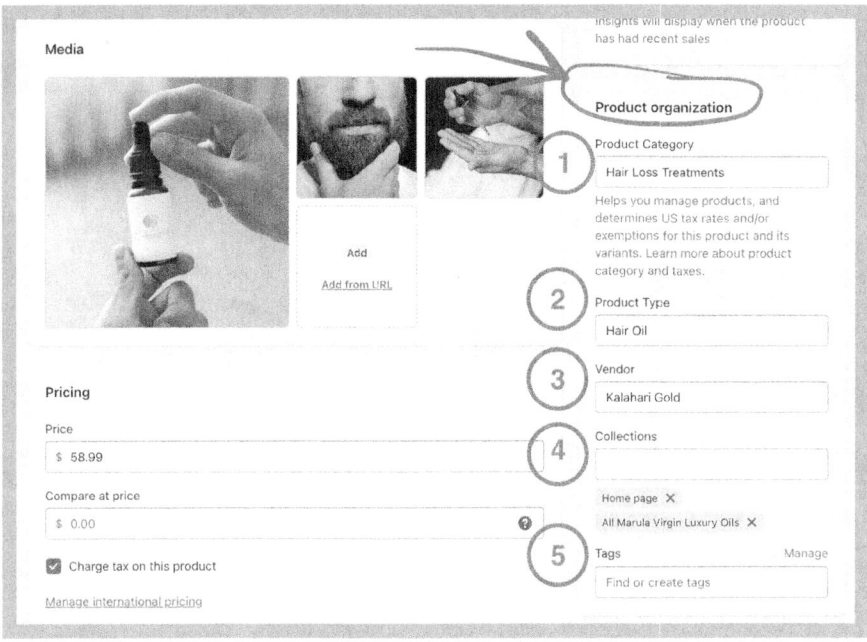

[2.3.76]

1. Product Category

The product category is only for USA stores because it affects the taxes charged on product purchases. Product categories influence what taxes customers are charged when they purchase a product. You are responsible for keeping track of the sales tax and paying the IRS. This is determined according to the state where you are registered as a business.

NOTE: *The tax settings are covered in my Shopify Made Easy book 1, 'Starting Your Online Business'.*

A product category is automatically created when you create a product, but it is only a suggestion. Each of your products can have only one product category.

This is an important step for you and your customer.

Step 1. Choose the category

Use the product category that best describes your product. Choose the category based on your product's main function, for instance, sculptures I know is under the category 'Home & Garden' and then to get more specific,

'Decor'. But this is still not describing my product in detail, so with further investigating I find 'Artwork' and eventually the exact description of what it is, under 'Sculptures & Statues'.

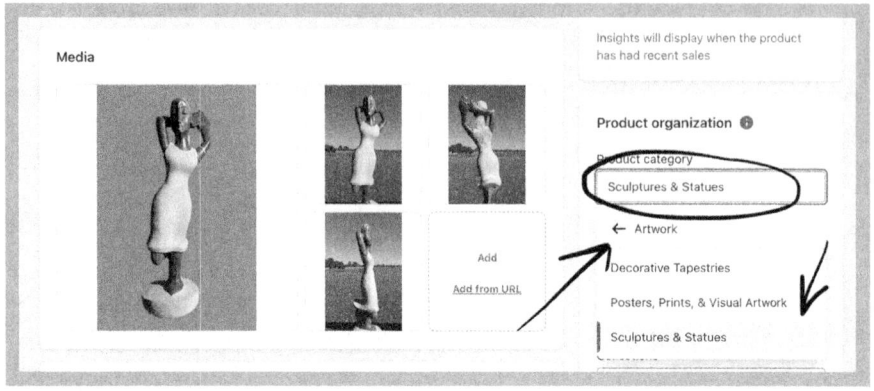

[2.3.90]

It is not always easy to get to the exact description of your product, but it is a good idea not to be as specific as you can.

Another example is Marula Hair Oil from KalahariGold.com. So this is the path I followed: 'Health & Beauty' > 'Personal Care' > 'Hair Care' > Hair Loss Treatments'. It is more than just a hair loss treatment but that is as close as I could get to what the product is. I could leave it at 'Hair Care', but I feel if I define it as a 'Hair Loss Treatment', the product will gain from searches by my customers and, ultimately, Google.

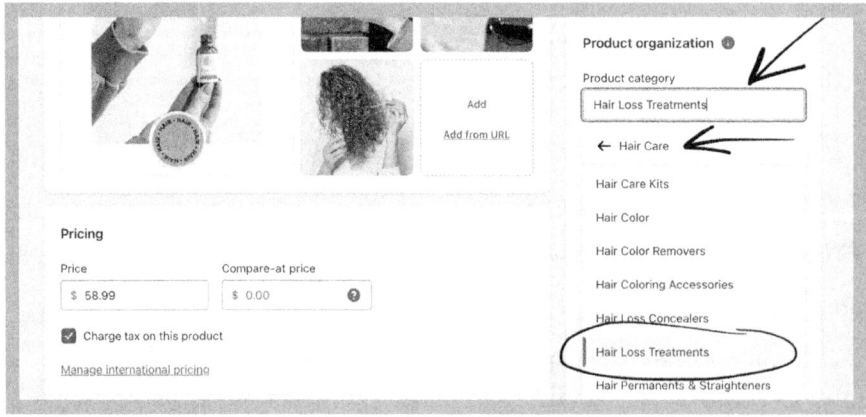

[2.3.91]

These product categories can be matched up to Google Product Category values.

I have a complete Product Category spreadsheet on my website resources page.

Another reason to get the product category as clearly defined as possible is the tax implications.

Here is an example from Shopify:

For example, if you sell t-shirts. In New York, clothing and footwear under $110 USD are exempt from New York City and New York State sales tax. If the correct product categories are set for your products, then these taxes are not charged when you sell your products to customers in New York. If the rules governing these products change in the future, then the way tax is calculated for your products is automatically updated, with no action from you required.

> Pro Tip: Research your product tax obligations in your local county or state and consult a tax advisor.

Step 2. Approve your product category

You need to approve the Shopify suggestions. If they are not correct, add the correct product category.

Shopify will give you a suggestion, but you have to approve the suggestion before it is active. The suggestions are in blue and once you click the checkmark, it means you agree with the suggestion.

If you don't agree with the suggestion, add the closest category that will fit your product.

Step 3. Digital product category

You might not need to charge sales tax if you sell digital products, which means you do not have to allocate a product category for your product. But because Shopify allocates a suggested product category, your product might be under the wrong tax category.

Unfortunately, you cannot delete the suggested category.

The products need to be in a manual collection to create a tax override for your digital products.

NOTE: *I will show you how to create these steps in the Chapter - Collections.*

> Pro Tip: Product Categories Taxonomy

Link to my website with updated Shopify & Google category taxonomy list:

https://veronicajeans.online/resources

2. Product Type

Product type is not a necessary identification, but it will help your customers find the right product in the right place.

Each of your products can have only one product type. For instance, in the online boutique, we have 'Boys', 'Girls, and 'Tween' as our type, and then in the 'Tags' section, we get more granular.

As you have already identified your product type in your storyboard, it is very easy to add information to your products.

See the following image as a reminder of what we discussed when you did your storyboard for your store.

COLLECTIONS & NAVIGATION							
BOYS >		Sizes/Tags For Products					
	Baby Boys	0, 3mth, 6mth, 9mth					
	Toddlers	1, 2, 3, 4					
	Kids	5, 6, 7, 8					
(Type)		(Where)	(Tags)	(Type)		(Where)	(Tags)
Boys				Girls			
Bottoms >	Long Pants	Collection	Boy Bottoms, Boy Long Pa	Bottoms		1 x Product	Girl Bottoms
	Shorts	Collection	Boy Bottoms, Boy Shorts	Tops		Collection	Girl Tops
Tops >	Long Sleeves	Collection	Boy Tops, Collar	Outerwear		1 x Product	Girl Outerwear
	Short Sleeves	Collection	Boy Tops, Tshirt				
Outerwear >		1 x Product	Boy Outerwear				

[2.1.2]

3. Vendor

In this section, you can add your brand as the vendor, or if you are selling other brands, add the appropriate brand name if you want to.

This information is not added to the product page unless you want it shown to your customers.

CREATE EFFECTIVE & CONVERTING PRODUCT PAGES 223

In the following image, the artist is depicted as the vendor for MoyoColletion.com.

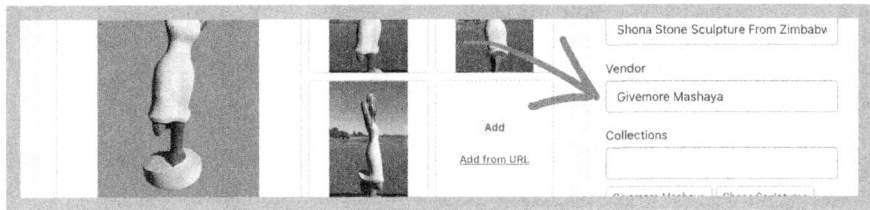

[2.3.77]

4. Collections

Collections will be automatically added by Shopify when you create your collections. You can see which collection your product will appear.

There are instances when you need to add a different collection per product, but the collection has to be already created before you can add it to the product information page.

[2.3.78]

NOTE: *In the chapter - Collections, we will create your collections. Then the collection will be automatically added to your products as you define them.*

5. Tags

Tags are the magic that can automate your products in your store. We have already identified the tags for your products, so now you can add the tags to each specific product.

The tags are manually added to your product information page.

See the following image as a reminder of what we discussed when you did your storyboard for your store.

BUILD YOUR SHOPIFY BRAND

COLLECTIONS & NAVIGATION							
BOYS >		Sizes/Tags For Products					
	Baby Boys	0, 3mth, 6mth, 9mth					
	Toddlers	1, 2, 3, 4					
	Kids	5, 6, 7, 8					
(Type)		(Where)	(Tags)	(Type)		(Where)	(Tags)
Boys				Girls			
Bottoms >	Long Pants	Collection	Boy Bottoms, Boy Long Pa	Bottoms		1 x Product	Girl Bottoms
	Shorts	Collection	Boy Bottoms, Boy Shorts	Tops		Collection	Girl Tops
Tops >	Long Sleeves	Collection	Boy Tops, Collar	Outerwear		1 x Product	Girl Outerwear
	Short Sleeves	Collection	Boy Tops, Tshirt				
Outerwear >		1 x Product	Boy Outerwear				

[2.1.2]

As seen in the following image, the tags are the artist, the specific type of sculpture - 'Woman' and 'LTL shipping', which we use as an internal tag for heavy products.

[2.3.79]

> 💡 Pro Tip: I know tags are a great keyword to add to your store. But don't overuse the tag identifier, which will confuse your customer if you have random keywords stuffed into this section.

Adding random keywords will serve no purpose even for a keyword search. The whole point of is making it easier to find the product. In the following image the keywords are already in the title, description, and type, so there is no reason to add tags to the product.

CREATE EFFECTIVE & CONVERTING PRODUCT PAGES

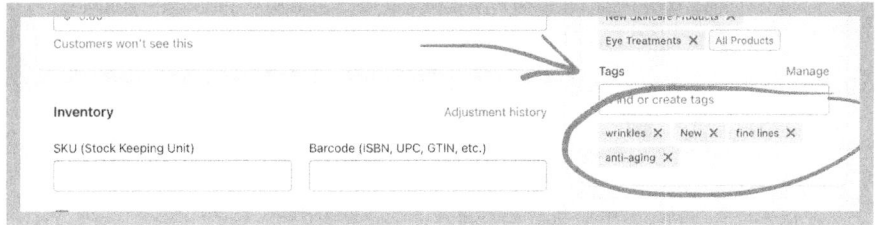

[2.3.80]

NOTE: *More about SEO, searches, and good practice is covered in Shopify Made Easy book 3 - Expand Your Shopify Store for Conversions.*

ONLINE STORE: THEME TEMPLATE

The default product page in your Shopify store is a **'default product'** template. The information that is added to the product page dashboard on the **'default product'** template will show on the browser window.

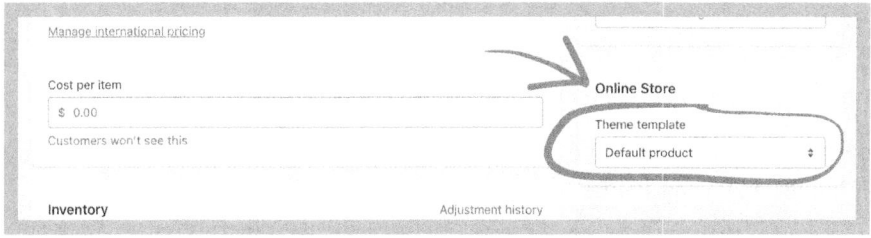

[2.3.81]

The product page the visitors will view is shown in the following image. The images, product options and variants and 'Add to cart' button are automatically added to your product page from all the details you have added.

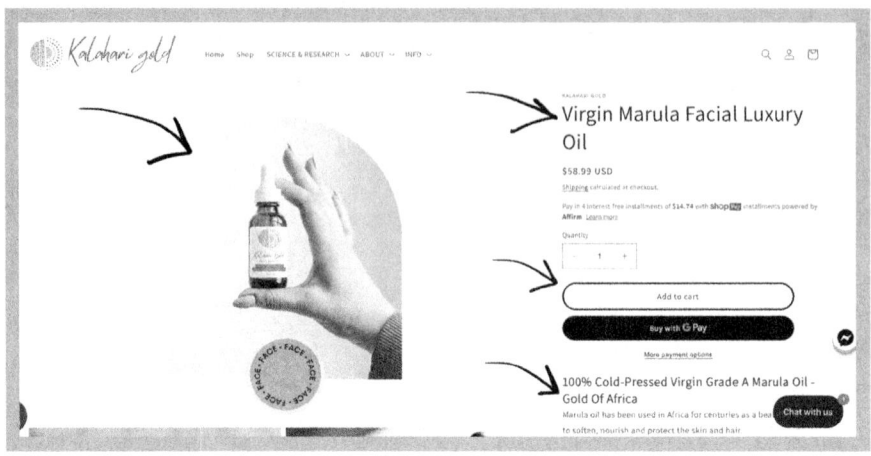

[2.3.84]

You can add more detailed information to your product pages in **'Themes' - 'Customization'**.

When customizing a product page with more detailed information, it will be displayed on every product page.

If you want to create different templates for different types of products, you need to create another product template in **'Customize'** editor. For example, in the product dashboard in KalahariGold.com there is a default product template and a 'for-your-face-hair' product template.

I created 2 different types product templates to create a different product detail page for each product.

In the following image you can view the different details that was added in the 'Customize' editor for the Marula oil for the face.

CREATE EFFECTIVE & CONVERTING PRODUCT PAGES

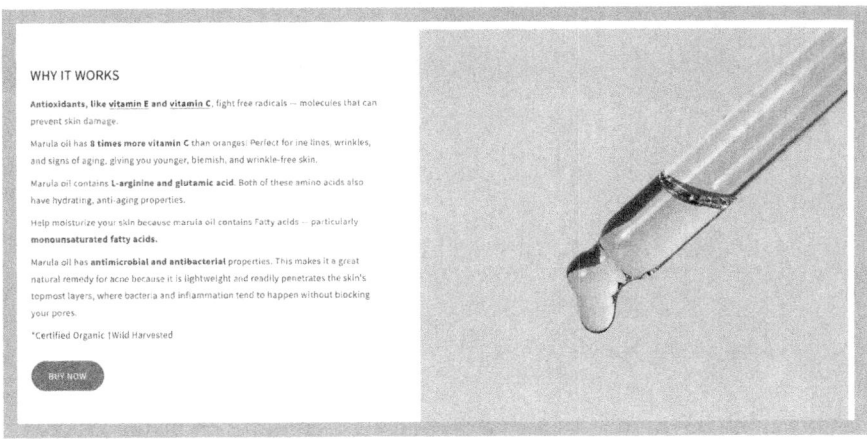

[2.3.85]

The default product template contains general information about Marula Face Oil, and I have more information and details about what the benefits, uses, and FAQ for the Marula Oil on the product page.

'Why it works' detail:

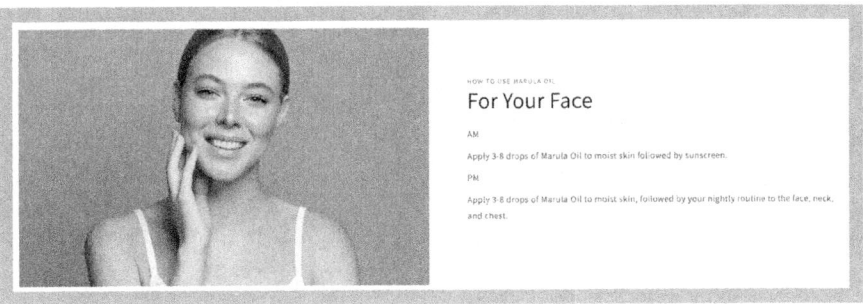

[2.3.86]

How to use the product:

[2.3.87]

Frequently Asked Questions (FAQ) section for any questions the customer might have:

[2.3.88]

NOTE: *You will learn more about how to customize your pages in the Shopify Theme chapter.*

The following image shows how I added digital products with different templates to my Shopify store. Again, creating different product sales pages in Shopify is easy.

CREATE EFFECTIVE & CONVERTING PRODUCT PAGES 229

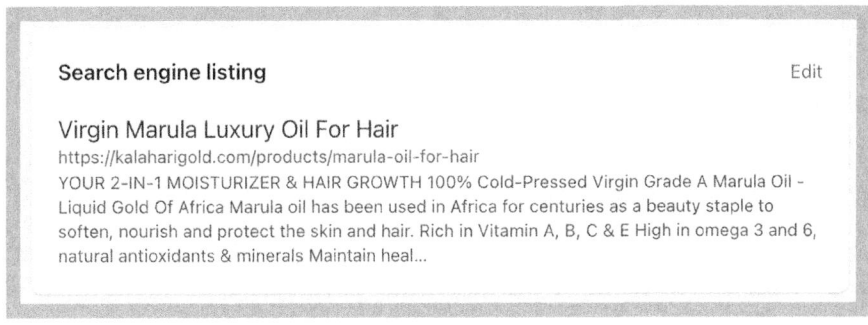

[2.3.83]

SEARCH ENGINE LISTING PREVIEW

Your product's title and description will be automatically added to this section. This section shows how you will be viewed on any search engine.

[2.3.89]

When you search on Google, you will see other people's websites and stores or pages displayed on the search page. So, optimizing each product information page is a great idea. Many people neglect this very important part of the product detail page; it is a great source for creating excitement and information for your product and brand.

NOTE: *See full description and steps on how to optimize shown in my Shopify Made Easy book 3 - Expand Your Shopify Store 2023. We will cover good SEO practices and keyword research.*

RESOURCES:

Here is a link to my TOOLS page:

Product Category spreadsheet

Breakeven Analysis

Price Widget

https://veronicajeans.online/resources

Copy.ai is a fabulous extension for content for your pages and information - **https://veronicajeans.online/copy-ai**.

Bold Options: **https://apps.shopify.com/product-options?ref=shappify**

Information in Shopify Help:

Adding Variants

https://help.shopify.com/en/manual/products/variants/add-variants

Changing Variants

https://help.shopify.com/en/manual/products/variants/edit-variants

More information on Shopify

https://veronicajeans.online/help-shopify

CHAPTER 7
GIFT CARDS

**WHERE TO FIND THIS IN SHOPIFY? PRODUCTS > GIFT CARDS

ADDING gift cards to your Shopify store will increase sales, encourage repeat business, introduce new customers, improve cash flow, and provide a flexible gifting option. By offering gift cards, you can provide your customers with a convenient way to shop, while also increasing your store's revenue.

WHAT TO EXPECT IN THIS CHAPTER:

- *Gift Cards*
- *Issue a Gift Card*
- *Keep Track of Gift Cards*
- *Redeem a Gift Card*

Gift cards are either physical or digital products. This means, are you going to ship your gift cards physically to your customers or email the information to your customers.

Here are benefits of adding gift cards to your Shopify store:

- Gift cards allow customers to buy products they may not have been able to afford otherwise or allow them to give gifts to others.

- Customers who receive gift cards are more likely to return to your store to make additional purchases and become repeat customers.
- When customers purchase gift cards, they may introduce others to your store who may not have otherwise known about it.
- Gift cards improve cash flow by providing revenue upfront, even if the customer doesn't redeem the card right away.
- They can be used for any product or service in your store, making them a versatile gift option.

To use Shopify Gift Card options depends on your Shopify plan. Your customers can use their gift cards to make purchases from your store both online and in person.

There are some restrictions to gift cards:

- Gift cards cannot be reloaded.
- Customers cannot check their gift card balance, but you, as the store owner, can, and you can email them the amounts.

These restrictions are being addressed by Shopify and may change in the future.

It is your choice if you want to offer gift cards or not. It is always a good option for gift ideas for your customers. Your gift cards can be physical cards or digital cards.

GIFT CARDS

All gift cards will be automatically issued with their own barcode. So, the cards cannot be used again once they are used by the gift card holder.

There are 2 types of gift cards:

- Digital Gift Cards
- Physical Gift Cards

DIGITAL GIFT CARDS

The 'Add gift card' product button automatically creates your Gift Card for your store. Gift cards are available as a digital product in your Shopify store.

You can optimize your gift card product with the same steps as in the previous Products chapter.

Step 1. Create a gift card image

Create a gift card image that suits your store and brand. I created a card in Canva.com - Canva is a free graphic design platform great for creating images for your store.

Here are some quick ideas on how to create a gift card: Create a template about 1000px x 500px and add text and nice gift card icons, as in the following image —this one I created for a Christmas gift card.

[2.4.2]

Download the image to your computer. Create another template 1000px x 1000px (sized the same as for all my product images) and upload the gift card image to Canva. Then, move it around and add a shadow to the card. Voila, you have a great gift card.

[2.4.3]

Step 2. Create a gift card product

**Where to find this in Shopify? Products > Gift Cards

Navigate to your dashboard's 'Products' and 'Gift Cards' sections. Click on 'Add gift card product', and a product is automatically created in Shopify.

[2.4.4]

Step 3. Optimize your gift card product

Now add a title and information for your gift card. As with all products, the product cannot be saved if you don't add a title.

The gift card product is automatically categorized as a 'Gift Card'.

Add information for the 'Product type', 'Collection', and if you name yourself as the 'Vendor'.

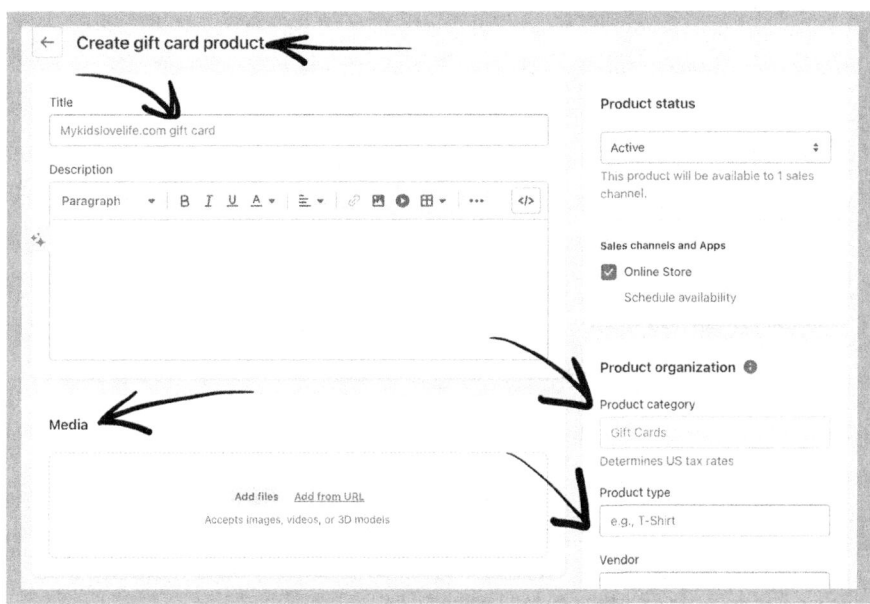

[2.4.5]

Upload your Gift card image to the 'Media' section.

Step 4. Fix denominations for the gift card

Shopify automatically creates a $10, $25, $50, and $100 variant. You can change the amounts or add more, depending on the pricing of your products in your store.

[2.4.6]

> Pro Tip 1: Shopify does not have an option for customers to add another name and email address, so this will have to be added by an expert. You can add a Shopify App to create this capability.

> Pro Tip 2: A suggestion is to add the information for your customers to the description so that they know to add the guest email in the checkout page.

PHYSICAL GIFT CARDS

Physical gift cards can be used in retail store with a Shopify POS system. You can buy physical gift cards from the Shopify Hardware Store in the United States, Canada, United Kingdom, Ireland, Germany, European Union, and Australia.

You can sell physical gift cards from a Shopify POS (Point-of-Sale) system. This will only work on your Android or iOS tablet or mobile phone.

Step 1. Add the Shopify POS app

Check on App Store for the Shopify POS app and install and follow the prompts.

GIFT CARDS

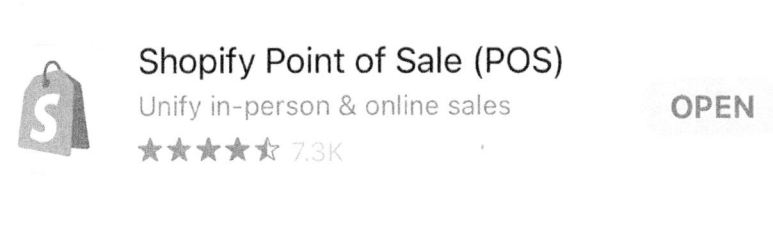

[2.4.12]

Activate your Shopify POS app.

Step 2. Sell your physical gift cards

If you're selling a physical gift card, then activate the gift card using one of the following options:

- Scan the card with the front-facing camera on your tablet or phone.
- Use a Shopify supported 2D-barcode scanner to scan the card's barcode. The ID scanner won't work.
- Enter the gift card's number

The following image shows the gift card on a mobile phone in the Shopify POS app.

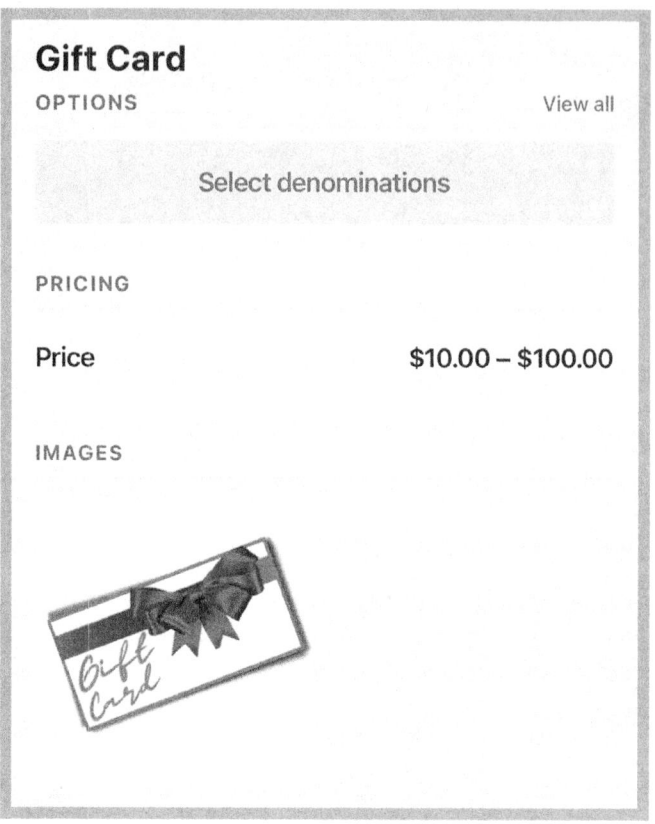

[2.4.13]

Once you create a gift card sale, the printed or emailed receipt for the gift card shows the following information:

- the name of your store
- the monetary value of the card
- the validation code
- a two-dimensional barcode.

NOTE: *When you exit this screen, you won't be able to retrieve the validation code for gift cards. This security feature prevents your gift cards from being exposed if your account is breached.*

ISSUE A GIFT CARD

You can send a gift card code directly to a customer with their email address. Shopify will randomly issue a gift card code, but you can edit this and add your own code.

**WHERE TO FIND THIS IN SHOPIFY? PRODUCTS > GIFT CARDS

Step 1. Issue a gift card

This is the method to use if you want to issue a digital gift card manually in your store

[2.4.7]

Step 2. Add a price value

Add a price to the gift card, and find your customer in your database. Otherwise, create a new customer - you only need an email address to create a gift card for them.

[2.4.8]

Step 3. Add an expiration date

You control the expiration date of the card.

There are two choices:

- No expiration date
- Set expiration date

[2.4.9]

> Pro Tip: Check with your state or country what the rules are for expiration dates. Some states don't allow an expiration date.

Step 4. Add a note

You can add information to notes which can be a reminder why you sent this gift card out for instance. Notes are private and is not seen by customer. Make use of the note option to keep track of why you issued a gift card.

Step 5. Edit gift card details

Once you activate the gift card, a preliminary order is created in the 'Gift cards' section. You can view the information for the gift card and also all the actions that have been initiated. The only parts that can be edited are the expiration date, customer information and notes.

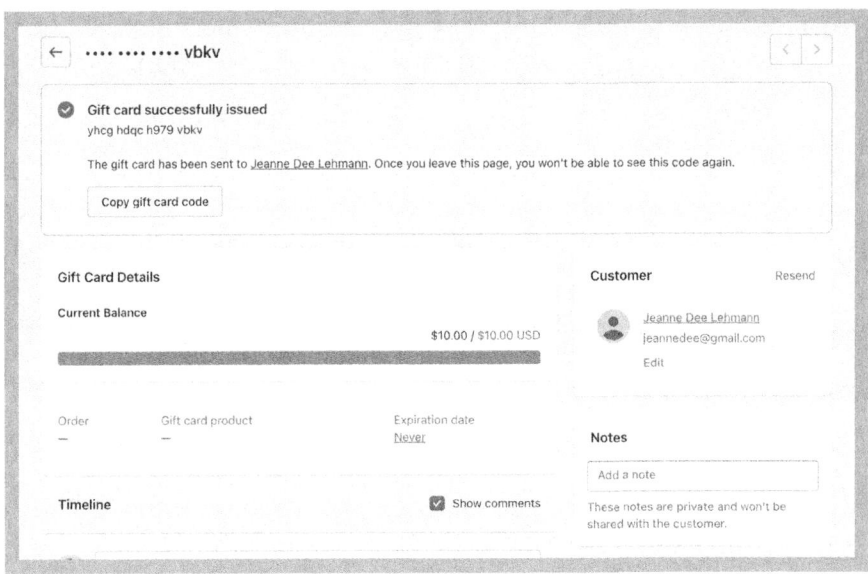

[2.4.10]

Step 6. Gift card orders

Gift cards will not be an order until the gift card is purchased. All gift cards issued will be in the 'Gift Card' section.

[2.4.11]

KEEP TRACK OF GIFT CARDS

The Gift card for customers will show in your dashboard's 'Products' - 'Gift Cards' section once activated. Your Gift card orders will show in your dashboard's 'Orders' section once used by the customer.

If you want to track the gift cards issued in your store, you will find this in your 'Reports' in your 'Analytics' section, as seen in the following image.

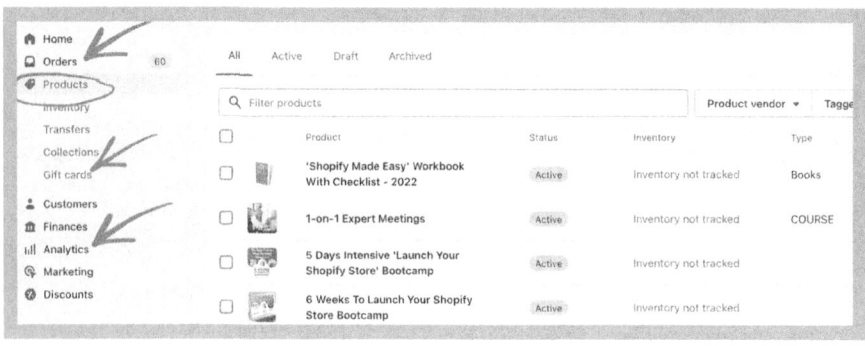

[2.4.14]

REDEEM A GIFT CARD

Customers can redeem their gift cards on any of your sales channels that use Shopify's checkout:

- Online Store
- Buy Button
- Pinterest
- Facebook Shop

- Messenger
- Shopify POS

Gift cards are not rechargeable at this moment. But it could change in the future. Keep an eye out.

Here are some frequently asked questions and the answers about Gift Cards from Shopify. This is a comprehensive list from Shopify help pages for Gift cards.

- Can a gift card be used more than once? - *Yes, provided there is still a balance remaining on the card.*
- Can more than one gift card be used towards a purchase? - *Yes. A customer can redeem another gift card during checkout.*
- Can a gift card be used to buy a gift card? - *No, you can't use a gift card to buy another gift card.*
- Can a gift card be used to pay for shipping and taxes? - *Yes, gift cards are applied to the final order total, which includes shipping and taxes.*
- Can gift cards be used in conjunction with a discount code? - *Yes, gift cards are a form of payment.*
- Can a customer pay for an order that includes a subscription with a gift card? - *Yes, you can use gift cards to pay for your first payment. However, you can't use your gift card to pay for recurring subscriptions.*
- Can I apply for a refund for a gift card? - *Yes. If your customer used a gift card to pay for the purchase, you can apply the refund to the gift card. If you only refund part of an order purchased using a gift card and other payment methods, you can manually change the refund amount applied to each payment method.*
- If I refund a gift card, is it automatically disabled? - *No. If you refund the purchase of a gift card, you must disable it, or it will still have a usable balance.*
- Can gift cards be reloaded? - *No, you can't reload a gift card.*
- How do customers check their balance? - *Customers can't check their gift card balance, but you can check the balance and send the information to the customer.*
- Can I customize the physical gift card redemption code? - *No, the 16-character redemption codes are randomized and printed by the gift card manufacturer.*

- Why can't I see the entire gift card code after I issue the card? - *Gift card codes are considered a currency, so only the customer can see the entire gift card code.*

RESOURCES

Here is a link to my RESOURCES & TOOLS page:

https://veronicajeans.online/resources

Check this link out for more information on Shopify Gift Cards FAQ:

https://help.shopify.com/en/manual/products/gift-card-products/faq#can-gift-cards-be-reloaded

Shopify Hardware store: https://veronicajeans.online/shopify-hardware

Canva.com - Canva is a free graphic design platform great for creating images for your store.

CHAPTER 8
COLLECTIONS

**WHERE TO FIND THIS IN SHOPIFY? PRODUCTS > COLLECTIONS

NOW WE ARE GOING to increase and optimize the customer journey in your Shopify store. With all your preparation, this chapter will be easy to implement.

The information you add to your collection pages depends on your type of customer and how your customer decides to buy your products.

WHAT TO EXPECT IN THIS CHAPTER:

- *Types of Collections*
- *Create Collections*
- *Collection Type*
- *Products*
- *Publishing*
- *Image*
- *Online Store: Theme Template*
- *Search Engine Listing*

CREATE COLLECTIONS

You will follow the guideline you created in your storyboard for your collections.

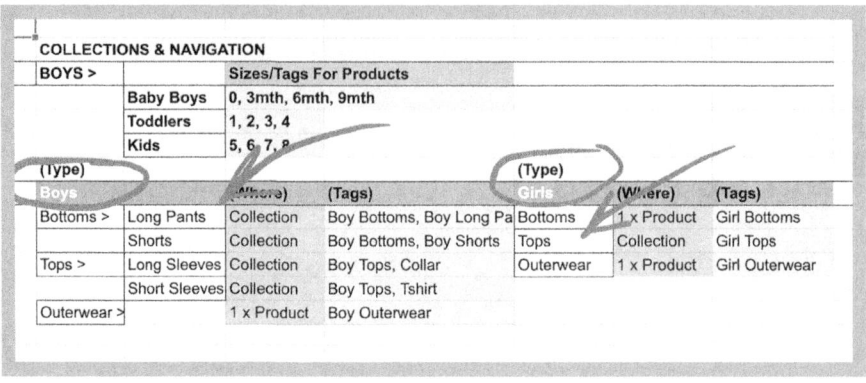

[2.1.2]

Create a collection for every department in your store as you have laid it out on your storyboard.

NOTE: *If you have only have one product for a collection do not add the product to a collection page. It will look really lonely on the page, and it makes more sense to send customer directly to the product page.*

There are two reasons for this:

- You don't want your prospective buyer to navigate too many pages unnecessarily to get to the product.
- If there is only one product, it is not a collection.

Step 1. Open 'Create collection'

You will find 'Collections' under 'Products' on the left of your Shopify Admin page or dashboard. The 'Create collection' button is at the top of the page.

COLLECTIONS

[2.5.1]

Step 2. Create a collection

When you open the 'Collections' dashboard, there is already one collection created by Shopify. Either rename this collection or create a new collection.

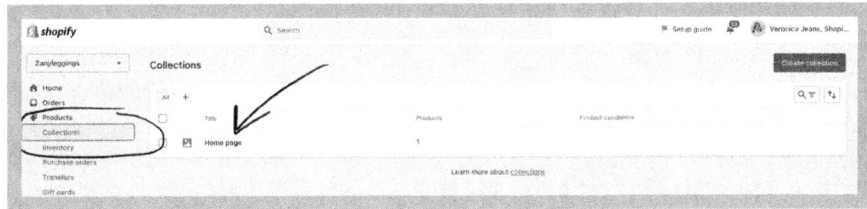

[2.5.36]

Now we can start adding information for your collections and here is the list of sections in your 'Collections' dashboard:

- Title & Description
- Collection Type
- Products
- Publishing
- Image
- Online Store: Theme Template
- Search Engine Listing

TITLE & DESCRIPTION

A new window opens for the new collection.

[2.5.2]

The title should clarify what the collection page is for to the customer.

This is an excellent opportunity to add some of your keywords. Please do not make the title too long because it will look odd and, more importantly, Google will truncate a long title.

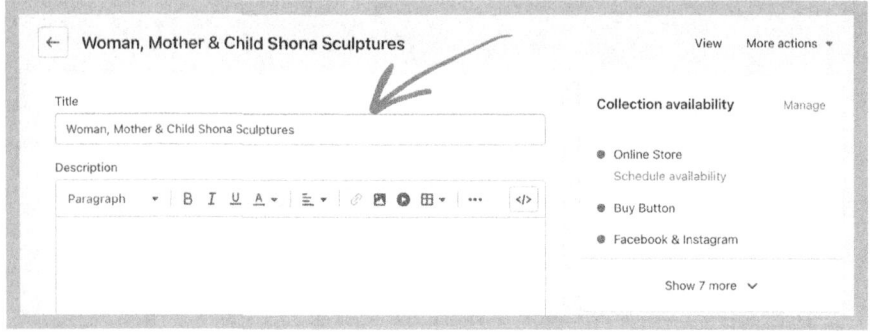

[2.5.3]

In the following image, you can see what it looks like in the browser on the website. The title is descriptive but not too long or short.

[2.5.4]

Step 2. Add your collection description

When you add a description on a collection page, keep these tips in mind:

- The information helps your customer immediately understand the collection's benefits.
- It is excellent for SEO (Search Engine Optimization). Google likes it.
- Keep it short because the description pushes the products lower in the browser window.

In the following image, for TheMissingPiecePuzzle.com collection pages, we created an accordion for the information. The customer can view the information if they want to, and it keeps the products at the top of the page.

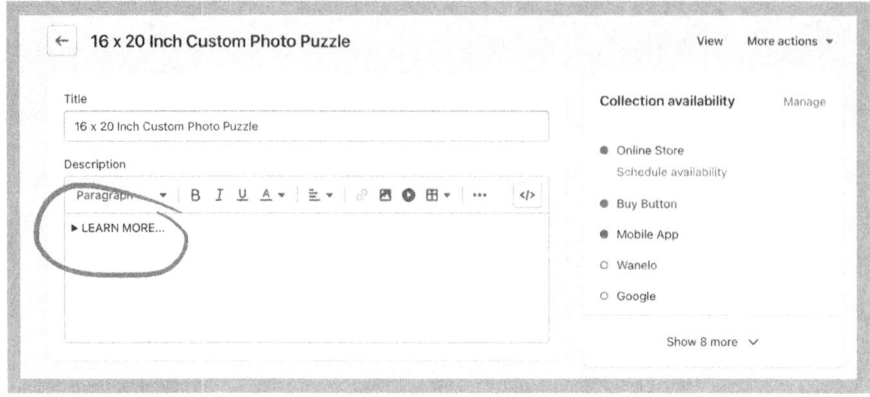

[2.5.5]

Pro Tip: Do not add too much information for your collection description, because this will push your products lower on the page for the visitor and you want your visitor to see your products. Keep is short!

COLLECTION TYPE

The first thing you need to realize about collections in Shopify is that there are **manual** and **automated collections.** You can have both types of collections in your store.

Manual (static) Collection

There are different reasons for creating manual collections:

- You want to add every single product to your collection manually.
- You want to create sub-collections which is a main collection with other collections on the same collection page. This is explained further in the chapter.
- You have a few products and are not going to expand your selections.
- You are selling digital products and there is a tax override on the products because your state or county does not require you to charge taxes. the products need to be in a manual collection to create a tax override for your digital products.

Manual collections must be updated manually when adding a new product to your store.

> Pro Tip: I would suggest using manual collections only if you have minimal products and do not plan to expand your product range.

You should still do Automatic Collections, just in case you want to expand your range of products.

Automated Collections

An automated collection uses selection conditions to include matching products automatically. You can add up to 60 selection conditions and specify whether products need to meet all conditions or any condition to be included in the collection.

When adding products to your store, you can allocate tags or the condition in your collection, and the product will automatically be added to the collection you identified.

> Pro Tip: Check out more prominent brands and see what they do. Remember, they have large teams of experts creating their pages and staying on top of trends. Don't just create your pages once and forget about them. Update all your pages regularly and know what is happening in your industry.

Step 1. Select Manual (static) Collection or Automated Collections.

I will walk you through all the steps, so you are comfortable executing them both.

```
Collection type

○ Manual
   Add products to this collection one by one. Learn more about manual collections.
● Automated
   Existing and future products that match the conditions you set will automatically be
   added to this collection. Learn more about automated collections.


Conditions

Products must match:   ● all conditions   ○ any condition

   [ Product tag      ▼ ]   [ is equal to    ▼ ]   [                ⇕ ]

   [ Add another condition ]
```

[2.5.6]

Step 2. To activate a Manual Collection

Choose 'Manual' in Collection Type. This selection has to be saved before it activates.

```
Collection type

● Manual
   Add products to this collection one by one. Learn more about manual collections.
○ Automated
   Existing and future products that match the conditions you set will automatically be
   added to this collection. Learn more about automated collections.
```

[2.5.7]

Now you can add your products to your collection page manually. Browse and find them in your Shopify store.

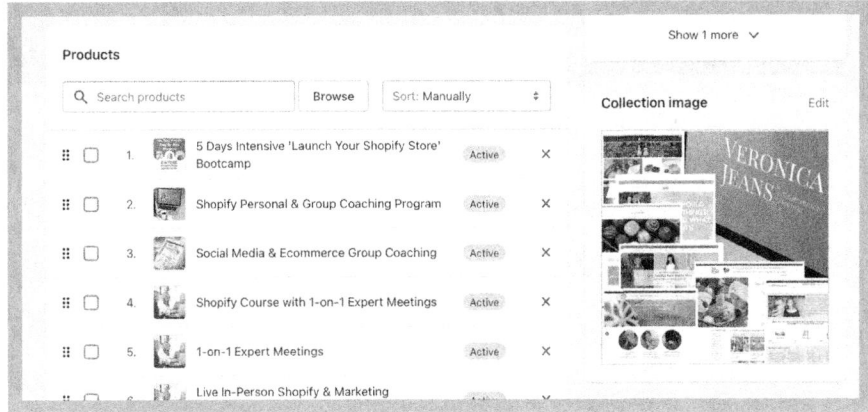

[2.5.8]

Once your browse for your products, all the products will pop up that you have in your store. If you search for a particular type of product, then those will be available. Check every product you want in these collections.

[2.5.9]

This is also a way of eliminating products from a collection. You can create a collection within a collection. This means, you have a main collection 'Boys', and your sub-collection can be 'Shirts', 'Pants', 'Outerwear'. Your main collection can be without any products or with products. In the following image, we have 3 sub-collections.

[2.5.10]

Your products in your collections can be manipulated in eight ways to appear in your store. You can sort your products in your collections as follows: 'Best-selling', 'Products A-Z', 'Products Z-A', 'Highest price', 'Lowest price', 'Newest' , 'Oldest',' Manually'.

[2.5.11]

> Pro Tip: if you use 'Manually' you can sort your products the way you want to and not randomly.

Step 3. To activate an Automated Collection

Choose Automated and you don't have to save before you can add your products automatically.

Collection type

○ Manual
Add products to this collection one by one. Learn more about manual collections.

◉ Automated
Existing and future products that match the conditions you set will automatically be added to this collection. Learn more about automated collections.

Conditions

Products must match: ◉ all conditions   ○ any condition

| Product tag ▼ | is equal to ▼ | ▲▼ |

[Add another condition]

[2.5.6]

Add conditions for your collection. Choose how you want to add your products to the collection. You can select from the following options to control how a product needs to match the condition value that you enter: You can automatically arrange your collection by 'Title,' 'Type,' 'Product category', 'Vendor,' 'Price,' 'Tag,' 'Compare at Price,' 'Weight,' 'Inventory Stock,' or 'Variant's Title.'

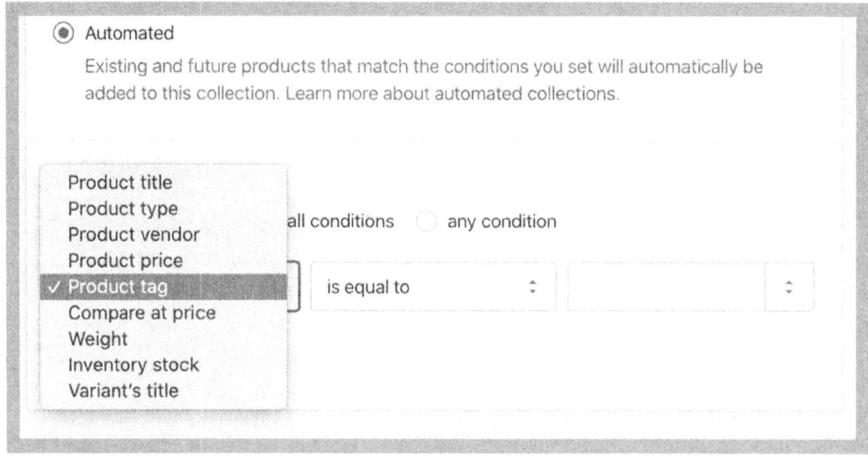

[2.5.12]

In this example, we will choose to arrange your collection by 'Product tag'. You can add more conditions, but I want to keep this quick and straightforward to get your Shopify store up and running. If you choose 'all conditions,' and add more than one condition (option), then every condition narrows the products to be added to the collection. So, for instance, if you choose two conditions, both conditions must be met to find the product. Only products that have both 'Courses' and 'Shopify' as tags will be added to the collection.

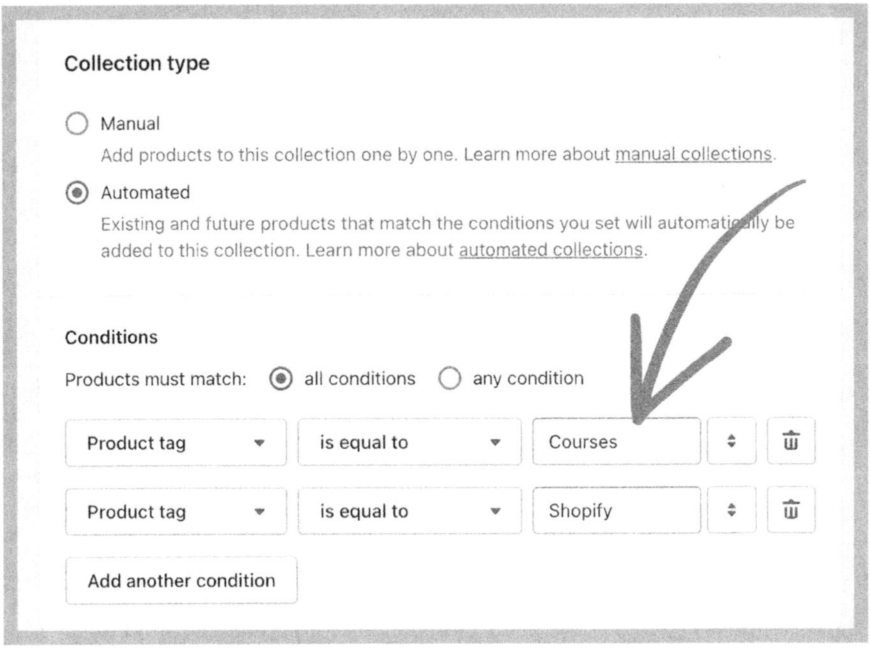

COLLECTIONS

[2.5.13]

If you choose 'any condition', all the products that match a tag as in the next case, will be added to the collection.

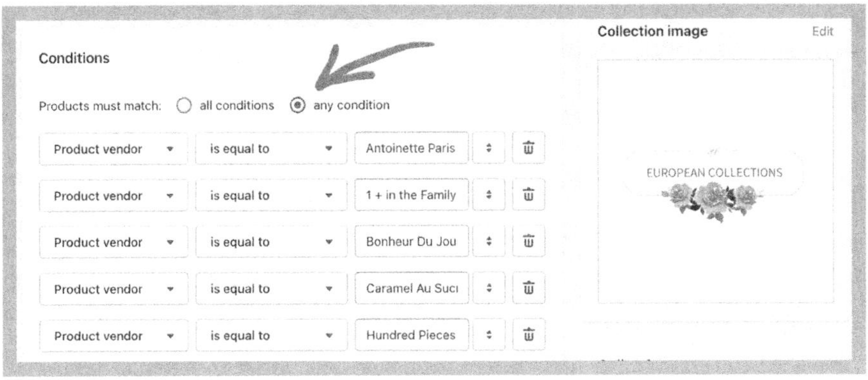

[2.5.14]

Add more conditions. Choose your second condition which will work with the first condition.

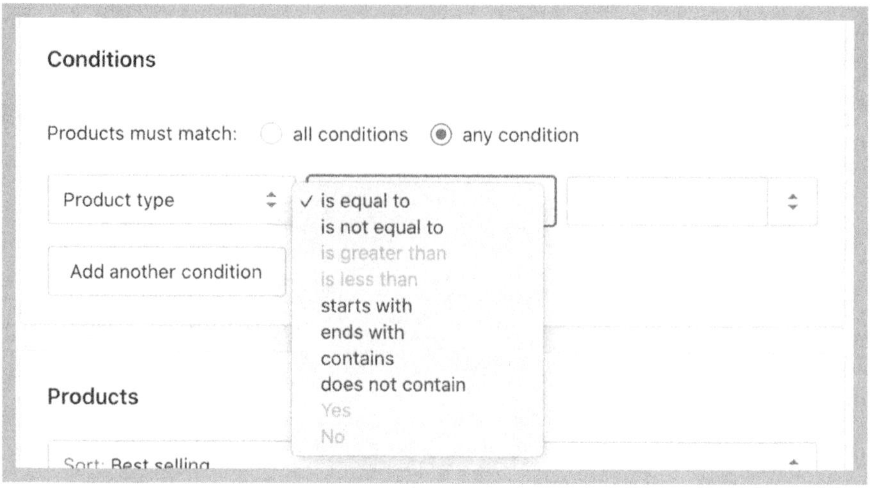

[2.5.15]

Add a value for the condition. Enter a condition value in the third field. So if your condition is a tag, you will add the tag value in this field as in the example, the tag was 'Woman'. All the products with a tag 'Woman' will be added to this collection.

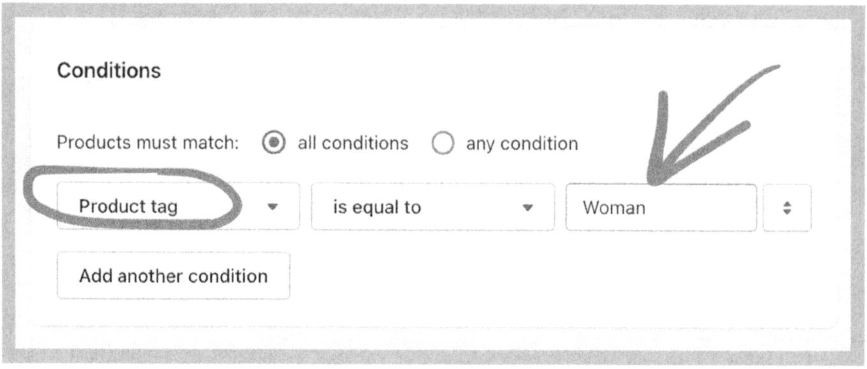

[2.5.16]

PRODUCTS

Once you decide what type of collection you need and you have saved your choice, now you can add your products manually if you have a manual collection, or if the collection is automatic, the products will be added automatically.

Step 1. Add your products

If you have a manual collection, search for the products that you want to add to this collection in the search bar or you can click on the 'Browse' button to view your products.

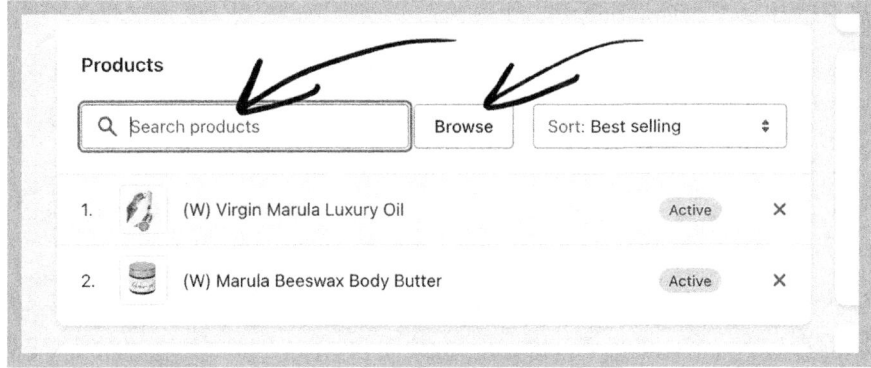

[2.5.31]

Step 2. Sort your products

Your products in your collections can be manipulated in eight ways to appear in your store. You can sort your products in your collections as follows: 'Best-selling', 'Products A-Z', 'Products Z-A', 'Highest price', 'Lowest price', 'Newest' , 'Oldest',' Manually'.

[2.5.11]

> Pro Tip: if you chose 'Manually' you can sort your products the way you want to and not randomly.

Now you know how vital 'TAGS' are. They can make it so much easier to add products to your collections in the future without adding another step to your process after adding products.

PUBLISHING

Depending on what sales channels you add to your store, your products can be selected to show on different sales channels.

Step 1. Manage Sales Channel

When you start your Shopify store, the collection will be automatically added to the 'Online store'.

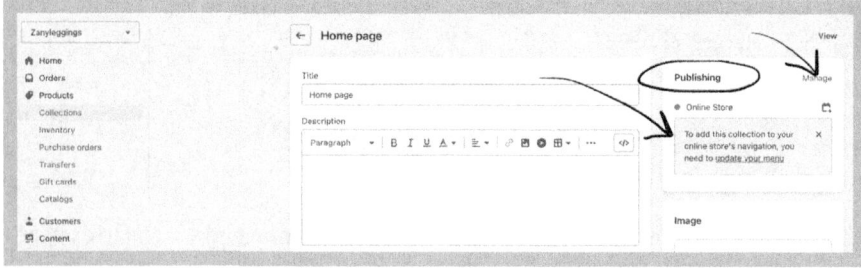

[2.5.37]

Availability on sales channels when you start will be '**Online Store**'. Your product must be online to show anywhere on your store or the internet. You will not be able to add it to your navigation or the 'Buy Button' app.

Once you add more sales channel, you can add them in the collection or add the sales channels in the 'Bulk' editor.

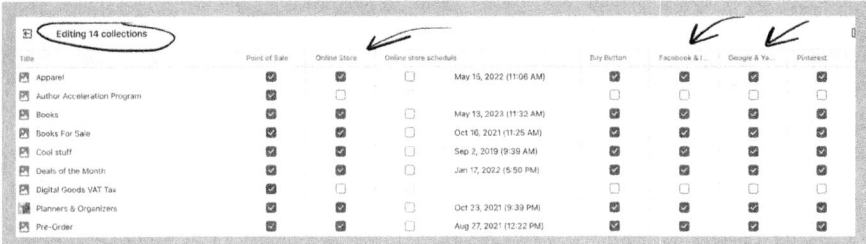

[2.5.38]

For the collection to be viewable in the browser, the collection needs to be added to the navigation.

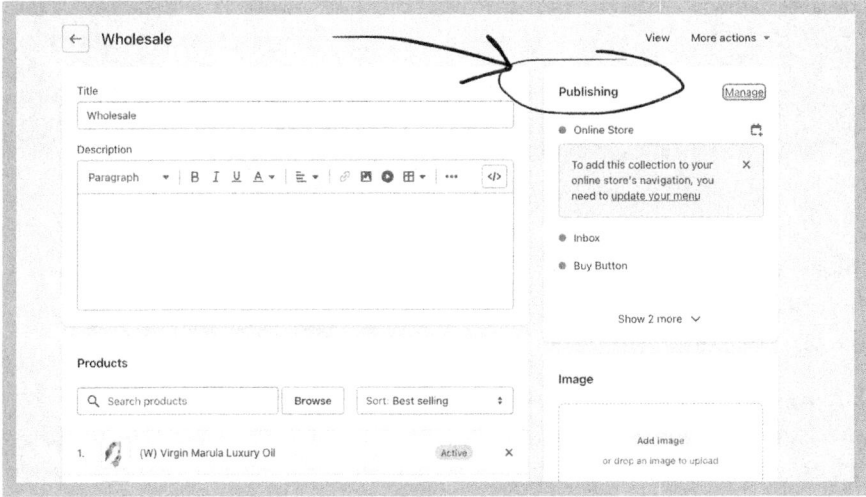

[2.5.34]

In the following image you can see what the 'Publishing' availability looks like in an active store.

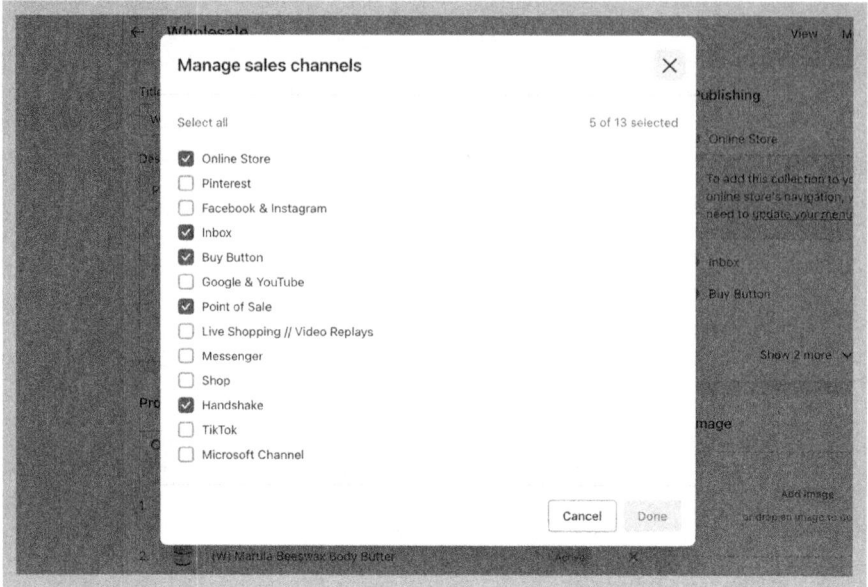

[2.5.33]

Once you have added more Sales channels, you can either add them or not to the collection. Then, the collection will be added to that particular category in the sales channel.

For **digital products**, you are restricted to where you can post your collections/products. I have not added them to Facebook, Instagram, Google. Etc. Sales channels will very quickly let you know if they don't like the type of product or collection.

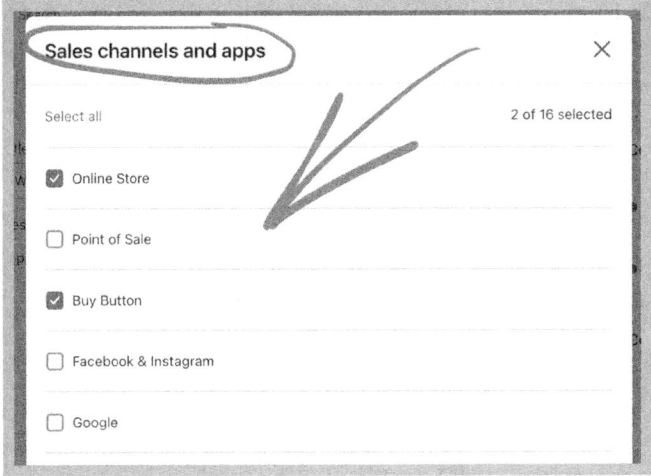

[2.5.20]

You can also control the visibility by date, as seen in the following image. The collection will only become visible online when you pick a date.

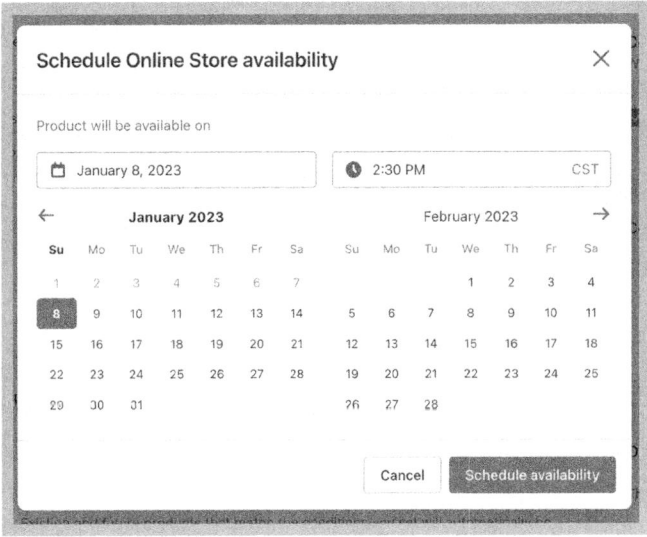

[2.5.21]

IMAGE

Collection images are essential if you want a banner image on your collection pages or a featured collection on your homepage. The size of your collection image will determine how it appears on your homepage and as a banner on your collection page.

In the following image I have added a square image because it is part of the sub-collection and I have added it to my homepage as a feature collection.

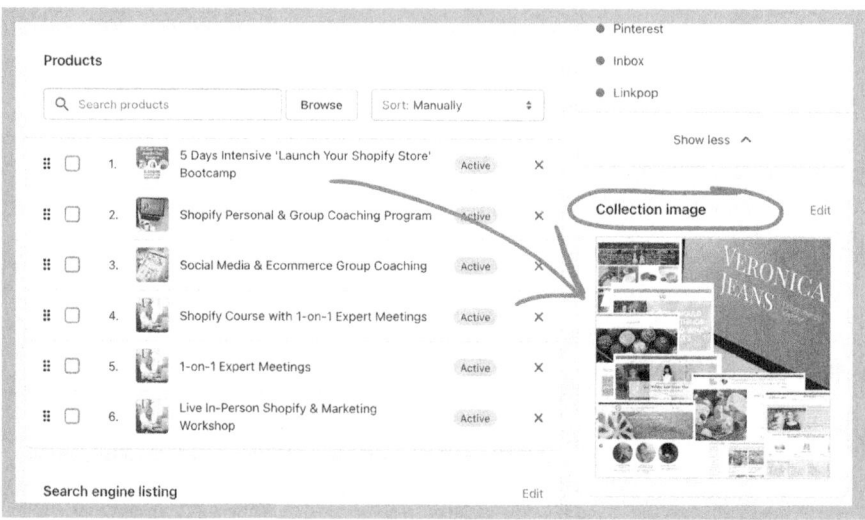

[2.5.22]

The size of the image you upload will affect the view of the banner image in your browser, as shown in the following image. In a lot of themes, you can control the banner size for the collection in 'Customize'.

Step 1. Create your collection image

Go to Canva.com and create a custom size image. I would start with 1600px x 600px for a banner, and for a feature image I use 1000px x 1000px, but you can create several sizes to try them out. In the following image we created a round image in Canva and added some pizzaz to the image to make it stand out.

[2.5.23]

Step 2. Add your collection image

Upload the image to the collection page. Click on 'Edit' - to change your image, remove the image, and add alt tags.

[2.5.24]

Add your 'Alt Tag' to the image - This is an explanation of what the image is about.

[2.5.25]

Step 3. View your page in the browser.

View your page in the browser. It is always a good idea to view how it looks because it really depends on your theme how your images show up.

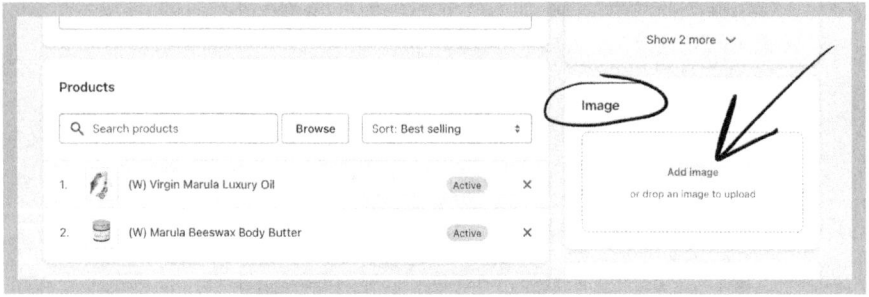

[2.5.35]

ONLINE STORE: THEME TEMPLATE

The default collection page in your Shopify store is a '**default collection**' template. The information that is added to the collection page dashboard on the '**default collection**' template will show on the browser window.

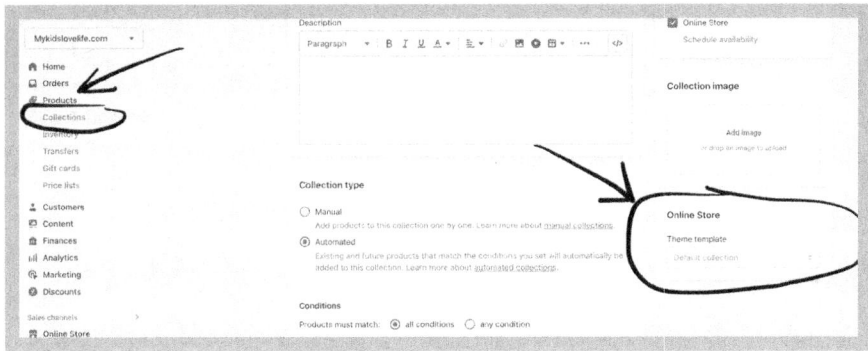

[2.5.26]

The collection page that visitors see is shown in the following image. They will see images, descriptions and all the products for the collection.

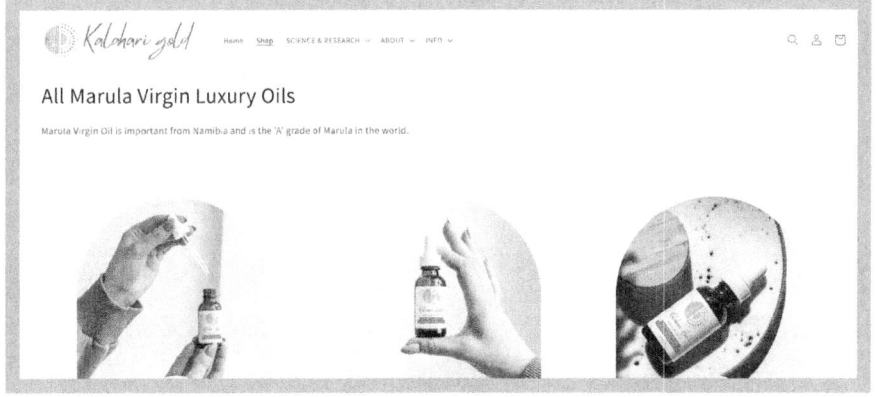

[2.5.27]

You can add more detailed information to your collection pages in **'Themes'** - **'Customization'**. When customizing a collection page with more detailed information, it will be displayed on every collection page.

For example: In the collection dashboard in KalahariGold.com there is a default collection template and an 'accessories' collection template.

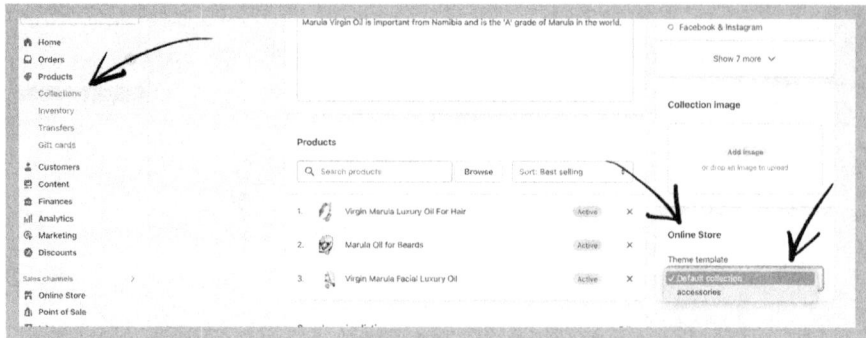

[2.5.28]

I created a different template for the accessories for my collaborators and wholesale customers. In the following image you can view the different sections that were added in the 'Customize' editor for the Marula oil for my collaborators. I wanted to show them a video how to use the website to shop for their wholesale products. This page is only for my wholesale customers and they can only get to the page by logging into their accounts.

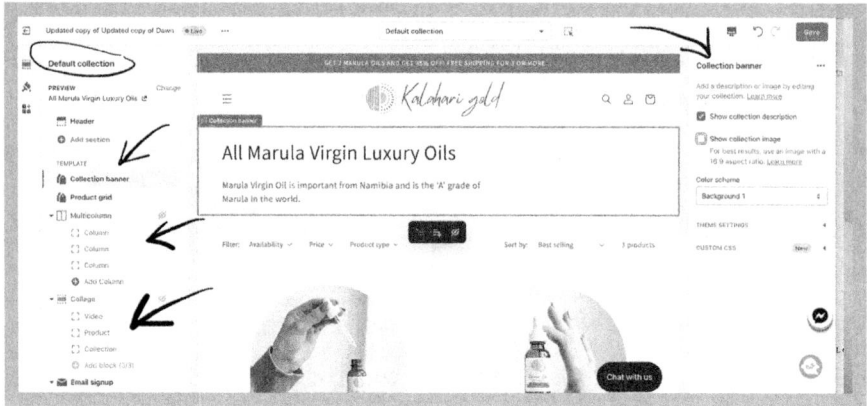

[2.5.29]

NOTE: *You will learn more about how to customize your pages in the Shopify Theme chapter. The following image shows how I added digital products with different templates to my Shopify store. Creating different collection sales pages in Shopify is easy.*

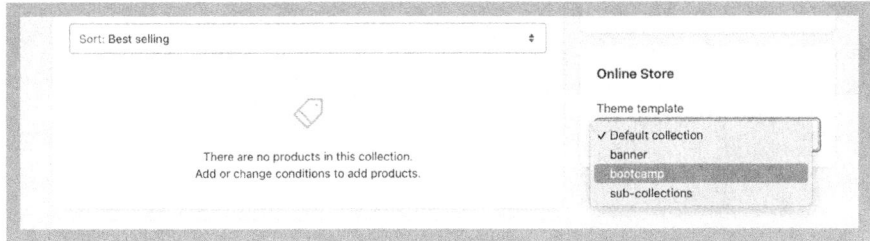

[2.5.30]

SEARCH ENGINE LISTING

SEO (Search Engine Optimization) determines how your collection page will show up on Google or any other search engine pages. You can change your information to your best advantage.

[2.5.17]

When you search on Google, you will see other people's websites and stores or pages displayed on the search page.

Optimizing each product information page is critical. So many people neglect this very important part of the product detail page; it is a great source for creating excitement and information for your product and brand.

NOTE: *See full description and steps on how to optimize shown in my Shopify Made Easy book 3 - Optimize Your Shopify Store 2023.*

RESOURCES:

Here is a link to my RESOURCES & TOOLS page:

https://veronicajeans.online/resources

Copy.ai is a fabulous extension to your content for your pages and information - https://veronicajeans.online/copy-ai

Automated Collections:

https://veronicajeans.online/collections

CHAPTER 9
NAVIGATION & MENUS

**WHERE TO FIND THIS IN SHOPIFY? ONLINE STORE > NAVIGATION

MENUS ARE part of the customer journey in your store and make it easy for your customers to get their information that they are searching for.

WHAT TO EXPECT IN THIS CHAPTER:

- *Navigation Menu*
- *Main Menu*
- *Sidebar Menu*
- *Footer Menu*
- *Main Menu navigation*
- *Footer Menu navigation*
- *Sidebar Menu navigation*
- *Collections & Filters*
- *Other Menus*

Here are some fundamental principles to remember for any website menu:

- **DISTINCT:** Make sure your main menu is visually separated and easy to find. Try not to make your main menu the same color, font, and size as your body text - your navigational text should always stand out.

- **SIMPLE:** Do make it easy for your customer to navigate your menu. It must be easy to find your products. Try not to be too different from other websites because this is a store, not a portfolio for an artist. Keep it simple.
- **CONSISTENT**: Keep your main menu the same on each page. This is not a hardship for an eCommerce store because the theme will help you keep your menu the same.
- **CLEAR**: Your products or collections must be clear to your customer. Use specific terms for naming your menu/product/collection. When setting up your navigation, you can change the name of your collection, product, or page.
- **CONCISE**: Be concise when naming your navigation. Do not make the menu title too long. Use only max two words if you have to. Otherwise, it doesn't look obvious.
- **INTERACTIVE**: When your customer hovers or clicks on a link, the color must change to indicate where and where they are going.
- **ORDERED**: Add your most important link in the first menu link, and 'Contact,' at the end of the navigation. I don't add an 'About' and 'Blog' link on the main menu because it takes valuable real estate. I add those to the footer menu.
- **STRUCTURED**: In your menu, you need to add your primary collection at the top tier of your navigation. The next level of menu links is part of that department. In Chapter 1, you created a storyboard for your departments/collections and products. Well, those departments are part of your navigation!
- **CLICKABLE**: All your menu links need to be clickable. Even if you have dropdown menus, your main menu link in the top tier of your navigation must be clickable. What I mean by that is that your menu link needs to be linked to one of your products, collections, or pages.
- **SHALLOW**: Do not have more than three levels. A dropdown menu makes it easier for your customer to find information, but I would limit the menu to 2 levels in a shopping cart.
- Unless you use a Megamenu (those extensive menus spread across the page), you should probably not use more than two levels.
- **STICKY**: It is better if your menu does not disappear when your customer scrolls down the page, so they know where they are, and also, it makes it easy to search.

- **RESPONSIVE**: Make sure your menu loads fast. You have seconds to keep your customer's attention, and your menu and website have to load fast.

> Pro Tip: Research the brand companies that you admire or that operate within the same niche market as your own. Take note of their website and their strategies. This exercise is great because it provides inspiration for what you should be doing, but on a smaller scale. Keep in mind that not all brands may be doing it correctly, but you can still extract valuable ideas to test and implement.

NAVIGATION MENU

A navigation menu is typically a horizontal or vertical bar with links that can be found on every one of a website's pages. With a navigation menu, visitors can easily navigate to the information that they need.

On a website, a **navigation menu** is a simple, organized list of links that help you find other pages, usually within the same site. You find these menus at the top, bottom, or side of a webpage.

The pages and content of your website and store will only be visible to your customers if you add them to any of your navigation menus.

You can add different types of information to the menus, i.e., an information page, collections, products, or blogs.

In Shopify, the navigation is a list of menus which consists of menu items. Each menu has a title and menu items.

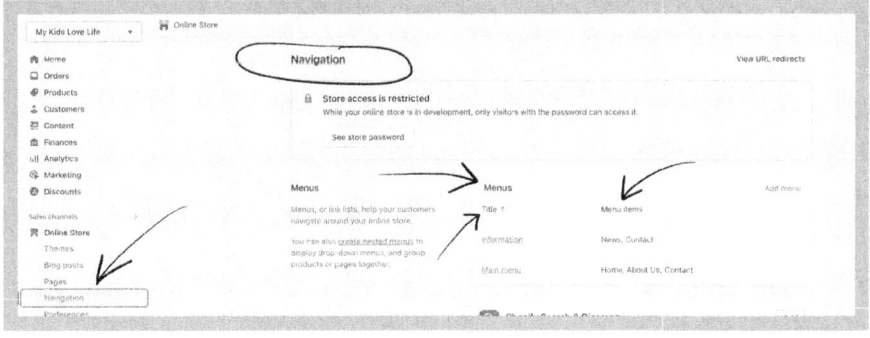

[2.6.24]

Each menu item has a name and a link. The link will connect to any page in your Shopify store.

If you have not created a particular page you want to connect, then it will not appear in the link search bar.

[2.6.25]

The handle will be automatically added to the menu correctly when add the menu title. The handle is part of the code used in Shopify.

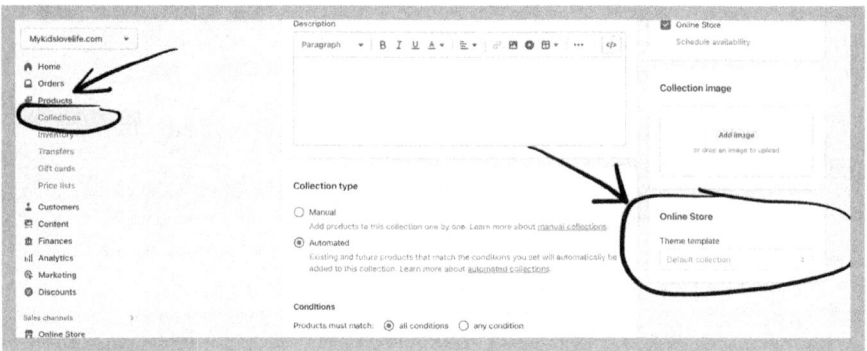

[2.6.26]

Good and Bad Practices

Too many store owners try and stuff as many menu links at the top of their pages, which only confuses a visitor to the website.

In the next image you can see what happens if you have too many menu links at the top of your page.

Here are the wrong aspects of this menu:

- Too many words in the menu name.
- No distinctive separation of each menu item.
- Navigation menu bar is in 2 main layers.
- Menu Names do not stand out.

The following menu is SEO rich - lots of great keywords but a confusing customer experience. Google is adamant that the user or visitor experience is optimized on every page and website.

[3.5.30]

In the next image is an example of a navigation menu that is clear and concise. You can easily find what you are looking for.

[3.5.31]

> Pro Tip: For the sake of SEO (Search Engine Optimization) and customer experience, I recommend keeping your main navigation menu at the top of the website limited to five to seven menu link items at most.

But as we see below, sometimes 7 is too much because the menu names are too long. Making the font smaller is not going to make the issue any better.

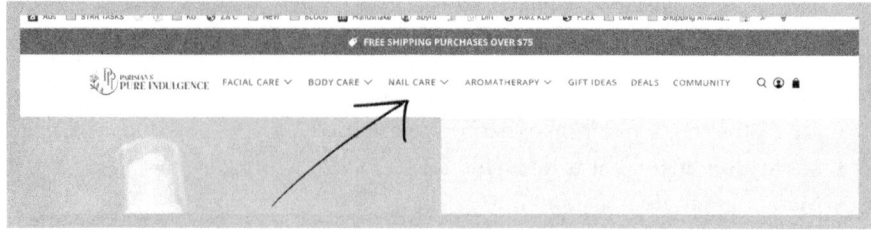

[3.5.30a]

As you can see in the following image, less and larger font is better for the customer experience in your store. Now customers can see the menu easier and it is not too confusing with too many choices.

[3.5.30b]

MAIN MENU

There are two types of main menus in the default Shopify theme:

- Dropdown Menu
- Mega Menu

These menus are generally for your collections, products and company information if possible, to be able to navigate the store easily. It is important to add information to your top navigation:

You can either add dropdown or a mega menu to keep the information nice and tight for easy navigation.

Here are two different top menus:

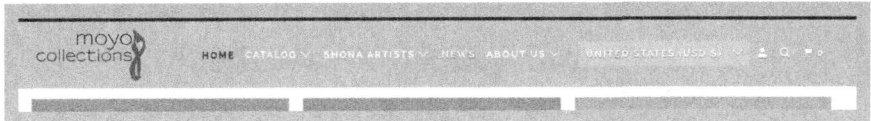

[2.6.1]

One main menu with a dropdown menu links from my website, VeronicaJeans.com as shown in the following image.

[2.6.2]

On Kalaharigold.com, we created a **mega menu** in a default Shopify theme. A mega menu stretches the full width of the browser with the nested menus in columns.

[2.6.2a]

The menu choices are in the 'Header' section in the 'Customize' dashboard - a dropdown or mega menu.

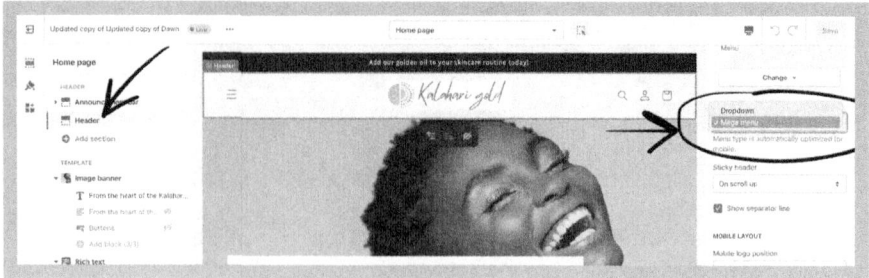

[2.6.2b]

The mega menu, as shown in the following image, has the 'Science & Research' as the main menu link visible on the page. Once the menu link is clicked, the mega menu opens up to the second level of menus. I have capitalized the menu link to distinguish them from the other links. Then added the third level of menus, that flow under the second tier as seen in image 2.6.2a.

[2.6.2c]

SIDEBAR MENU

The sidebar menu adds more details, such as prices, sizes, or elements for a specific page or collection. TheMissingPiecePuzzle.com has a sidebar menu on her homepage which is unusual, but experience showed her that her customers search for puzzles with the size of puzzle and pieces of puzzle.

[2.6.3]

We are constantly testing to see what works best for her customer to get to the product page as quickly as possible.

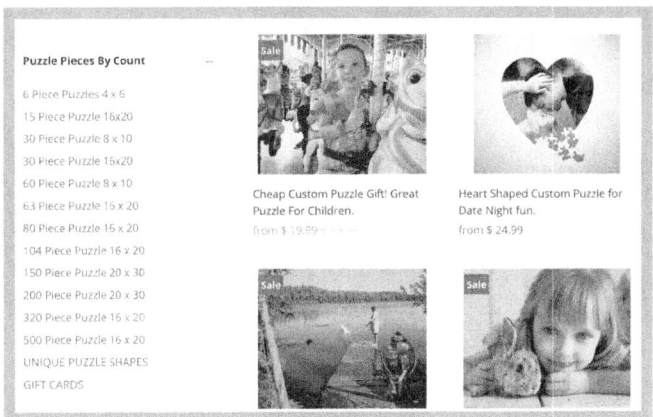

[2.6.4]

> Pro Tip: Do not add a sidebar menu to your product page. Your customer has already decided to buy the product when they land on the product page. A sidebar menu would only add a distraction for the customer.

FOOTER MENU

Your footer menu is for your company information, shipping information, Refunds, Privacy, blogs, and other relevant resources for your customer. Some of the menu links can be repeated in the Footer to help customers find information.

With most themes, you can add more than one menu.

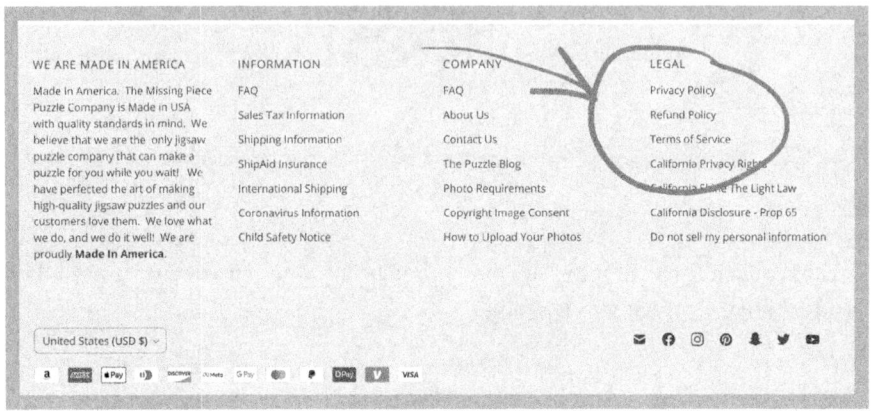

[2.6.5]

Other information can be added, for example:

- Login form or newsletter signup
- Company information
- Contact information

Social Icons and links can be added either to the Main menu, the footer menu, or both.

NAVIGATION & MENUS

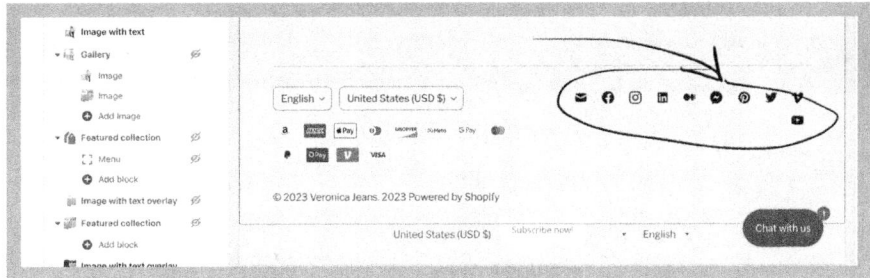

[2.6.6]

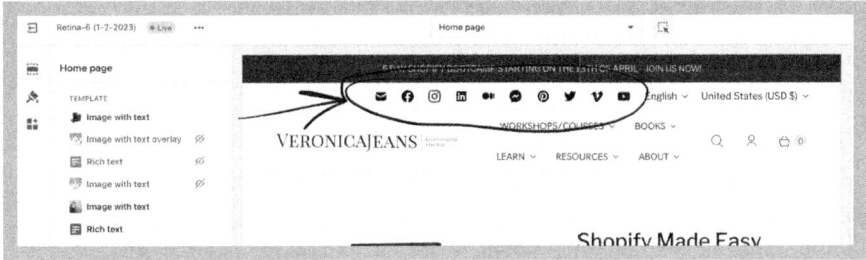

CREATE YOUR MENU NAVIGATION

Start with the storyboard your created for your products and collections. Your storyboard defines your navigation.

Step 1. Define your navigation

You created a logical and easy path for your products and your customers with your storyboard. Now you have an easy way to create your navigation for your store.

COLLECTIONS & NAVIGATION							
BOYS >		Sizes/Tags For Products					
	Baby Boys	0, 3mth, 6mth, 9mth					
	Toddlers	1, 2, 3, 4					
	Kids	5, 6, 7, 8					
(Type)		(Where)	(Tags)	(Type)		(Where)	(Tags)
Boys				Girls			
Bottoms >	Long Pants	Collection	Boy Bottoms, Boy Long Pa	Bottoms		1 x Product	Girl Bottoms
	Shorts	Collection	Boy Bottoms, Boy Shorts	Tops		Collection	Girl Tops
Tops >	Long Sleeves	Collection	Boy Tops, Collar	Outerwear		1 x Product	Girl Outerwear
	Short Sleeves	Collection	Boy Tops, Tshirt				
Outerwear >		1 x Product	Boy Outerwear				

[2.1.2]

Step 2. Navigation

When you open your navigation page, you will have some default menus, the main menu, and a footer menu that are automatically created for you by Shopify.

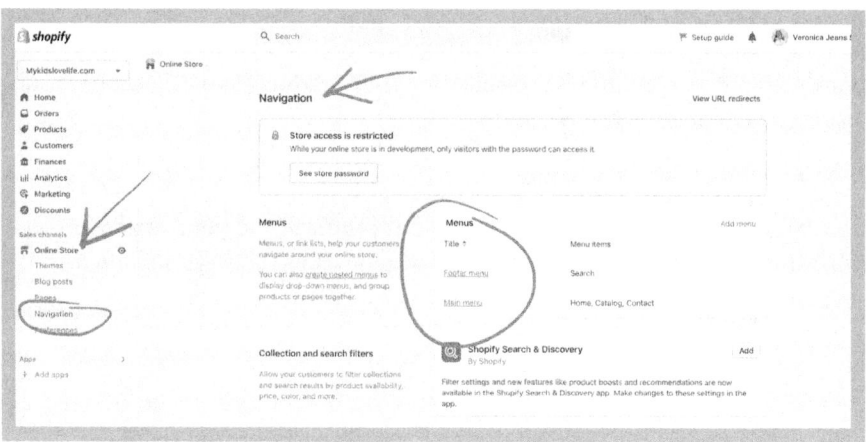

[2.6.8]

The name or the default title of the main menu will not appear on the website. Only the 'Menu items' will show on the online store.

NAVIGATION & MENUS

[2.6.9]

The default title of the 'Footer' menu may appear on the website, depending on your Shopify theme.

[2.6.10]

> **Pro Tip:** I like to rename the footer menu to 'Information' and leave the default for the 'Main' menu.

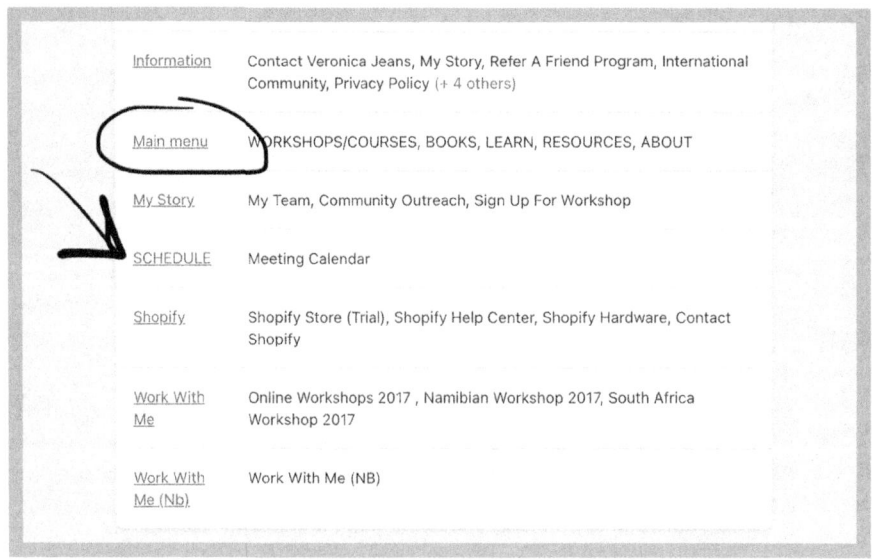

[2.6.11]

As you can see in the following image it is easier to see which menu is the main menu when you start creating different menus for your store.

[2.6.11a]

Step 3. Add a main menu

Now we start your main menu navigation.

Shopify has automatically added some default menu items which you can either edit or remove. Add a menu item to your main menu by clicking the **'+Add menu item'** link.

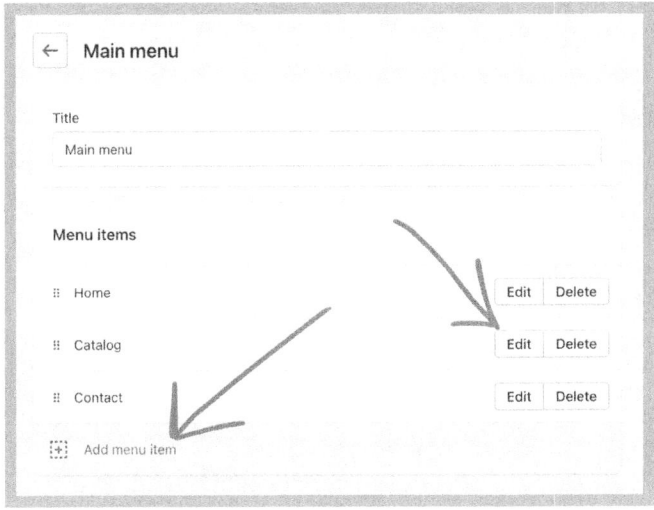

[2.6.13]

A sidebar on the right will appear in your window. Now you add your cursor to the 'Link' box, and all your options for products, collections, pages, blogs, etc., will appear. You can search and find the item you want to add to your menu.

[2.6.14]

> 💡 Pro Tip: If your name for your collection or product or page is long, do not add the complete title to your menu. The menu title should only be one or two words. Resist adding a long title. It looks messy, and your customer will be confused. This will be detrimental to your customer journey.

Now you can choose the collection you want to add to your main navigation menu. As you can see, it is a long title for the collection. You can rename your collection for your menu, and it will not affect your collection page.

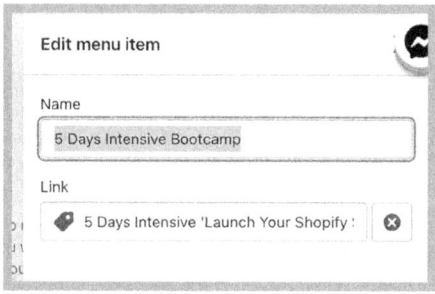

[2.6.15]

Add the menu item to your navigation menu.

In Shopify navigation, you can create a dropdown menu for your main menu. These are called nested menus.

The main menu in the following image shows you nested menu items. The top level menu item is 'Workshops/Courses' and the **nested menu item** is 'Launch Your Shopify Store', etc.

NAVIGATION & MENUS

[image of Main menu edit screen]

[2.6.12]

Or as you can see in the next image, the 'About Us' is the main menu item, and then 'Our Story', 'Community', and 'Contact Us', are nested under the main menu item.

[2.6.12a]

And here is what the main menu will look like in the browser window.

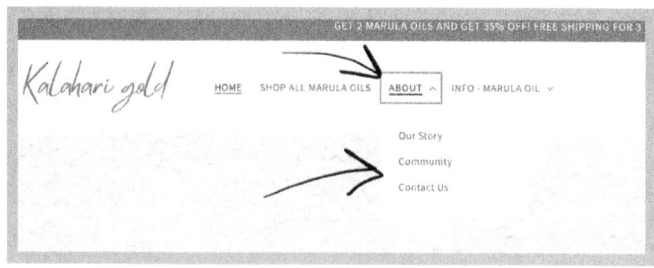

[2.6.12b]

Step 4. Add tags to the menu

You can add some tags to the menu item, but that is optional. You have to save the menu item first to the navigation, before you can add a tag. Stick to the tags you already created for your collections on your storyboard.

Step 5. Edit menu items

Now you can move that menu item into a different position on the menu list.

> Pro Tip: Some basics about your cursor. If your cursor has a full-hand display, you can drag and drop the section you are on where you need it to be. If you move your cursor over the six dots on the left side of the menu item, you will see a hand appear. If your cursor has a finger, it means it is pointing to a link.

[2.6.12e]

When the full-hand display of the cursor is over the 6 dots on the left, you can move the menu item to any position you want to in the main menu.

In the following image you can see that once you click on the menu item you want to move, a blue line appear where the menu item is presently. The menu item will pop up over the position it was and now you can move it. The blue line will show you where you are placing the menu item.

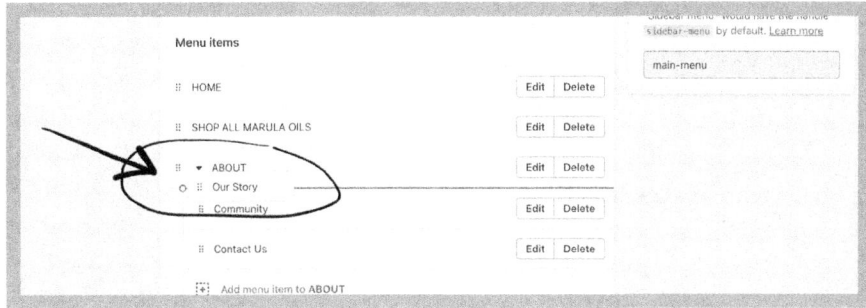

[2.6.12c]

If the menu item is not in the position you wish it to be, move it or discard.

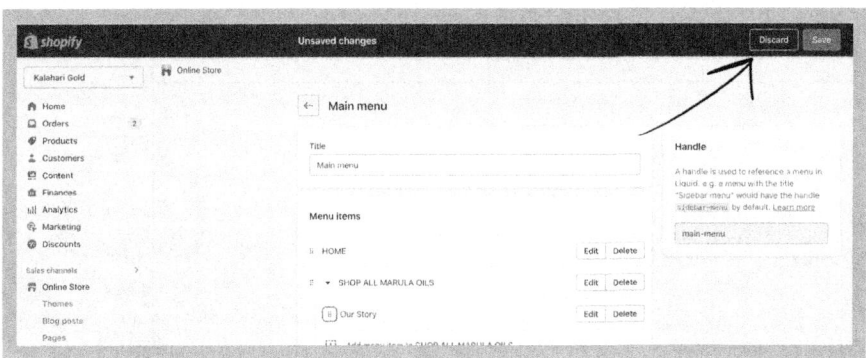

[2.6.12d]

Step 6. Create your footer menu

Why is this different from your main menu? Your main menu can have several drop-down levels, but your footer menu has a vertical link list - no nice menu buttons or anything fancy. You add a footer menu to your store for customers to find **additional information** they might need.

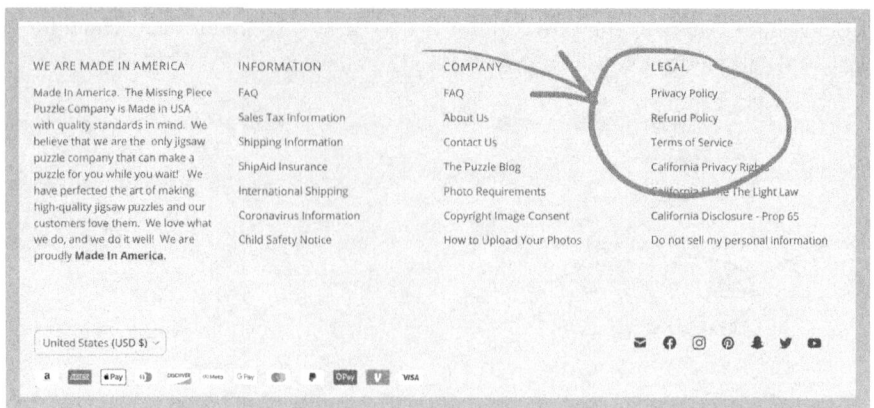

[2.6.5]

Add all your information pages, like FAQ, Shipping, Privacy, Terms of Service, Refund Policy, etc. to these menus.

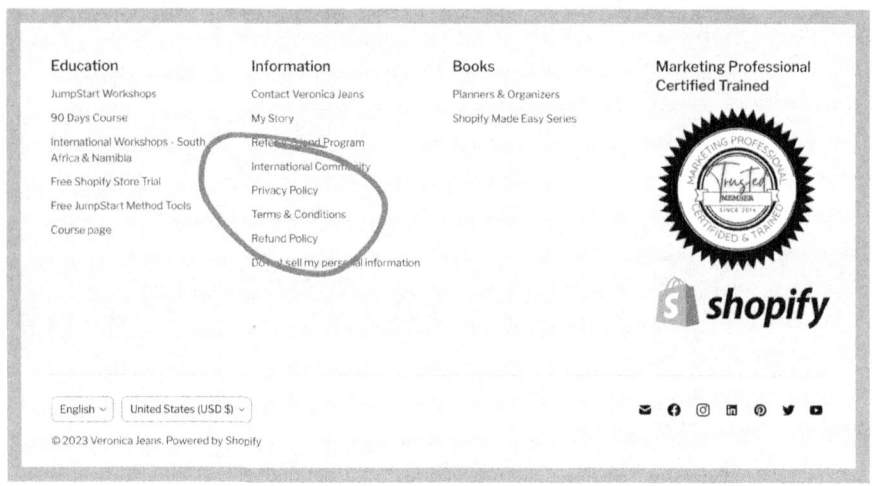

[2.6.6]

Sometimes the theme only allows one menu list, although another menu could be manually added where the address of the company is.

In the following image you can see that the footer menu is added horizontally to the Shopify theme and these are the policies mainly.

NAVIGATION & MENUS

The only other position to add another menu is where the address is – the left content box if necessary.

[2.6.7]

If you need more than one menu for the footer section of your page, you need to create a menu for each list as shown in the following image.

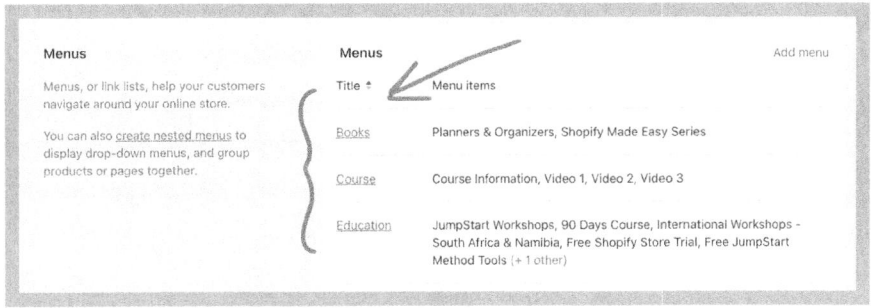

[2.6.17]

Step 7. Create sidebar navigation

Depending on your Shopify theme, you might be able to add a sidebar to your collection or home page. Your sidebar navigation can have different menu lists in two levels, which will be added as a link list menu. If your theme is capable, it allows you to filter some information on the collections page. For instance, vendors, sizes, prices, and ages, as in the example below, are all different menus.

[2.6.18]

In the next image, I have added text sections for the sidebar to show my own advertising.

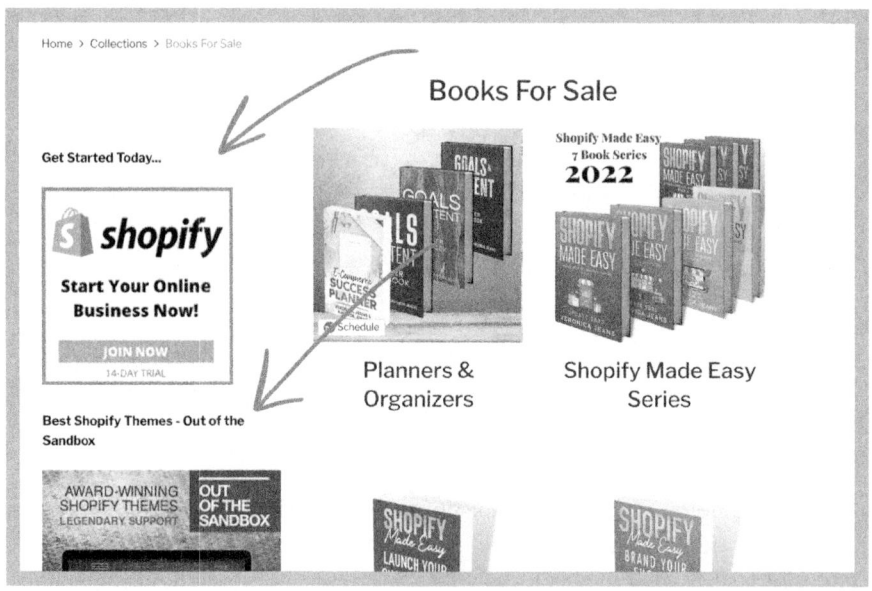

[2.6.19]

In the next image, we have added different menus to the sidebar navigation.

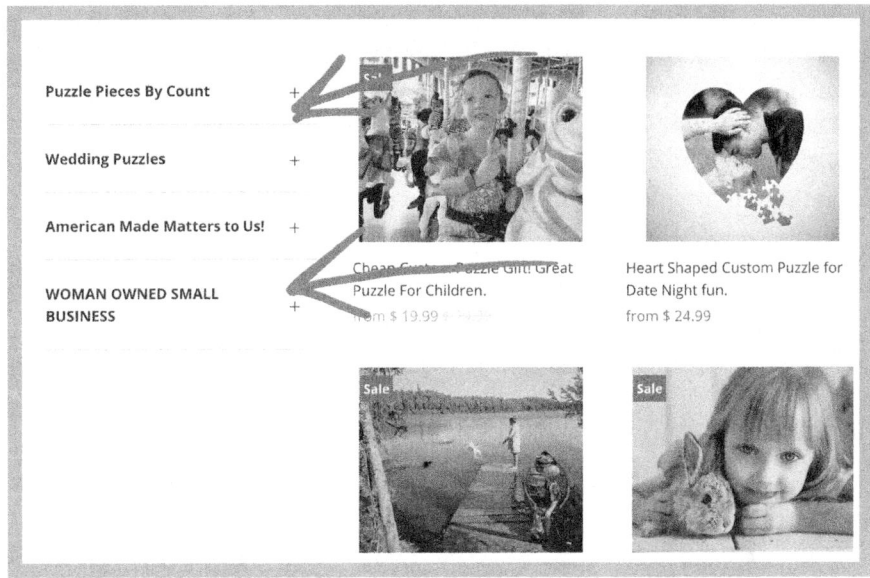

[2.6.20]

Follow the previous steps to add more menus to your store.

You will add your sidebar menu options in your THEMES and 'Customize.' We will add sidebar navigation in the chapter Themes.

OTHER MENUS YOU CAN CREATE

You can create three optional types of menus.

- Mega menu
- Breadcrumb navigation
- Sub-Collection Menu

Mega Menu

The same principles apply to creating a mega menu as to the main navigation menu. You need to create different menus to add them to the mega menu sections in THEMES, 'Customize'.

If your template does not accommodate mega menus, and you want one, you might need an App or a paid template, or only have 2 levels on your main menu and create a selection on your collections description page.

In the following image you can see the 'Navigation' setting under 'Online Store'. I have nested the menu links in 3 levels. The SCIENCE & RESEARCH menu link is on the main menu bar on the website. Then the next level, MORE ABOUT MARULA OIL & TREATMENT & USES, are the next level and I capitalized the text because I want it to stand out and appear as a header link. Then the third level menu links are just normal text.

[2.6.21]

In the next image you can see what it looks like on the website for Kalaharigold.com.

[2.6.22]

> Pro Tip: Do not try to do a Mega menu if you do not have enough pages or links to add. I create the Mega menu because a dropdown menu would go too far down the page.

Breadcrumb Navigation

Breadcrumb navigation is to enable users to visualize where they are in your store and be able to retrace their steps back to where they started. It doesn't take up much real estate. This secondary navigation bar is typically made up of text links separated by the "greater than" symbol (>) and placed below the header.

[3.5.32]

Your theme should have this automatically integrated into the theme. Or it could be an option to add in Themes > Customize > Theme settings. In addition to helping customers understand where they clicked from, it also helps with SEO (Search Engine Optimization).

Sub-Collection Menu

Sub-collection menus are a collection within a collection. Either your template creates this option or you have to code this into your collection page.

If you have this options in your Shopify theme, now we create the menu for the sub-collection.

IDEA: *This is an option in the Out Of The Sandbox Themes or other paid themes.*

Step 1. Get the URL handle

First you need the handle for the collection which is part of the chosen sub-collection.

Go to the 'Collections' section under the 'Products' section, and on the 'Products' dashboard.

Check the 'Online store' section, if the sub-collection' template has been allocated. Then you know your collections and sub-collections have been created.

Find the 'Search engine listing' at the bottom of the dashboard and copy the visible 'URL handle'. This will only be part of the 'URL handle' as shown in the following image.

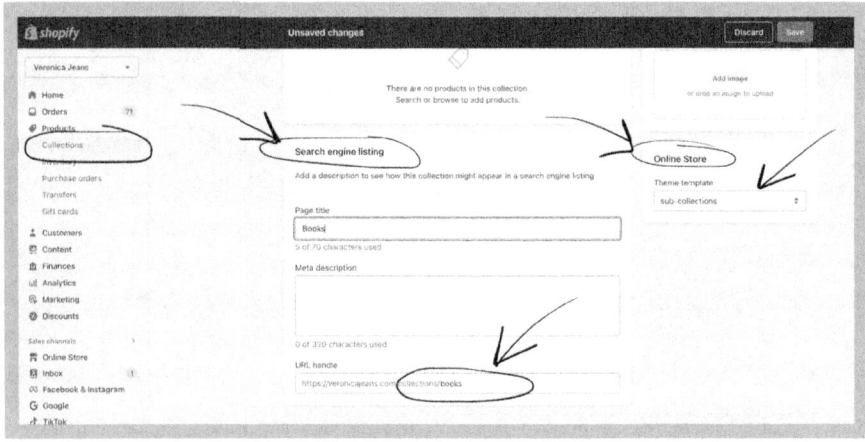

Step 2. Create the menu

Go to the 'Navigation' section and create a new menu.

Add the 'URL handle' you copied from your collections in the 'Handle' section. This has to be the same as the collection otherwise the link will for the sub-collections will not happen.

NAVIGATION & MENUS

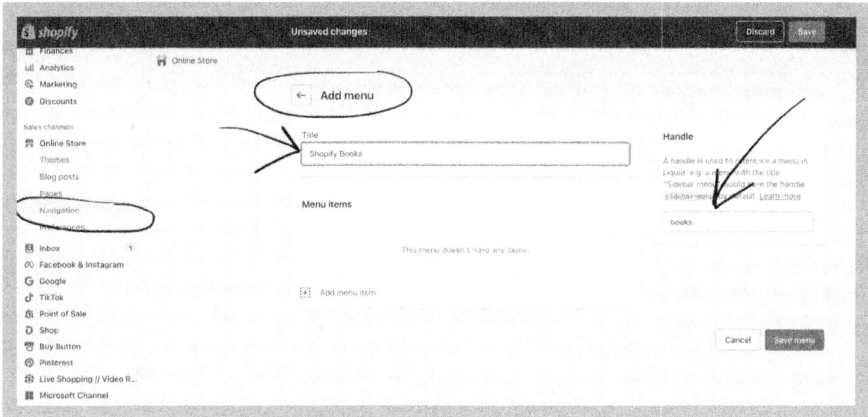

[2.6.28]

You can add any title to your menu, it will not affect the link.

Step 3. Add your menu items

Now you can add all the sub-collections that you want to show in your main collection.

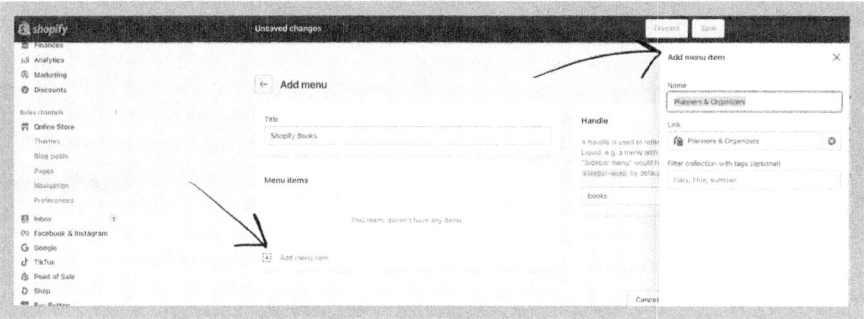

[2.6.29]

Done!

> 🌟 Pro Tip: A good idea is to add a lifestyle image for the main image in the collection or give it a border to distinguish the collection image from the product image.

RESOURCES:

Here is a link to my RESOURCES & TOOLS page:

https://veronicajeans.online/resources

Out Of The Sandbox Chrome Extension: https://veronicajeans.online/OOTSB-chrome

Navigation menu: https://blog.hubspot.com/website/main-website-navigation-ht

What Is Next?

In the next chapter, we will connect The Dots in your Shopify store and social media.

CHAPTER 10
SHOPIFY THEME

 "Design is the silent ambassador of your brand." – Paul Rand, In his book, A Designer's Art.

**WHERE TO FIND THIS IN SHOPIFY? ONLINE STORE > THEMES

SHOPIFY THEMES IS the visual branding of your online store and the representation of your brand, products, and story. In this chapter, we will learn how to implement and use the Shopify Theme 'Customize' editor.

This chapter will only cover the basics for your theme, what each section or area means, and how to use them. In the following chapters, I will show you how to implement the different parts of your store into your branded Shopify theme.

WHAT TO EXPECT IN THIS CHAPTER:

- *What Is a Shopify Theme?*
- *Choose a Theme*
- *Customize Your Theme*
- *Customize Settings*
- *Pages: Dropdown Options*
- *Customize Editor*
- *View Your Store*

WHAT IS A SHOPIFY THEME?

A Shopify theme is a template of pages already designed for you. All you have to do is add the content. You don't need to know HTML or how to code a website. This means you don't need a web developer to get your store up and running. There are no significant expenses upfront.

A Shopify theme, including its layout, is a ready-made design for your branded Shopify store. Changing your theme changes how your site looks on the front end, what visitors see when they browse your site from the web.

You can change and update the store pages yourself.

You also don't need a separate website to create your store. **Shopify and most other shopping platforms** have a home page and different types of pages to add more information to your store. It includes a blog section, so you do not need to create a different website for your blog.

You can add different types of themes to your store. Shopify has free themes and paid themes. Each theme has a demo to see the store in action, including active stores that use the themes.

> Pro Tip: First, check out some brands you like. Create a list of items you want for your store. Then start looking for a theme.

CHOOSE A THEME

It is not easy deciding what you need in a store because it all sounds the same. Here are some main items you need in your store that the free themes might not have:

- Fonts: more fonts are available.
- Product: More image positions
- Sections: Extra sections
- Mega Menu:
- Footer Menu:
- Improved speed

> Pro Tip: It is relatively easy to choose a free theme at the beginning and, later, change to a different theme. The one big task when changing to a new theme will be to re-customize your homepage for the new theme and some pages if you have used the 'Customize' editor. The store information, collections, products, etc., will not change. All your information will be added to the new Theme.

> Pro Tip: When choosing a paid Shopify theme, ensure that they theme will be updated on a regular basis. Shopify and other platforms like Google, change all the time and themes need to be capable of updating without interruption to your business.

Step 1. Select your theme

Find a theme you like the look of in the Shopify Themes store. The default theme in Shopify is 'Dawn'. This will be indicated on the theme when viewing the Shopify website. These are free, and you can find more free themes in the Shopify Theme store

Another option is to use a paid Shopify theme by different developers in the Shopify Theme store.

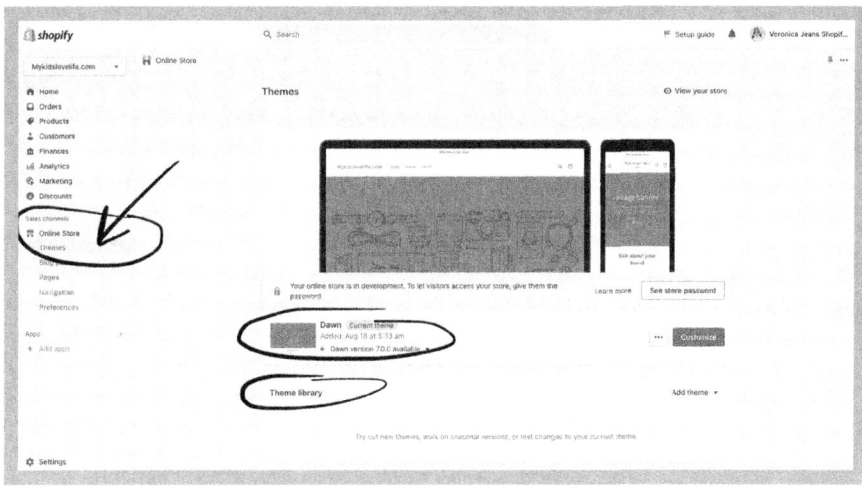

[2.12.0]

Step 2. Upload your theme

You can also upload a theme to Shopify, but it must be from a Shopify-approved developer. Make sure the theme is 2.0 compliant, which means they have the new features that Shopify has added to the Shopify platform.

[2.12.1]

CUSTOMIZE YOUR THEME

Now we get to the good stuff, setting up and customizing your store theme. The setup and customizing of your theme will require all of your branding and tools, including your content and products.

What is the primary purpose of the 'Customize' editor for your theme? You can customize any page in your store and add features and content in the 'Customize' editor dashboard without knowing any HTML language or coding, except for the checkout page. You can choose, add, and configure sections with images, text, and brand colors.

Theme content is built using sections. Sections are customizable blocks of content that determine the layout and appearance of different pages on your online Shopify store.

The sections are on the left of the theme editor, and the editable sections are on the right of the theme editor.

There are different areas in the 'Customize' dashboard for your Theme where you can add or change your visual branding and information for your store.

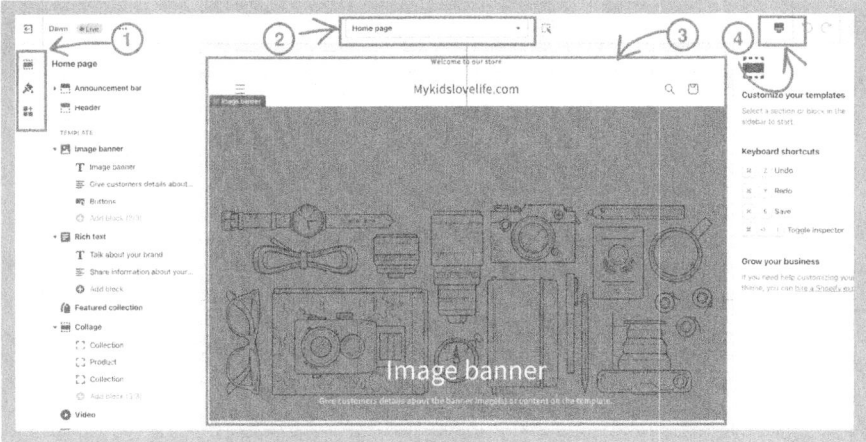

[2.12.2]

'Customize' Settings: There are 3 areas in the editor to customize the theme: the **Sections, Theme Settings, and Apps Embeds** areas. These settings will access the different pages, create the brand elements of your pages, and add the relevant Apps to the pages. This is controlled by the 3 icons on the far left of the dashboard, as shown in the following image.

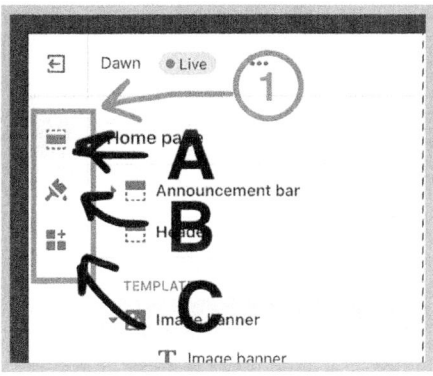

[2.12.2a]

Pages: Dropdown Options: You can navigate to each different area and page in your store, i.e., the home page, product page, collections, blogs, cart, checkout, etc. from the dropdown, you can navigate to a different type of page and create or access templates of each page.

[2.12.2b]

The editable page options will show on the sidebar. I will show you in detail what each theme section and block means and how to use it.

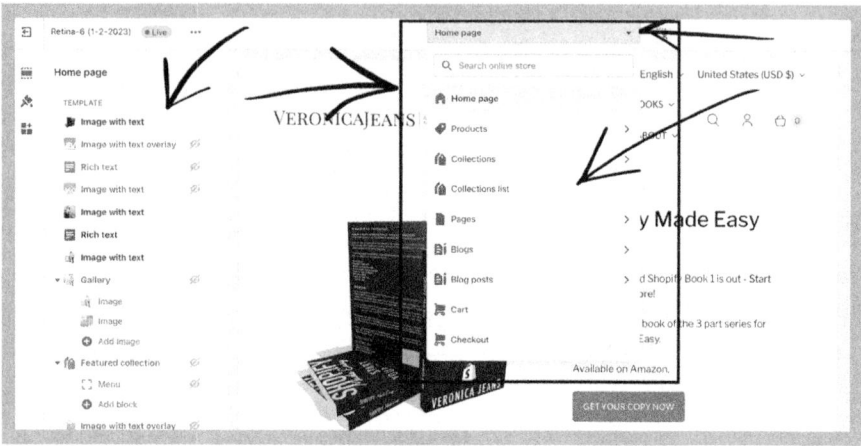

[2.12.2c]

Customize Editor: 'Customize' editor - this is your main page dashboard - here, you can view your page and the edits as you create them.

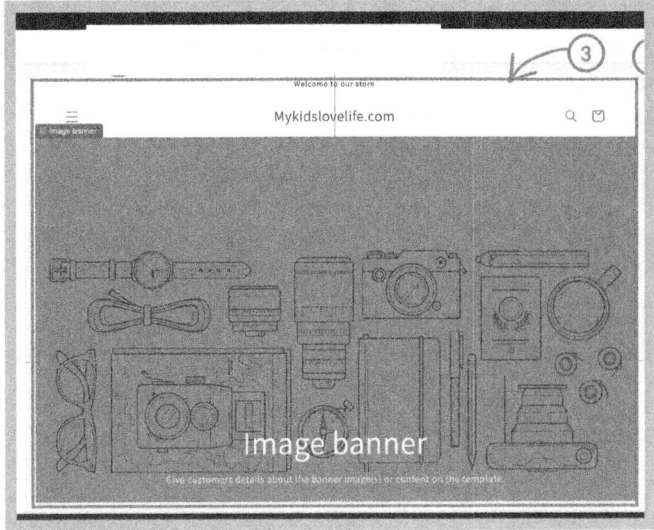

[2.12.2d]

View Your Store: On the top right of the dashboard is a computer icon that will show the store as seen on a mobile, small, or wide device view.

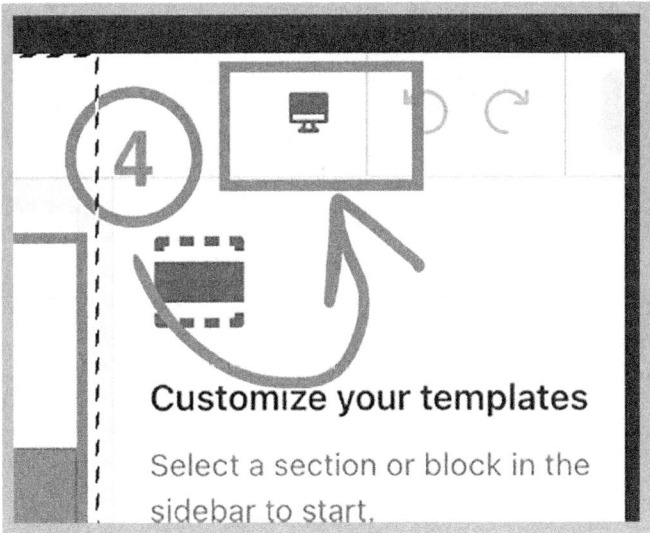

[2.12.2de]

> **Pro Tip:** It is important to view your store on all types of devices to see how your content, like images, text, videos, etc., will appear to visitors. For instance, if you add text directly on your image before you upload it to a page, the text might get cut off in a mobile view because the text is not responsive.

Next, to understand how to use the 'Customize' editor here is a complete detailed explanation of each area and how to use it.

NOTE: *You can use this part in any of the pages you create in the editor. The detailed edit information will not be repeated with each different page we set up after this chapter.*

CUSTOMIZE SETTINGS

You must understand each type of section before adding them to your different pages.

The following will explain the theme sections, blocks, and features and how to use each.

- Each **theme section** can have different content **blocks** to add to your theme setting. These are visible when you add a particular theme section.
- Each **block** can also have more features. These are visible if you click on the block, and either the left or the right sidebar will open with different features.
- Each theme section also has different **features** that can be different for each Shopify theme. I have added different Shopify theme features to the explanation. The different features are visible if you click on the theme section, and either the left or the right sidebar will open with different features.

NOTE: *There are 'Check' options with the information in the feature descriptions. This does not mean you need to check the options. It is your choice to check them.*

On the left side of your dashboard, you will see 3 icons.

- Sections (rectangle with dots icon)
- Theme settings (paintbrush icon)

- App embeds (3 squares and + icon)

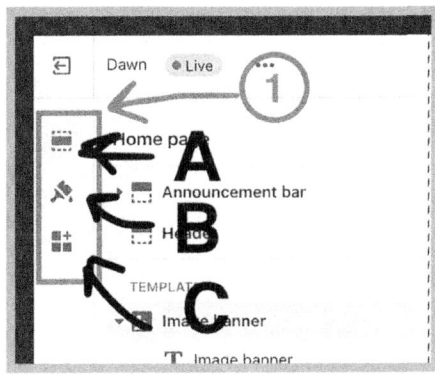

SECTIONS

The 'Sections' are features you can add to any page of your online store. The features are called sections. The sections are how to add more information to your page with images, text, brand colors, and more.

Some page will have the default sections automatically added which are the 'Announcement bar', the 'Header', and the 'Footer'.

The 'Sections' dashboard starts with your home page. In the 'Sections' area for the home page, you will see all the **theme sections** automatically added to your home page template, for instance, an image banner, rich text, featured collection, collage, video, and multicolumn. This depends on the Shopify theme you chose for your store.

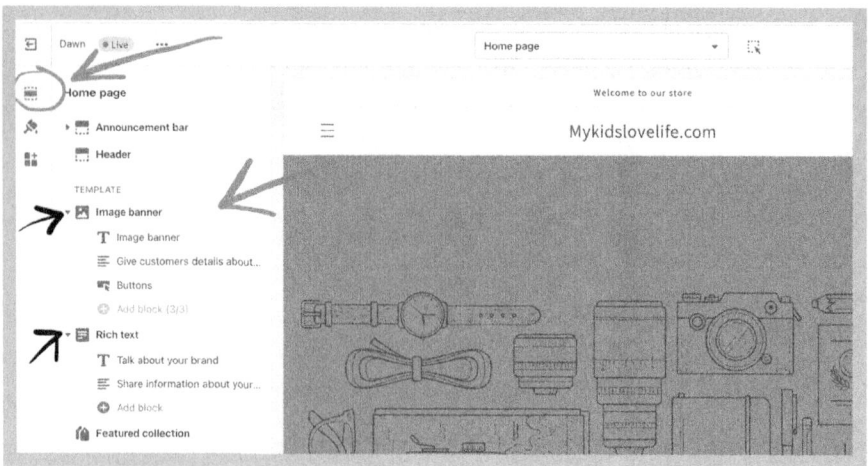

[2.12.3]

To make it less confusing when you start, close the theme sections with the small triangle on the side of the title. Now you can see clearly what sections have been added by default. The sections can be removed or edited, or you can add more sections, depending on your brand design.

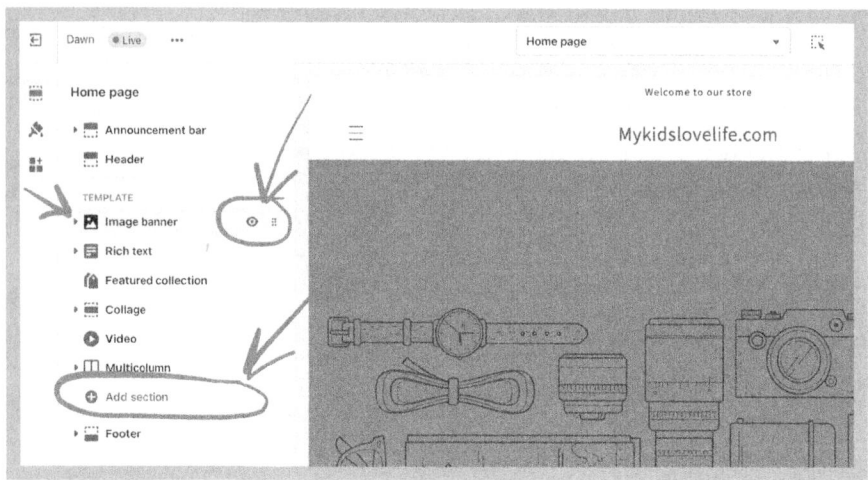

[2.12.4]

Each type of page will have different sections available to add more information and content. There are two ways to add more sections to the pages:

Step 1. Add sections

Then add information, images, pages, videos, etc., at the bottom of the home page area, with the 'Add section' link.

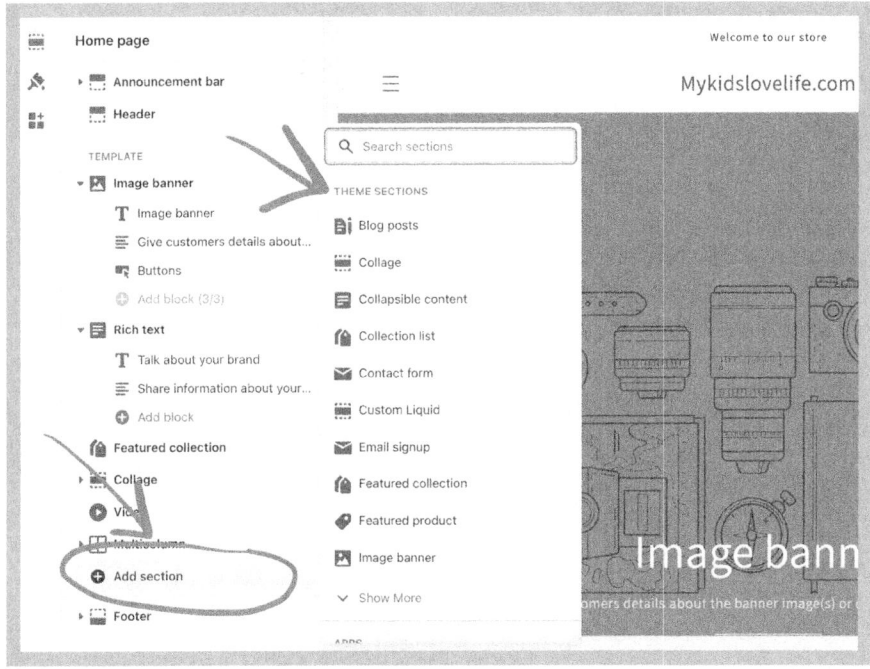

[2.12.5]

Step 2. Add or edit theme section

To add or edit a theme section, you need to activate the 'Inspector' at the top of the dashboard.

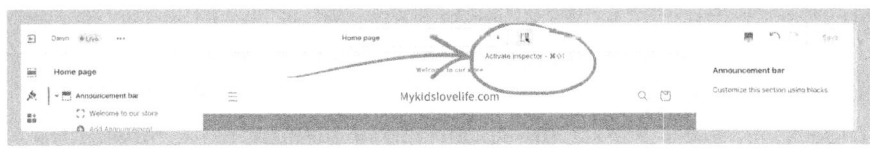

[2.12.6]

Now, you can either add a theme section on the left side of the dashboard or add it with the '+' sign in the editor.

If it is a theme section you want to add to the page, the button 'Add section' will give you various options.

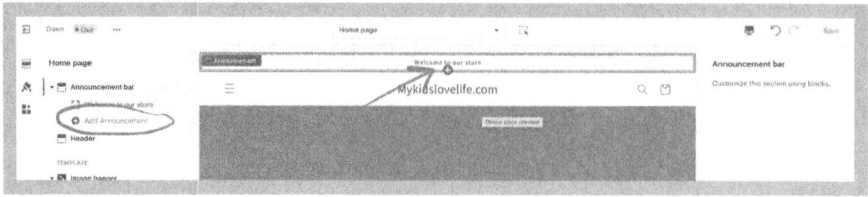

[2.12.7]

Once you are in a theme section, you can add more blocks to the theme sections. The blocks are the same type of detail as the theme sections. But they are restricted to the number of blocks you can add. It is either a button 'Add block' or the '+' sign in the editor.

> Pro Tip: When you add your sections and features, view them in all the possible devices with the right top button on the dashboard - Mobile, Desktop or Fullscreen. 'Desktop' is what you will view in your Theme editor and 'Fullscreen' us what your visitor will see in their browser on a desktop. Remember, this is also not the complete view for the visitor because everybody has a different size desktop.

[2.12.7a]

DIFFERENT SECTIONS

Depending on your Shopify theme, the following options are available in the 'Template' sections. These are available in the free Shopify themes:

- Blog Posts
- Collage
- Video

- Collapsible Content
- Collection List
- Contact Form
- Custom Liquid
- Email Signup
- Featured Collection
- Featured Product
- Image Banner
- Image with Text
- Multicolumns
- Page
- Rich Text
- Slide Show
- Video

Blog Posts

This section will add your blog posts to your page. You can add as many blogs as you want. This will be the blog's image cover and the blog's title.

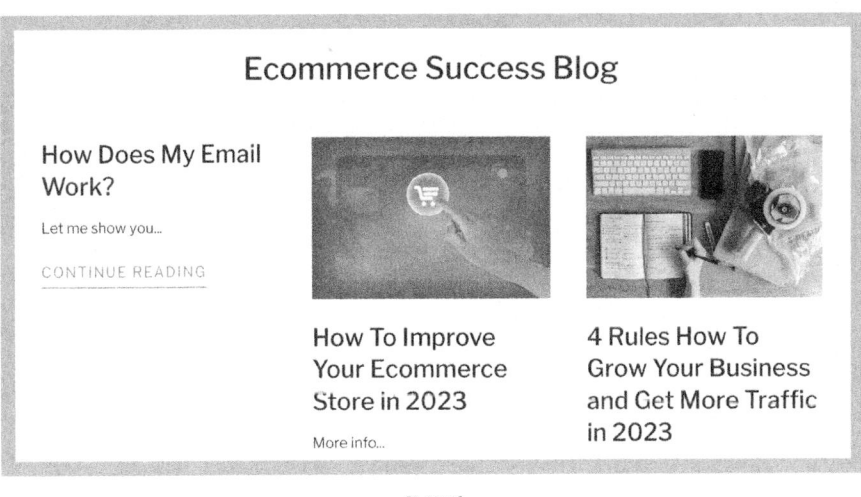

[2.12.8]

The different features to edit for the blog post setting:

- Heading: Name your blog post.
- Blog: Add your blog to the page.

- Blog posts: You can add 1 - 4 blog posts to the page.
- Color scheme: Accent 1, Accent 2, Background 1, Background 2, Inverse. The color scheme changes the background colors.

> Pro Tip: This feature changes the content background and set up in 'Theme settings' under 'Colors' or 'Cards', depending on your Shopify theme.

The next features can be checked to add them to the theme settings:

- Show featured image - this is your hero or main image you add to your blog post.
- Show date.
- Show author - the author is one of the staff or owner of the Shopify store.
- Enable 'View all' button if blog includes more blog post than shown.
- Section padding: Top and bottom padding. This is the space between the blog posts and other information on the page.

Collage

With a collage, you can add different blocks like images, a product, collections, or a video in various combinations. The default in the collage only shows one combination.

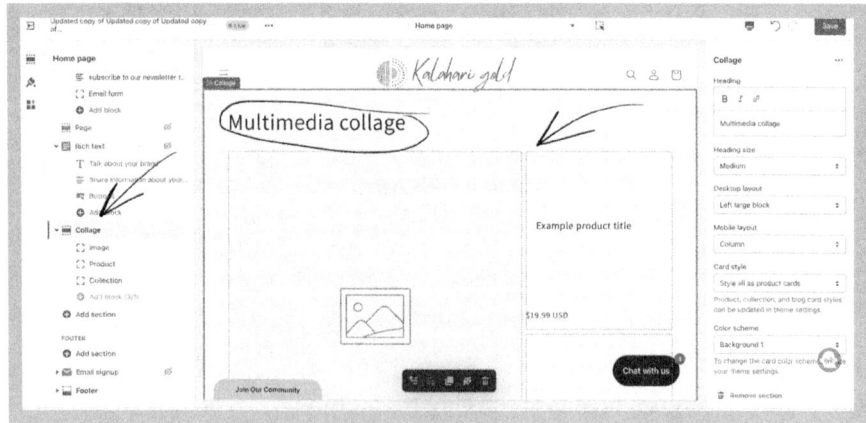

[2.12.62]

The different features to edit for the collage setting:

- Heading: Name your heading.
- Heading size: Small, Medium or Large - choose the size you want your heading to be.
- Desktop layout: Left of Right large block.
- Mobile layout: Collage or Column.
- Color scheme: Accent 1, Accent 2, Background 1, Background 2, Inverse. The color scheme changes the background colors.
- Section padding: Top and Bottom padding. This is the space between the blog posts and other information on the page.

Video

Check 'Use original image ration' if you don't want your image to be cropped.

- Cover image: The cover image is for your video and the normal thumbnail image for a video is 1280 x 720px 1920 x 1080px. When I design my thumbnails, I use the larger size.
- URL: The URL is the web address of your video. Your video needs to be hosted on another site like YouTube, Vimeo, Wave.video, Wisteria or others.
- Video alt text: Add a description for your video.
- Check 'Use original image ratio' - Select this option if you do not want your image to be cropped.
- Product: choose any product in your store.
- Collection: choose any collection in your store.
- Image: Select an image to show in the collage.

Collapsible Content

This is an accordion for all sorts of possibilities. Each block is a collapsible row to add more information to the page.

One of the big uses is as a FAQ (Frequently Asked Questions) for your pages. The question will be the heading or title; the answer is the text or row content. You can also select to add a page for the row content. For each block, you can add an icon to indicate what the FAQs are. I will not list them here because there are so many icon options.

[2.12.63]

> 💡 Pro Tip: If you are adding the FAQ for a page, be very intentional about the information. The information must be relevant to the product of the page or to the content of the page. Do not add too many FAQs because you want your customer to get to their information quickly and hopefully decide to buy.

The different features to edit for the collapsible content:

- Caption: Sub-title for the collapsible content which appears above the heading.
- Heading: Name the collapsible content.
- Heading size: Small, Medium or Large - choose the size you want your heading to be.
- Heading alignment: Center, Left or Right.
- Layout: None, Row container or Section container - these are different types of backgrounds for your content.
- Color scheme: Accent 1, Accent 2, Background 1, Background 2, Inverse. The color scheme changes the background colors for the collapsible content - the overall container.
- Container color scheme: Accent 1, Accent 2, Background 1, Background 2, Inverse. The color scheme changes the background colors for the collapsible content just for the information content.

The next features can be checked to add them to the theme settings:

- Open first collapsible row - this will show the text in the first row if it is checked.
- Image layout: Add an image to the side of the collapsible content.
- Image ratio: Adapt to image, Small or Large - 'adapt to image' is the image size you have uploaded.
- Desktop layout: Image first, Image second -
- Theme settings: Color: Accent 1, Accent 2, Outline button, Text - these are the colors in the 'Theme setting'.

Collection List

The different features to edit for the collection list:

- Heading: Name the collection list.
- Heading size: Small, Medium or Large - choose the size you want your heading to be.
- Color scheme: Accent 1, Accent 2, Background 1, Background 2, Inverse. The color scheme changes the background colors for the contact form.
- Section Padding: Top and Bottom padding for the collections on the website. This will add space before and after the collections.

Here, you can add several collections one at a time. You have control over what collection you have on a page. Each collection block is for one of the collections you have in 'Collections'. As you add another collection block, the collection images will be reduced.

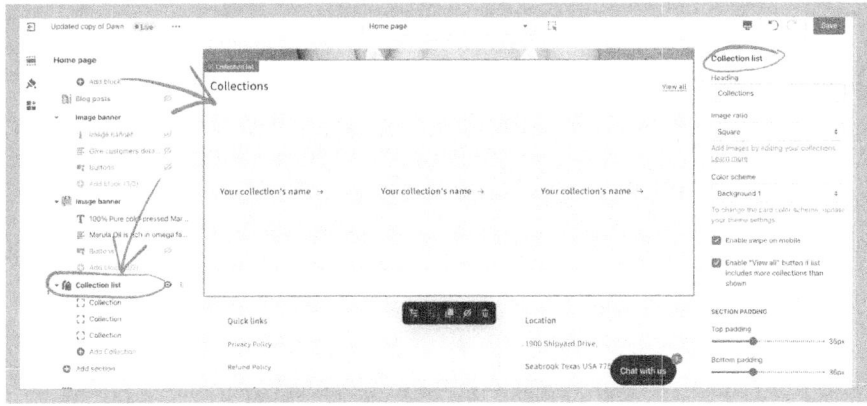

[2.12.10]

> 💡 Pro Tip: Do not try to add all your collections or too many. Make it simple and easy for people to get what they want and need. Create different parts of your page with different types of collections so customers can quickly choose what they want to buy.

The different features to edit for the collection list:

- Heading: Name the collection list.
- Heading size: Small, Medium or Large - choose the size you want your heading to be.
- Image ratio: Adapt to image, Portrait or Square - 'adapt to image' is the image size you have uploaded.
- Number of columns on desktop: 1 - 5 - the more you columns you add, the smaller the collection image will be.
- Color scheme: Accent 1, Accent 2, Background 1, Background 2, Inverse. The color scheme changes the background colors behind the collection list.
- Check 'Enable View all button…' if you have more collections to show.
- Mobile layout: 1 column, 2 columns - these are the columns that will show on mobile.
- Check 'Enable swipe on mobile' - visitors can swipe the images from the side of the mobile window.

Section Padding:

Top and Bottom padding for the collections on the website. This will add space before and after the collections.

Theme settings:

- Style: Standard or Card - these are the options you chose in the 'Theme setting' but you can override it in the theme sections.
- Color: Accent 1, Accent 2, Outline button, Text - these are the colors in the 'Theme setting'.

Contact Form

A 'Contact' page has been automatically created in your Shopify store with a form under 'Online store' and 'Pages'. The contact form has the basic information for customers to email you. Your email in your 'Store details' will be used. You will not need to add any extra blocks.

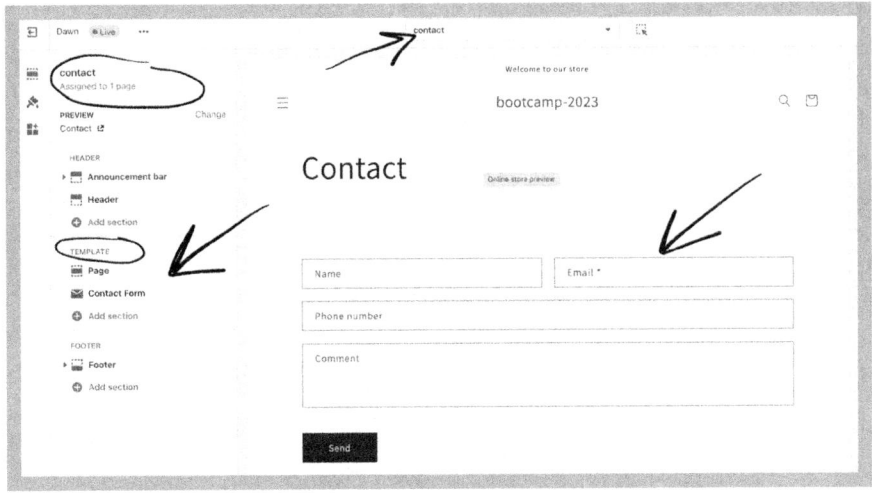

[2.12.11]

This is not the same as an 'Email signup' form.

> 💡 Pro Tip: I would not add the contact form to your home page unless you have a very good reason. People are used to finding the contact page if they want to get your attention. Adding the contact form to your home page make it unnecessary longer. Rather add more information about your products or promotions to your home page.

Custom Liquid

Liquid is the code language Shopify uses. These are expert-level additions to your store.

Email Signup

Email signup is a form you are familiar with. This is where your visitors can sign up for your email newsletter. This form is embedded in your page. The title and message can be edited in the section blocks. You cannot add more text boxes in the Shopify free theme.

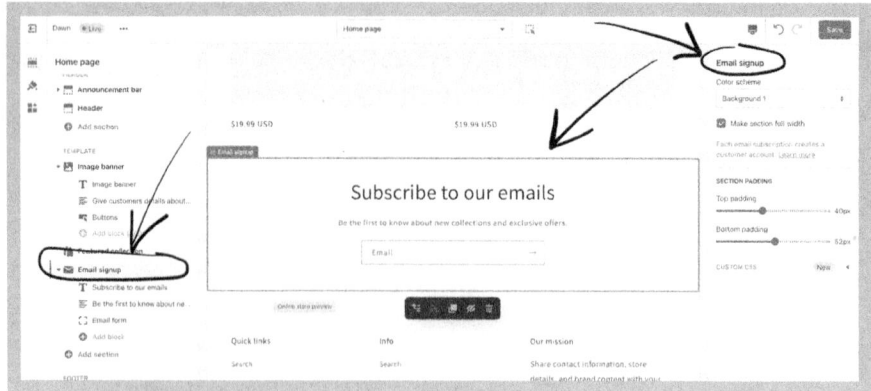

[2.12.12]

> *Pro Tip:* The reason to add a required first and last name for email signups is so that spamming can be curtailed. If you only add the generic signup, spam bots can sign up for your email newsletter, and the biggest reason to stop that is the restriction on free emails you get before you start paying a subscription fee.

You can also add an email newsletter sign-up form from your email provider.

Block sections:

- Heading: Add a title which is will entice visitors to sign up.
- Subheading or Text: Add a message for your visitors why they should join.
- Email form: This is a default form or you can add extra features depending on the Shopify theme.
- Color scheme: Accent 1, Accent 2, Background 1, Background 2, Inverse. The color scheme changes the background colors for the contact form.
- Check 'Make section full width' if you want to background to be the full width of the browser.
- Section Padding: Top and Bottom padding for the newsletter form on the website. This will add space before and after the collections.

Featured Collection

This is a specific collection you want to show on your home page. All the products will show up that are allocated to the collection.

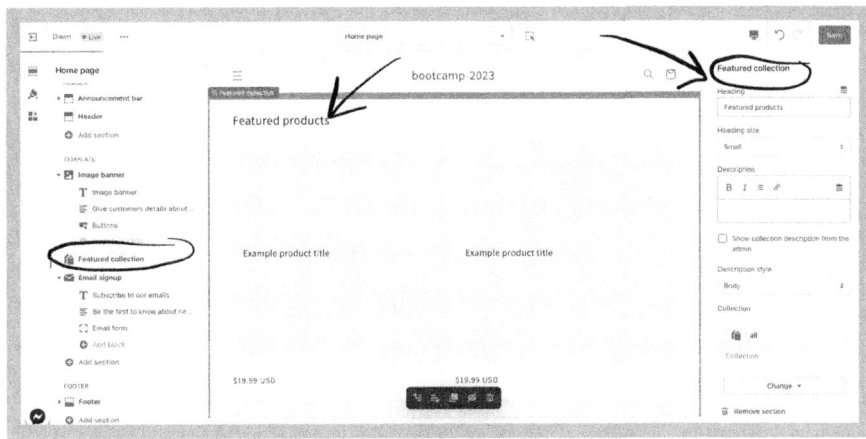

[2.12.12]

> Pro Tip: This is a great way to show new arrivals, sales, or closeouts.

The different features to edit for the featured collection:

- Heading: Name the collection list.
- Heading size: Small, Medium or Large - choose the size you want your heading to be.
- Description: This is a description of the featured products/collection.
- Check "Show collection description from the admin'
- Description style: Body, Subtitle, Uppercase.
- Collection: Here you add the collection you want to showcase on your page. Maximum products to show: 2 - 4 - the more you columns you add, the smaller the collection image will be. If you only want to show 1 product, then you can add the 'Featured Product' theme section.
- Check 'Make products full width'
- Check 'Enable View all button...' if you have more collections to show.
- 'View all' style: Solid button, Outline button, Link.
- Check 'Enable carousel on desktop'
- Color scheme: Accent 1, Accent 2, Background 1, Background 2, Inverse. The color scheme changes the background colors behind the collection list.

- Check 'Enable View all button...' if you have more collections to show.
- Product Card: ???
- Image ratio: Adapt to image, Portrait or Square - 'adapt to image' is the image size you have uploaded.
- Mobile layout: 1 column, 2 columns - these are the columns that will show on mobile
- Check 'Enable swipe on mobile' - visitors can swipe the images from the side of the mobile window.

Check choices:

- Show second image on hover: This will show the second image you have added in the product page setting.
- Show vendor: If you have different vendors in your store, this is a great way to highlight that feature.
- Show product rating: If you wanted to show ratings, you need to add a rating app.

Section Padding:

Top and Bottom padding for the collections on the website. This will add space before and after the collections.

Theme settings:

- Style: Standard or Card - these are the options you chose in the 'Theme setting' but you can override it in the theme sections.
- Color: Accent 1, Accent 2, Outline button, Text - these are the colors in the 'Theme setting'.
- Page width: 1000px - 1600px (which is fullwidth of a browser window)
- Product card position: Bottom left or right, Top left or right. - ???
- Sale bade color scheme: Accent 1, Accent 2, Background 2 - these are colors you have allocated to the 'Theme settings'.
- Check 'Show currency codes' - Add your currency of choice.

Featured Product

This will show one product you choose on the page. You can add different blocks of information to the product, e.g., Text, title, price, variant picker, quantity selector, buy buttons, product rating, custom liquid, and share.

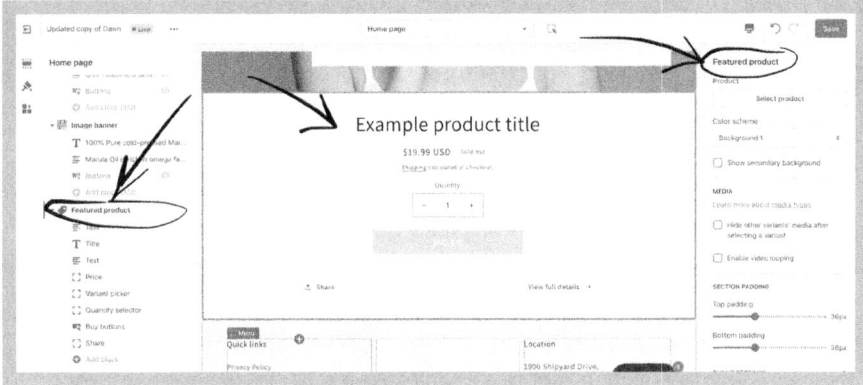

[2.12.14]

The product information added on the product page in the 'Product' dashboard will show on the page when you add the product. You can hide some of the information if you want to. In the following image, you can see the product and some of the variants of the product I have hidden to the section.

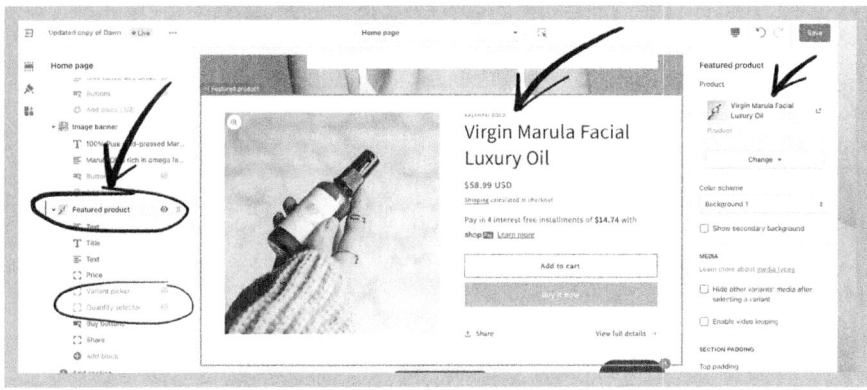

[2.12.15]

Block Sections:

- Text: This is some text above your title, which could be the vendor or other semi important text which is part of the information for your product.
- Title: The title or heading cannot be changed. This is the title of your product. The heading size can be changed to Small, Medium, or Large.
- Text: This is an extra text for a description of your product.

- Price: Price is not customizable - it will show the product price.
- Variant picker: the variant picker is how you want your product variants to show on the page - Pills or Dropdown.
- Quantity selector: The quantity selector is not customizable - it will show as a standard Shopify quantity selector.
- Buy buttons: Here, you can check the 'Show dynamic checkout buttons', and customers will see their preferred payment options.
- Product rating: If you want to show a product rating, you will need to add a rating app.
- Custom liquid: This should only be used by an expert.
- Share: If you posted a link in a social media post, the page's featured image will be shown as the preview image. The store title and description are included in the image.

You will find this in 'Online Store' and under 'Preferences' - Social sharing image.

The different features to edit for the featured product:

- Product: Add a product from your products in your Shopify store.
- Color scheme: Accent 1, Accent 2, Background 1, Background 2, Inverse. The color scheme changes the background colors behind the collection list.

Check 'Show secondary background' - this will add the second background color, Background 2, to the background of the complete container of the product.

Media:

- Check 'Hide other variants' media after selecting variant
- Check 'Enable video looping'

Section Padding:

- Top and Bottom padding for the collections on the website. This will add space before and after the collections.
- Page width: 1000px - 1600px (which is fullwidth of a browser window)
- Check 'Show currency codes' – if you are selling internationally, then you would check this box.

- Sale badge color scheme: Accent 1, Accent 2, Background 2 - these are colors you have allocated to the 'Theme settings'.
- Sold out badge color scheme: Background 1, Inverse

Image Banner

> 💡 Pro Tip: Do not add too much text in your banner. If you add more text this should be 1 short sentence only. It has to add to the value of the title on the banner and to the message.

The image banner will be the full width of the website. In the image shown, we have added some information about the product. View this as more advertising about how wonderful your products are.

[2.12.16]

Or, as in the following image, advertise your special services to your customers.

[2.12.17]

The blocks for the image banner are the title, text, buttons. You can only add 3 blocks from any of the blocks available.

Block Sections:

- Heading: The heading is the title of the banner. Add a heading size that can be changed to Small, Medium, or Large.
- Text: You can add a description on the banner image. Text style is Body, Subtitle or Uppercase.
- Button: Adding a button and CTA (call to action) to your banner is a great idea. The choices are:
- First button label: Add a label that your visitors will react to.
- First button link: Add your link to the button, which is where you want your visitors to go.
- Check 'Use outline button style' - if you don't check this, your button will appear as your main button style.
- Second button label: This is an option to add 2 buttons on the banner.
- Second button link: Add your link to the button, which is where you want your visitors to go.

Check 'Use outline button style' - if you don't check this, your button will appear as your main button style.

> Pro Tip: Test your images with different sizes. It depends on the Shopify theme and how the image appears on the page. I start with 600 x 1600px and adjust it to another size if it is not what I like.

There are different features to edit for the image banner:

- Images: 2 selections of images.
- Image overlay opacity: this will darken the image so the text will show better.
- Banner height: Small, Medium, or Large
- Check 'Adapt section height to first image size' - which means that the second image will resize to the first image size.
- Desktop content position: Top - Left, Middle, Right, Middle - Left, Middle, Right, Bottom - Left, Middle, Right.

- Color scheme: Accent 1, Accent 2, Background 1, Background 2, Inverse. The color scheme changes the background colors behind the collection list.
- Mobile Layout: Center, Left or Right.
- Check 'Stack images on mobile'
- Check 'Show container on mobile'
- Desktop content position: Top left, center, and right. Bottom left, center or right.
- Show container on desktop: check means you have a background for your text.
- Color scheme: Accent 1, Accent 2, Background 1, Background 2, Inverse.
- Mobile Layout: You can change the content alignment and how the images show up on your mobile devices.

Image with Text

This is exactly what it is - the image on the one side with the text on the other side of the image. The blocks shown are only for the text features. In the following image, the information is about the process of natural oil extraction.

[2.12.18]

Block Sections:

- Title: Add the heading and choose the Heading size.
- Text:
- Buttons: Add a button label and the Button link to a page, collection, or product.

- Caption: Text is short and focused, Text Style is Subtitle or Uppercase, and Text size is Small, Medium, or Large.

In the next image, I have 2 'image with text' sections, but to make it visually better, I have changed the image from left to right on the next section. And added a different color background to the text.

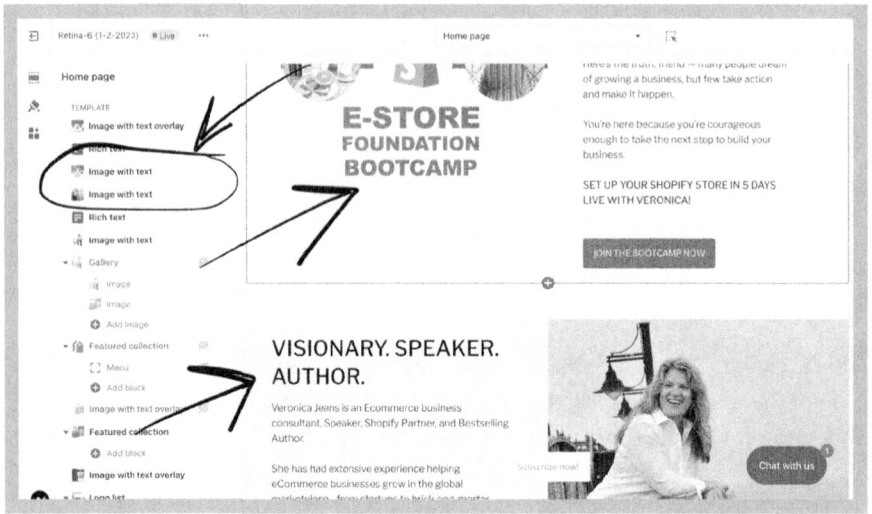

[2.12.19]

There are different features to edit for the image with text:

- Image: Select an image and be aware of the size of the image. That will influence how the image shows. If you don't have a lot of text, create an image with less height. If you have a lot of text, create a more square image or even portrait style.
- Image height: Adapt to image, Small or Large. The best way is to size the image correctly otherwise the image will be cropped.
- Desktop image width: Small, Medium or Large - the image will automatically be optimized for mobile devices.
- Desktop image placement: Image first or second - you can choose which image you want to see first, which is the default mobile layout.
- Desktop content position: Top, Middle or Bottom - if you don't have enough text in the content area, you can position your content.

- Desktop content alignment: The content (text) will either be centered, left or right aligned.
- Content layer: No overlap or Overlap - this is when the image overlaps or moves over the content.
- Color scheme: Accent 1, Accent 2, Background 1, Background 2, Inverse. The color scheme changes the background colors for the image and text background container.
- Mobile Layout: The content (text) will either be centered, left or right aligned.
- Section Padding: Top and Bottom padding for the collections on the website. This will add space before and after the image with text section.
- Theme Settings: In this section you can add the page width of your store which I recommend the full width version.
- Thickness: This is a border around the image and or the text.
- Opacity: This means that the background will show as the opacity settings are changing.
- Page width: 1000px - 1600px (which is fullwidth of a browser window)

Multicolumns

With this section, you can add images and text in different columns to the page.

[2.12.21]

> Pro Tip: Make sure your images are the same size. Otherwise, it looks unprofessional.

Block Sections:

- Column: In each column, you can select an image and add a heading and description for each column, including a Link label and Link to any page, product, or collection.

There are different features to edit for the multicolumn:

- Heading: Name your multicolumn.
- Image width: The image will be - Full width of column, Half width of column or one-third width of column.
- Image ratio: Adapt to image, Portrait, Square, or Circle - 'adapt to image' is the image size you have uploaded.
- Column alignment: Left or Center - your content will be aligned.
- Secondary background: None or 'show as column background' - this is part of the Theme settings.
- Button label: Give your button a label.
- Button link: Link your button to a page, product or collection.
- Check 'Enable swipe on mobile'

- Color scheme: Accent 1, Accent 2, Background 1, Background 2, Inverse. The color scheme changes the background colors for the multicolumn section.
- Section Padding: Top and Bottom padding for the collections on the website. This will add space before and after the multicolumn section.

Page

This is an opportunity to add any page information to your pages. This might sound counter intuitive. The reason is that, unless you know HTML, it is hard to create a very professional page with images and text.

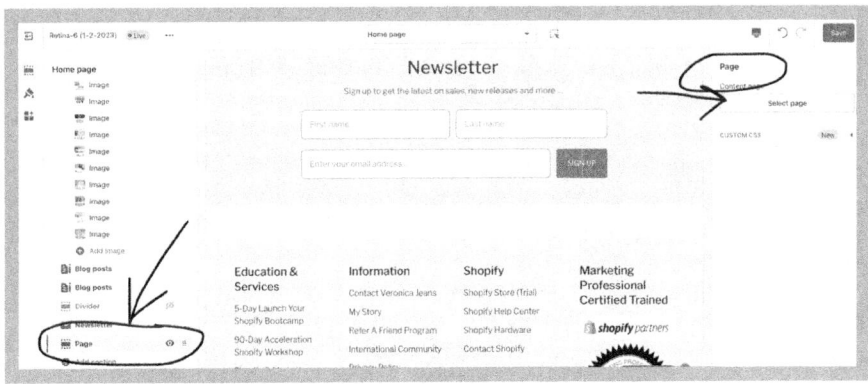

[2.12.22]

It is a great idea to add small amounts of content to a page and add that to your page features. There are different features to edit for the page section:

- Page: Select a page to add to your page.
- Color scheme: Accent 1, Accent 2, Background 1, Background 2, Inverse. The color scheme changes the background colors for the page section.
- Section Padding: Top and Bottom padding for the collections on the website. This will add space before and after the page section.

Rich Text

This is an easy way to add a brand message to your store. This is an important message to let visitors know your USP (unique selling proposition or message).

[2.12.23]

As in the following image, I have only added the title, not the text, to get my main message on the page. I will change the message when I have my next event or whatever I want to promote.

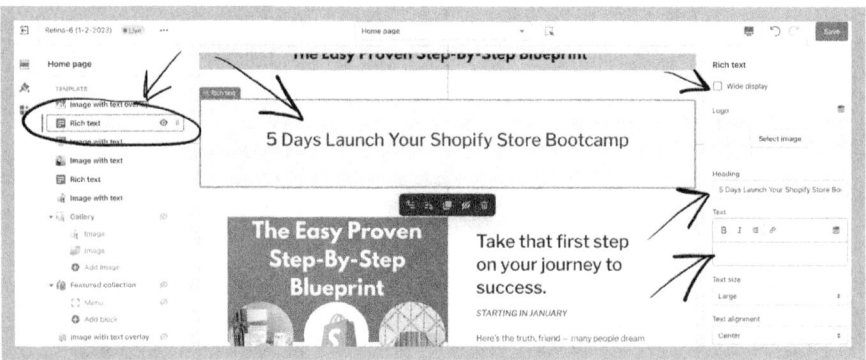

[2.12.24]

Block Sections:

- Title: Add the heading and choose the Heading size.
- Text: This is a description that you want to add to the page.
- Buttons: Add a button label and the Button link to a page, collection, or product.

And you can check the 'Use outline button style'.

There are different features to edit for the rich text section:

- Color scheme: Accent 1, Accent 2, Background 1, Background 2, Inverse. The color scheme changes the background colors for the contact form.
- Check the 'Make section full width.
- Section Padding: Top and Bottom padding for the collections on the website. This will add space before and after the Rich text section.

Slide Show

This was very popular for showing different promotions and information for a website. With more people shopping and visiting from their mobile devices, it has lost its importance. Static images or videos are better now. The limit is 5 images per slideshow.

This is only available for some themes and every theme is different.

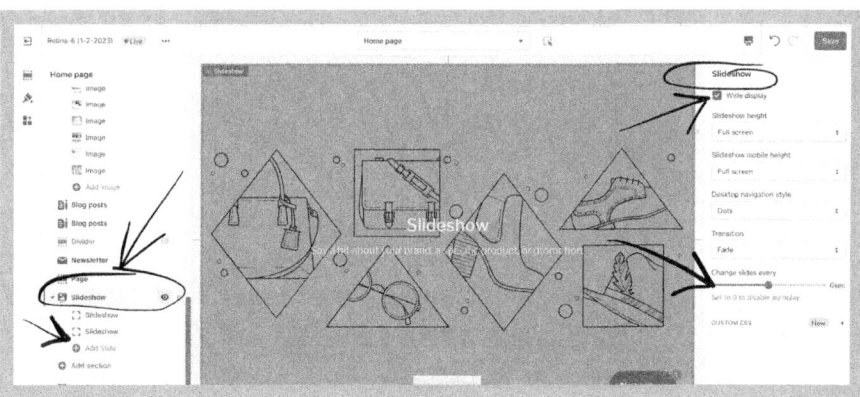

[2.12.25]

Block Section:

Image Slide:

- Heading: Add text and the text size will be what you chose in 'Theme settings'.
- Subheading: Add text and the text size will be what you chose in 'Theme settings'.
- Button label: Give your button a label.
- Slide link: Add your destination for every image you add to the slide.
- Text position: Choose from left, center, right to top, middle and bottom.

There are different features to edit for the slideshow:

- Layout - 'Full width', is as wide as the browser window or 'Grid', which will be only the website width, which means in the middle with white or space on either side.
- Slideshow height: Small, Medium, Large, Full Screen, Original
- Slideshow mobile height: Small, Medium, Large, Full Screen, Original
- Pagination style: Dots, counters, or numbers.
- Check - "Auto-rotate slides"
- Change slide every: timing of the slides.
- Mobile layout: the images will show stacked
- Check - 'Show content below images on mobile'

Accessibility:

- Slideshow description: Describe the slideshow to customers using screen readers.

Video

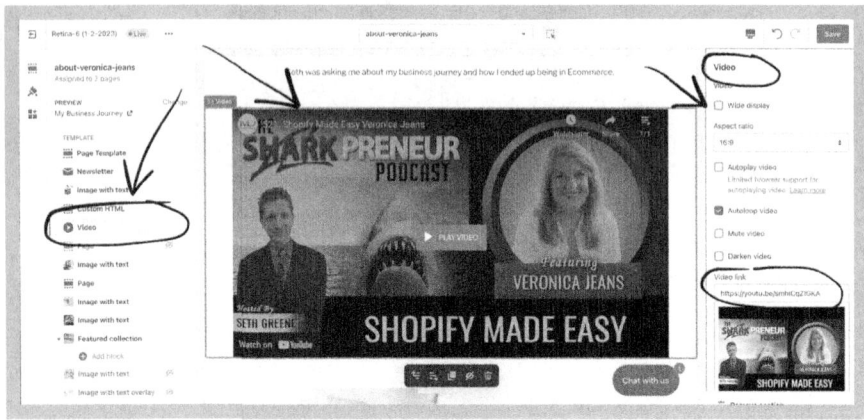

[2.12.26]

There are different features to edit for the video section:

- Heading: The heading is the title of the section on the page.

- Cover image: The cover image is for your video and the normal thumbnail image for a video is 1280 x 720px 1920 x 1080px. When I design my thumbnails I will use the larger size.
- URL: The URL is the web address of your video. Your video needs to be hosted on another site like YouTube, Vimeo, Wave.video, Wisteria or others.
- Video alt text: Add a description for your video.
- Check 'Make section full width'
- Color scheme: Accent 1, Accent 2, Background 1, Background 2, Inverse. The color scheme changes the background colors for the video background around the video.
- Section Padding: Top and Bottom padding for the collections on the website. This will add space before and after the video.

THEME SETTINGS

NOTE: *More sections and features are available in paid Shopify themes, which will vary. To see what is available, you can check out the demo or sometimes even upload a demo to your store to see them all.*

Under the 'Theme settings' section, is where your brand information is added. Although the information was added to the 'Brand' settings, sometimes you can override them here. If the 'Brand' settings are incompatible with your theme, they must be added manually in this setting.

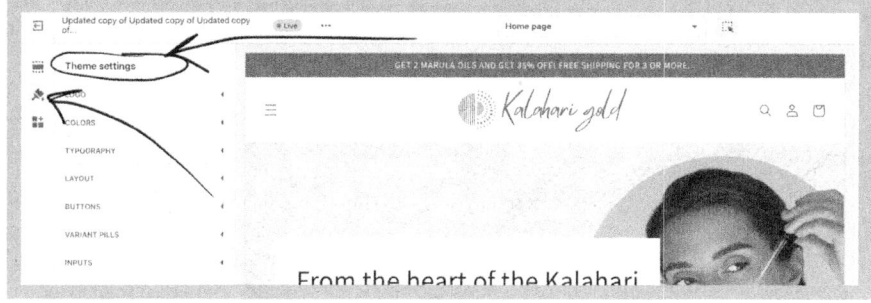

[2.12.64]

Depending on your Shopify theme, the following options are available in the 'Theme settings'. These are available in the free Shopify themes:

- Color

- Typography
- Layout
- Buttons
- Variant Pills
- Inputs
- Cards
- Content Containers
- Media
- Dropdowns and Pop-ups
- Drawers
- Badges
- Social Media
- Search Behavior
- Favicon
- Currency Format
- Cart
- Checkout
- Theme Style

COLOR

In the free Shopify theme, you do not have an extensive list of colors. Add the colors you want to various selections. Depending on your theme, you can change colors for your header titles, buttons, titles, etc.

SHOPIFY THEME

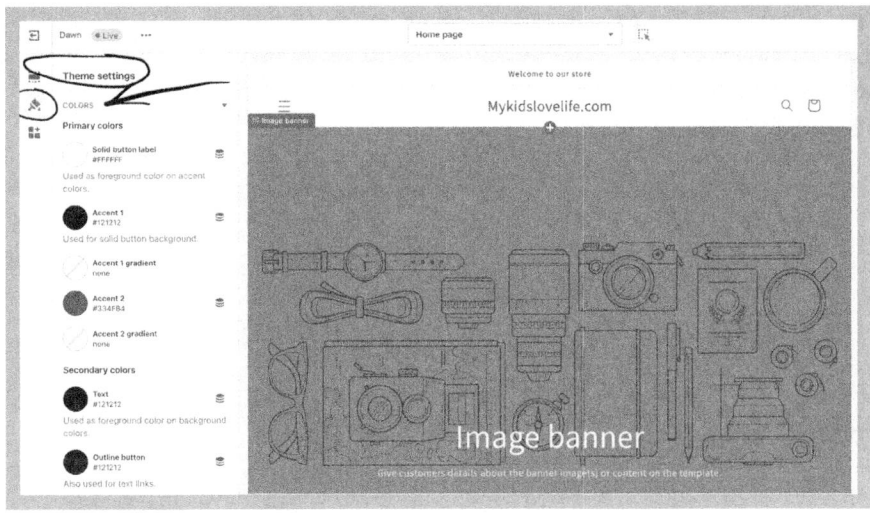

[2.12.27]

The color options are '**Primary colors**' and '**Secondary colors**'.

Primary Colors

Solid button label - the text color on your main buttons or accent colors for the content area's background.

Step 1. Choose colors

Select from the color picker pop-up or add your HEX codes to the text box.

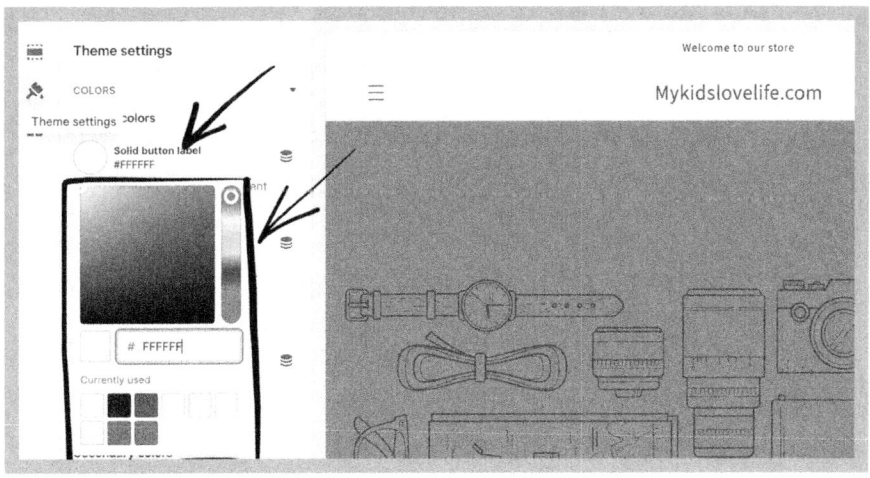

[2.12.28]

Hex codes (#123456) are a hexadecimal format for **identifying colors**. This is a system used in HTML. Each hex code refers to a very specific color, which allows for two designers or a designer and developer to be on the same page about what exact light blue (or any other color) they are referring to.

> 💡 Pro Tip: Once you identify the HEX codes of your brand, write them down on your branding list. You can download the list from my resource page on my website.

Step 2. Choose accent colors

Click on the three disks in the sidebar as shown in the following image, and the colors you added to the 'Brand' settings will appear.

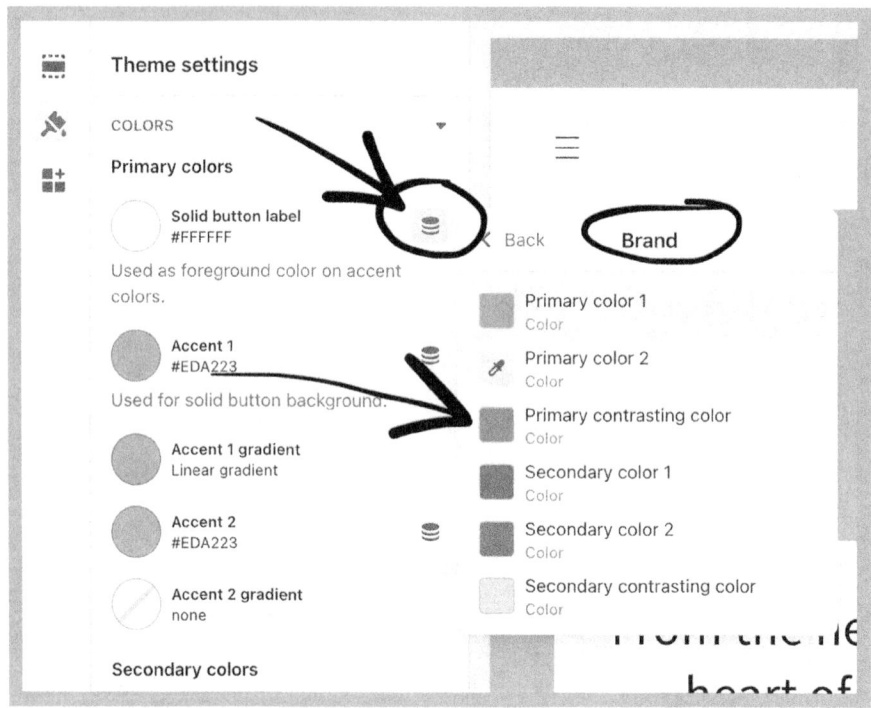

[2.12.29]

The next colors to identify are:

Accent 1 - the main button background color.

Accent 1 gradient - is the primary color for a content area's background with the Accent 1 button colors if buttons are available in the section. Shopify themes will suggest random gradient colors if you have no colors added yet.

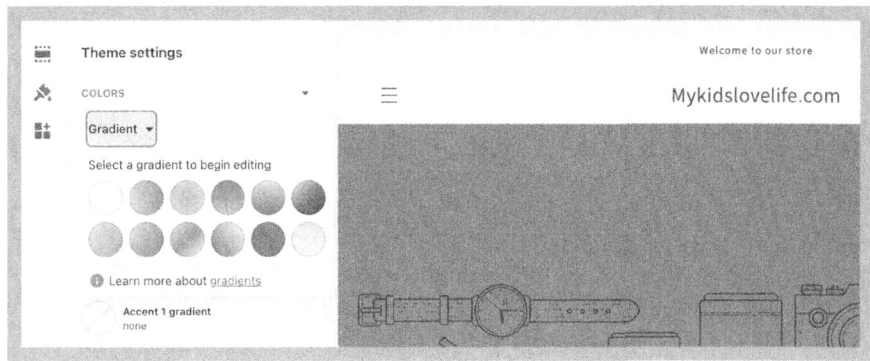

[2.12.30]

If you have your brand colors in your theme, then the gradient color picker pop-up will give you the opportunity to choose a linear or radial gradient, the angle of the gradient, and the color gradient saturation.

[2.12.31]

This is not obvious, but if you want to remove the gradient color option, scroll to the bottom of the gradient color pop-up, and you can see the 'Remove gradient' button.

Accent 2 - is the second primary color for a content area's background.

Accent 2 gradient - is the secondary color for a content area's background with the Accent 1 button colors if buttons are available in the section. Shopify themes will suggest random gradient colors if you have no colors added yet.

Secondary colors

Text is used as text color on the background colors.

Background 1 and **Background 2** - these are secondary colors for a content area's background.

Inverse - the color scheme changes the background colors for the page section.

> Pro Tip: Don't go too wild and make your store confusing for customers with an array of colors. Less is best.

The color scheme can be allocated in sections with a background and text. Each choice will change the background color and text color accordingly.

[2.12.32]

> Pro Tip: Try out different colors, but the best is not to get too crazy with your choice colors unless you understand the relationship.

TYPOGRAPHY

You can use the typography that is in your Shopify theme or you can add a custom style typography.

Custom typography is added as a link or page in the code.

Font Type

In your Shopify theme, you can control your font type and size. The font types are system fonts familiar to your customer's devices.

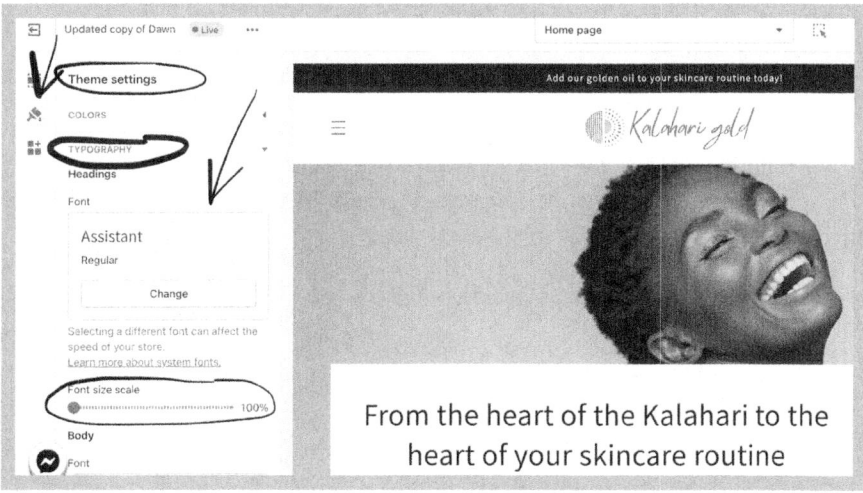

[2.12.33]

You can use your own font type to your Shopify theme by uploading in the 'Code' editor from 'Theme' settings. Once you click on 'Edit code' the font type file can be uploaded. If you don't know much about coding, I recommend asking an expert.

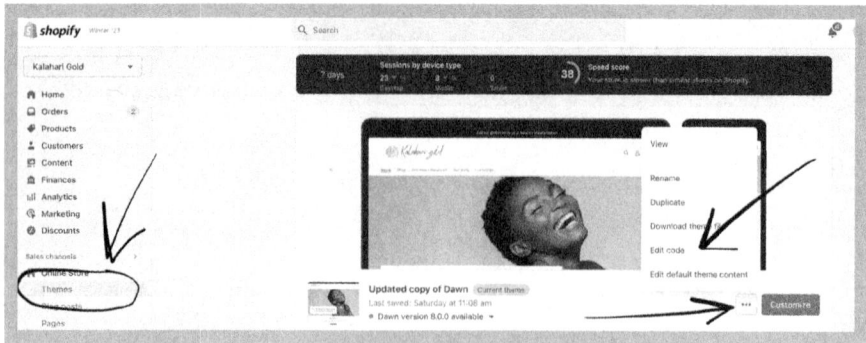

[2.12.34]

> Pro Tip: If you upload your own font type, it will negatively affect the download time for your website.

In the following image, you can see an uploaded font type in the store for PMComforts.com. This is a custom style typography added to the Shopify theme.

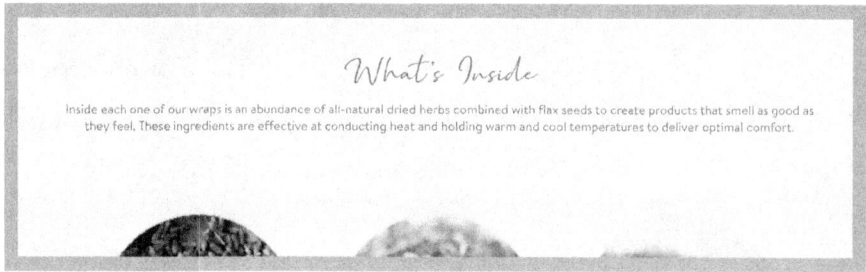

[2.12.35]

There is a difference of choices for the typography between the free and paid Shopify themes:

Free Theme

Choices are headings, buttons, and body text.

Paid Theme

Choices are logo, headings, main menu, dropdown menu, buttons, regular text, banner headings, banner sub-headings, banner text, footers, etc.

Font Size

The font sizes can be changed in the Shopify themes by increasing the percentage size. The increase is by increments of 5%.

In some Shopify themes, the font sizes are changed by increasing the size of pixels (px).

Both types of size options work the same. Test the sizes that fit your brand and check them in the mobile device view in your 'Customize' editor on the top right of the dashboard.

> Pro Tip: Make it easy for people to read on all devices.

To make your fonts readable, make sure to:

- Use commonly used Sans Serif fonts such as Arial, Verdana, Lato, etc. for the body text. It's best to not use serif typeface fonts for the web.
- Avoid using too many decorative font types for header text. No decorative font types for body text.

In the following image, you can see a decorative system font type in NaughtyGoodBites.com.

[2.12.36]

- For the body text, use no less than 12px. Use larger-size fonts if you have an older audience.
- For the headings, use larger than your body text.

- Avoid using capital letters too much.
- Set line-height property larger than your current font size. Texts that are very tight together can be hard to read.
- Be consistent with your font type, sizing, and spacing.
- Avoid using more than 2 types of fonts.

LAYOUT

Use a range slider to choose between a page width of 1000px or 1600px. The default setting is 1600px, meaning any content will fill the browser window.

Add **vertical space between sections** with the range slider as shown in the following image. You can add a maximum of 100px between sections.

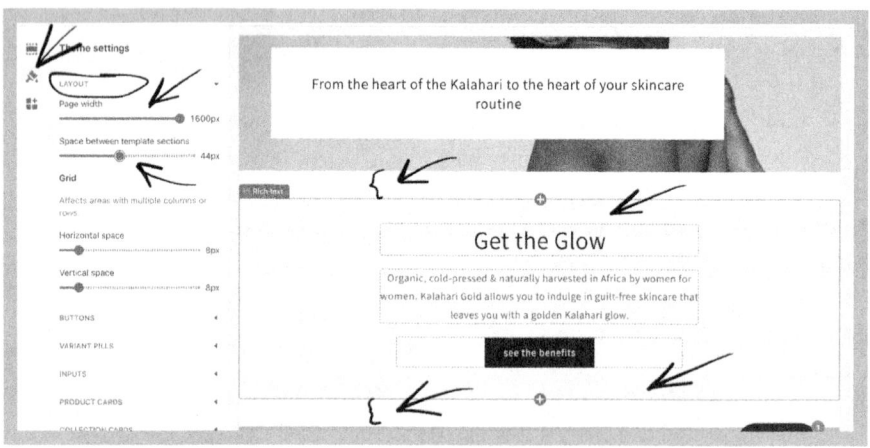

[2.12.37]

> Pro Tip: I like to use the automatic white space already in the sections so the content flows better. White space is always good, but too much is not because it will force your visitor to find the next section. This is part of making the customer journey as smooth as possible.

If you have a **Grid** layout, use the 'Horizontal space' and 'Vertical space' range sliders to add space between grid content. Adding horizontal space will add a maximum of 40px of space to your rows, whereas adding vertical space will add a maximum of 40px of space to your columns.

BUTTONS

This section controls the look of the buttons.

Border: The border **thickness** of the buttons ranges between 0 and 12px.

Opacity: The richness of the color is between 0 and 100%, where the largest percentage is the full color.

Corner radius: This will change the button corners from 0 to 40px radius, as shown in the following image.

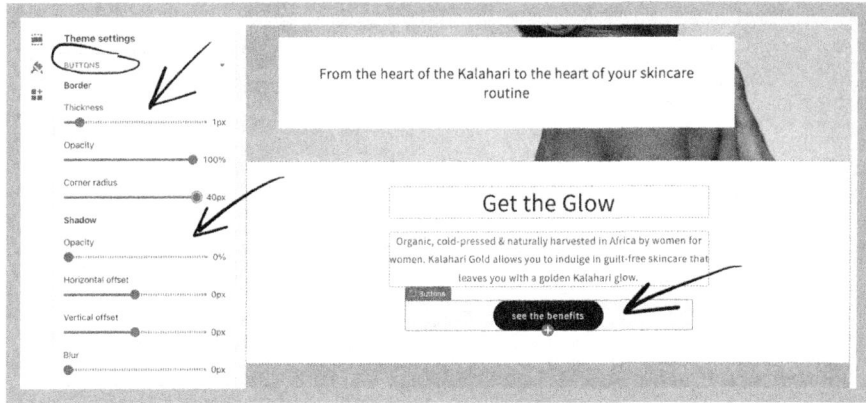

[2.12.38]

In some themes, the buttons are controlled in 'Color' setting in 'Theme Settings' with a few choices, not as many as in the free Shopify theme in some cases.

[2.12.39]

Shadow Opacity: The richness of the color is between is between 0 and 100%, where the largest percentage is the full color.

Horizontal and vertical offsets: These will affect where your shadow will be behind the button.

Blur: These options will spread the shadow behind the button.

VARIANT PILLS

Variant pills allow you to display the variants of a product on a product page or a featured product section. Customers can select the desired variant to add the product to their cart without changing product pages.

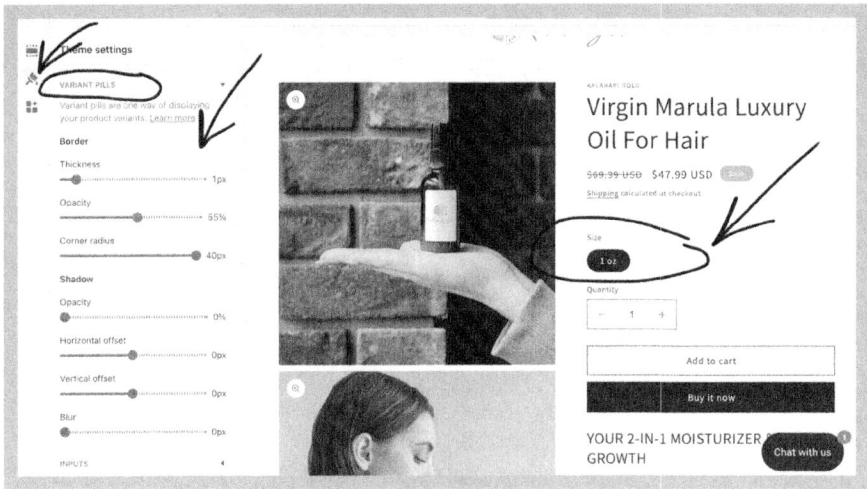

[2.12.40]

One of the options for the '**Variant pills**' in some Shopify themes is to add a color swatch as shown in the following image. In this theme, you can choose custom colors for the products.

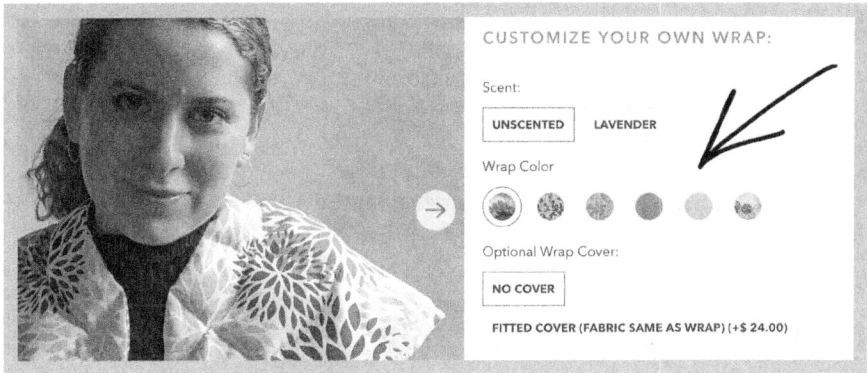

[2.12.41]

If you don't want the basic theme colors, i.e., blue, yellow, etc., have your own colors, as in the following image for Hugpatrol.net, with her material color swatches.

You can choose the 'Color swatch' options in the 'Theme Settings' in the 'Product Grid' setting in this particular theme from Outofthesandbox.com.

[2.12.42]

To use your own colors, there are extra steps to create an image size 50 x 50px of the color you need and to add it in 'Assets' in your 'Code editor'.

You can also activate the **color swatches** in the 'Metafields' setting under 'Settings'. This will be covered in my book 4 - Optimize Your Shopify Store.

INPUTS

Inputs are interactive areas requiring customer input, such as a quantity selector, an email signup form, or cart notes. You can adjust the appearance of your online store inputs in theme settings.

Border: The border **thickness** ranges between 0 and 24px, on the outside of the product image and text. This thickness will be added to your **image padding.**

Opacity: This is between 0 and 100%, where the largest percentage is the full color.

Corner radius: This will change the button corners from 0 to 40px radius, as shown in the following image.

[2.12.43]

Shadow Opacity: This is between 0 and 100%, where the largest percentage is the full color.

Horizontal and vertical offsets: These will affect where your shadow will be behind the input.

Blur: These options will spread the shadow behind the input.

PRODUCT, COLLECTION & BLOG CARDS

Cards are container areas in sections that allow you to display multiple items, for example, product cards, blog cards, collection cards, or collage cards. You can customize your section cards' shape, style, color, alignment, and image padding.

The **standard** card is the standard view for a container showing the product image and text, or for the blogs, the blog image and title.

This option shows the product with the product image and title below the image.

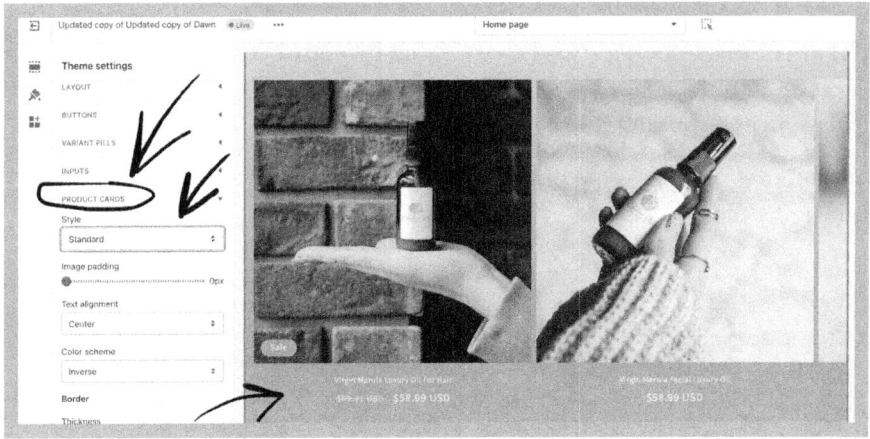

[2.12.44]

This option is with the product image and the title below, highlighted in the **color scheme** of your choice for the title text background.

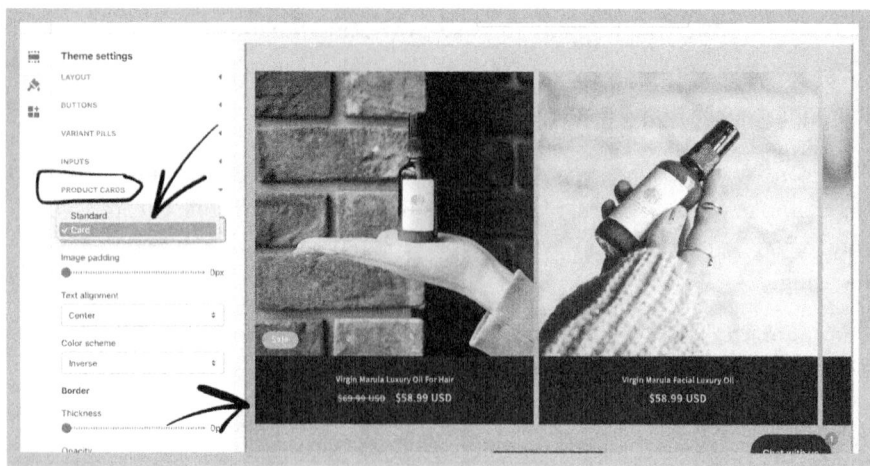

[2.12.45]

Image padding - the padding occurs within the image container and will add a space around the image from 0 - 40px as shown in the following image including the 'Text align'.

Text align - the options are **center, left and right,** which positions the product title under the image.

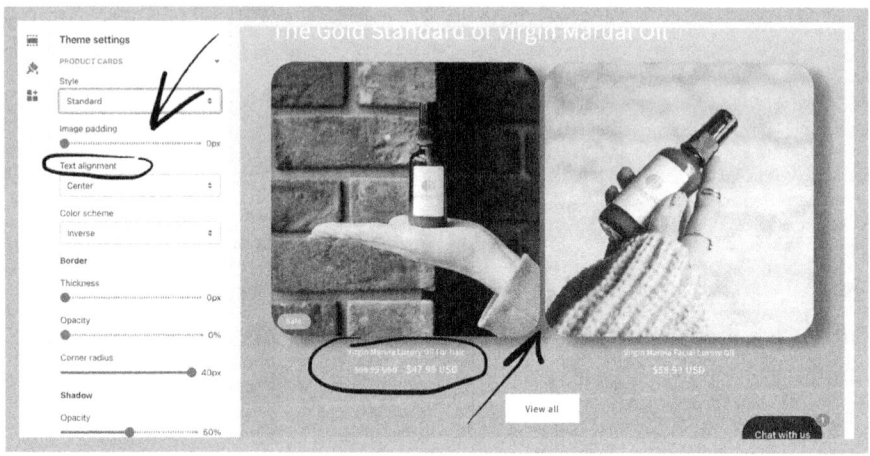

[2.12.47]

Color scheme - these options were allocated in the 'Color' setting and will change the background behind the product image and text.

Border - the **thickness** of the buttons ranges between 0 and 12px.

Opacity is between 0 and 100%, where the largest percentage is the full color.

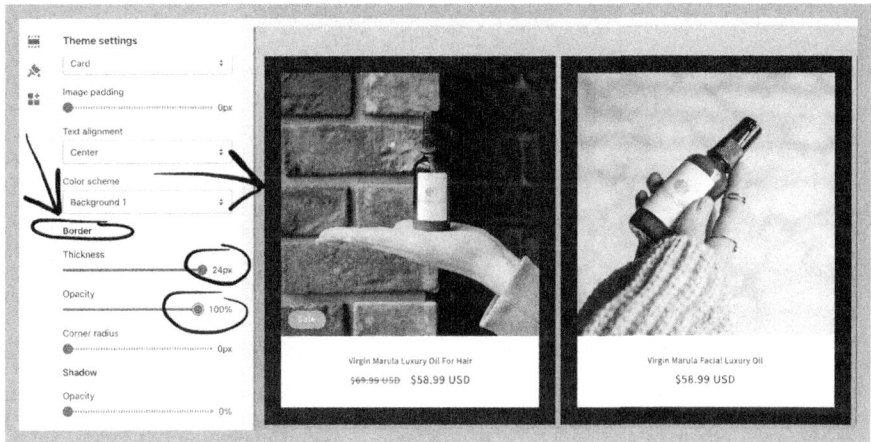

[2.12.48]

The corner radius will change the button corners from 0 to 40px radius, as shown in the following image with the shadows.

Shadow

The shadow option will add a shadow behind the product images – related products for instance as seen in the image 2.12.49 which can be shown with various degrees of opacity and thickness.

Opacity is between 0 and 100%, where the largest percentage is the full color.

Horizontal and **vertical offsets** will affect where your shadow will be behind the product image and text container.

Blur options will spread the shadow behind the input.

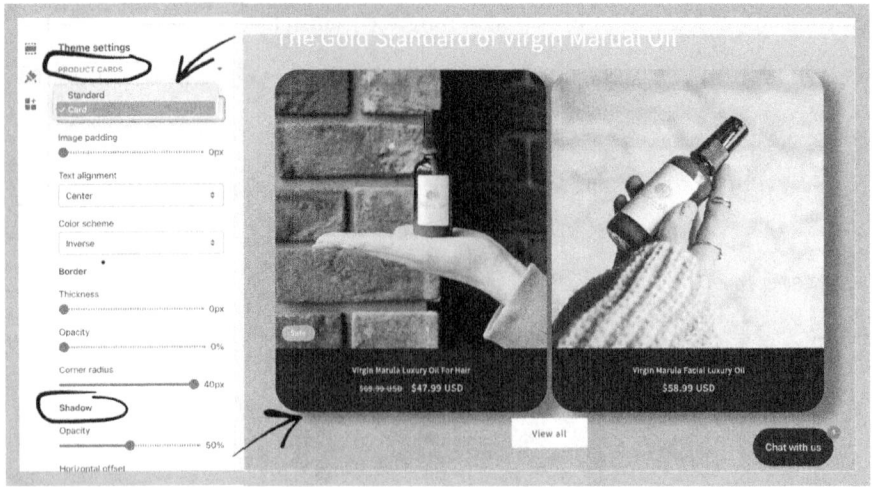

[2.12.49][2.12.49]

In the following image, you can see how the background of the blog post change on the blog page.

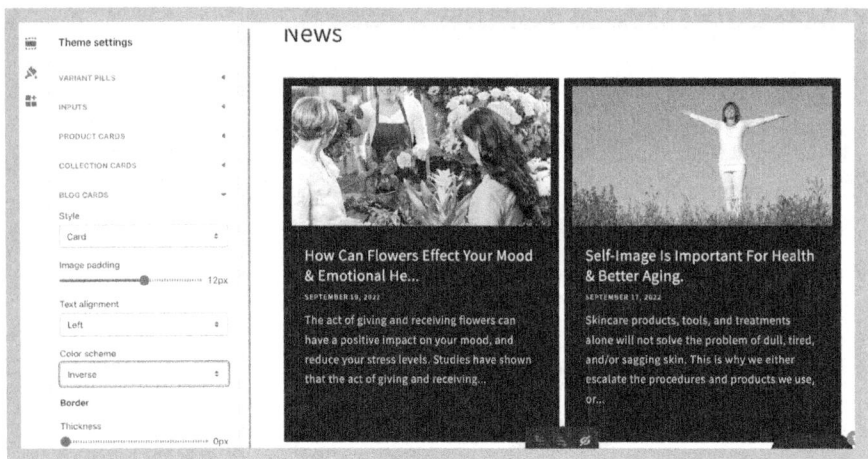

[2.12.50]

Content Containers

Containers are the text portion of content sections, for example, the text box on a slideshow, an image banner, or the columns in multicolumn sections. You can customize the appearance of content containers for your online store.

This action changes all of the containers, as seen in the next image.

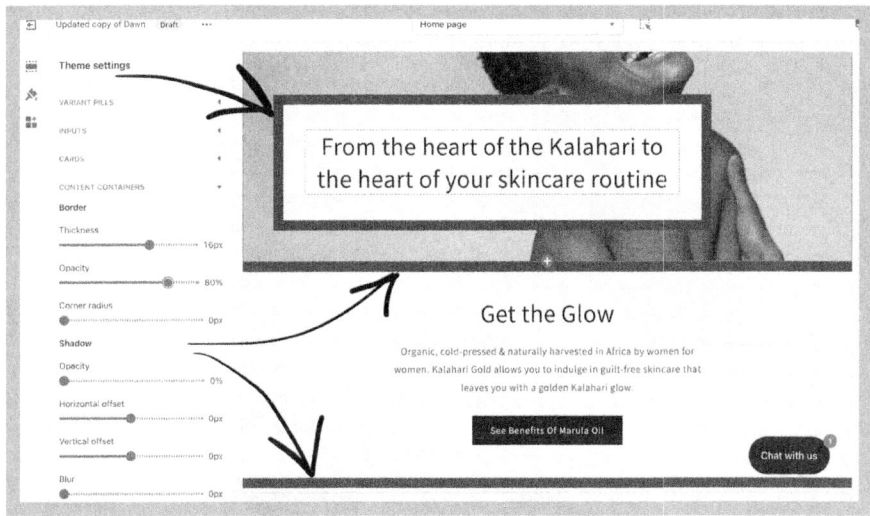

[2.12.51]

Border - The border's **thickness** ranges between 0 and 24px on the outside of the product image and text. This thickness will be added to your **image padding**.

Opacity is between 0 and 100%, where the largest percentage is the full color.

The corner radius will change the button corners from 0 to 40px radius, as shown in the following image.

Shadow

The shadow option will add a shadow behind the content containers which can be shown with various degrees of opacity and thickness.

Opacity is between 0 and 100%, where the largest percentage is the full color.

Horizontal and **vertical offsets** will affect where your shadow will be behind the input.

Blur options will spread the shadow behind the input.

Media

Media is the visual component of sections, for example, product media or the image in Image with Text sections. You can add borders and shadows to your media.

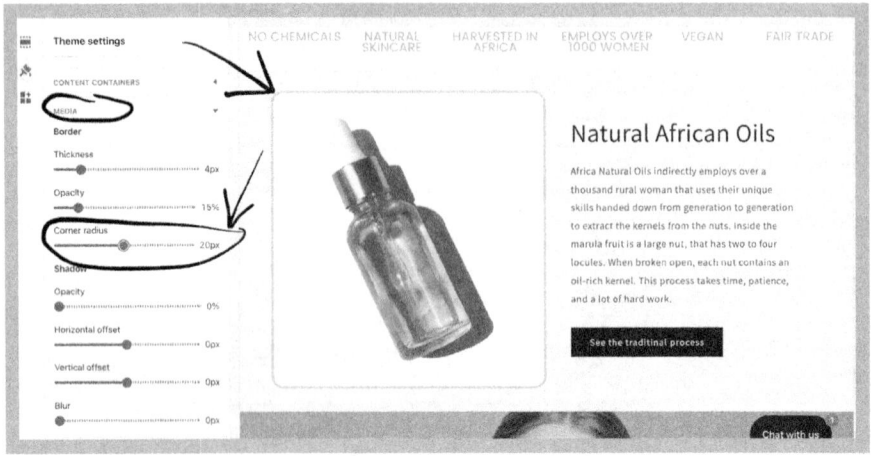

[2.12.52]

Border - The border's **thickness** ranges between 0 and 24px on the outside of the product image and text. This thickness will be added to your **image padding.**

Opacity is between 0 and 100%, where the largest percentage is the full color.

The corner radius will change the button corners from 0 to 40px radius, as shown in the following image.

Shadow

Opacity is between 0 and 100%, where the largest percentage is the full color.

Horizontal and **vertical offsets** will affect where your shadow will be behind the input..

Blur options will spread the shadow behind the input.

NOTE: *The action will affect all the media in the store except if the image is in the multi-column, collection list, collage sections, and blog posts. The media in the following image is on the product page.*

[2.12.53]

Dropdown and Pop-Ups

Adjust the appearance of navigation dropdowns, pop-up modals, and cart pop-ups.

[2.12.54]

Border - The border's **thickness** ranges between 0 and 24px on the outside of the product image and text. This thickness will be added to your **image padding**.

Opacity is between 0 and 100%, where the largest percentage is the full color.

The corner radius will change the button corners from 0 to 40px radius, as shown in the following image.

Shadow

The shadow option will add a shadow behind the dropdown and popups which can be shown with various degrees of opacity and thickness.

Opacity is between 0 and 100%, where the largest percentage is the full color.

Horizontal and **vertical offsets** will affect where your shadow will be behind the input.

Blur options will spread the shadow behind the input.

Drawers

Drawers are hidden, interactive containers that appear and disappear when tapped or clicked, for example, a collapsible navigation menu or filter options.

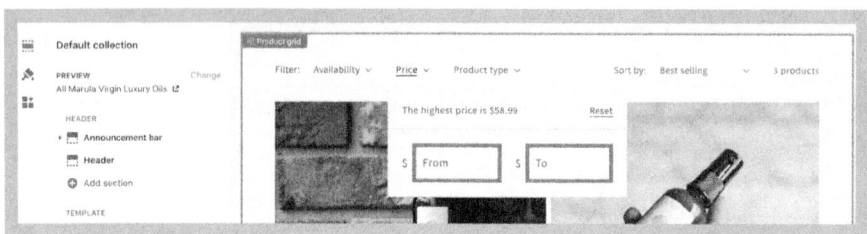

[2.12.55]

Border - The border's **thickness** ranges between 0 and 24px, on the outside of the product image and text. This thickness will be added to your **image padding.**

Opacity is between 0 and 100%, where the largest percentage is the full color.

The corner radius will change the button corners from 0 to 40px radius, as shown in the following image.

Shadow

Opacity is between 0 and 100%, where the largest percentage is the full color.

Horizontal and **vertical offsets** will affect where your shadow will be behind the input.

Blur options will spread the shadow behind the input.

Badges

Sale and Sold out badges are automatically added to your product images when the price drops, or when the inventory count reaches 0. You can adjust the position, shape, and color of your badges. In the free Shopify theme, you can only have access to a few main colors.

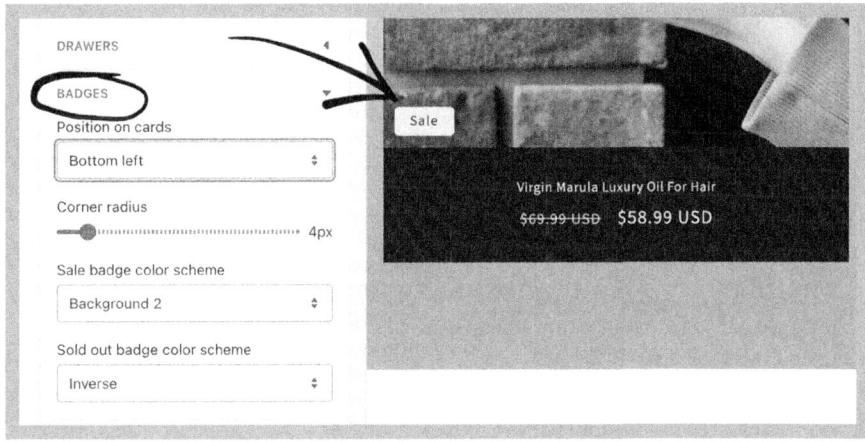

[2.12.56]

In the following image you can see the extra colors I can allocate to each of the badges and sales price in the collection and product pages.

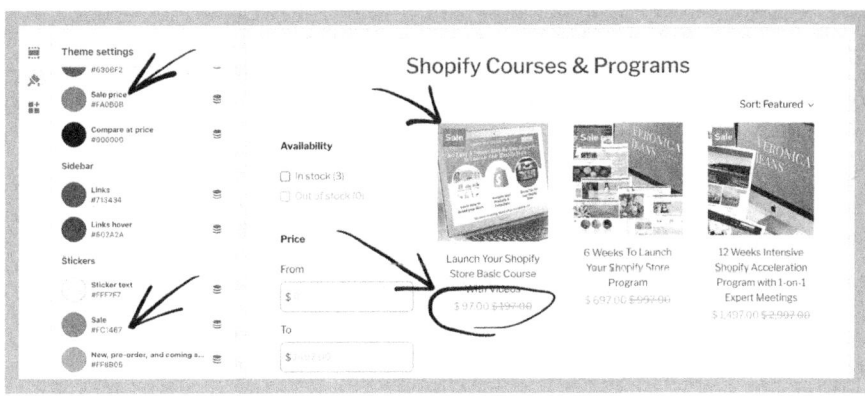

[2.12.57]

Icons

Icons are small images that can be added to certain sections or blocks. Set the color scheme for your icons in Theme settings.

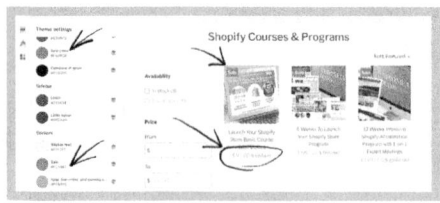

[2.12.58]

Social Media

You can add social sharing buttons for your products and blog posts, and links to your social media accounts. Links to your social media accounts show in the footer of your online store.

- Social Sharing Options - Products
- Social Accounts
- Social Sharing Image

You can add an image you would like to appear on social media when there is no image available on your shareable link from your website. This would happen; your hero image will not always pop up if you post your blog immediately.

Social Sharing Options – Products - These are the social media icons on your product page for your visitors to share. In the free theme, you do not have a large selection. But really, a small selection is better so that your customer does not get sidetracked when buying. The social media options are available in 'Themes > Optimize > Theme Settings > Social Media'.

Social Accounts - In the text box, you can add your complete social media address for any of your social media accounts. Example: https://www.facebook.com/veronicajeansshopifyqueen for my Facebook Business page.

Search Behaviour

Online Store includes predictive search, which shows suggestions when customers start typing into the search field. Search suggestions can help customers articulate and refine their search queries, and provide new ways for them to explore an online store. They can also let customers quickly browse matches without having to leave their current page to see a separate list of search results.

Favicon

All you have to do is add your Favicon to your theme editor. The tiny logo will be automatically added to the correct position for your online presence.

You can only load your favicon in the 'Customize' part of your theme settings, located at the left side of your theme dashboard, once you are in the theme customization area.

In the 'Favicon' option, add your image.

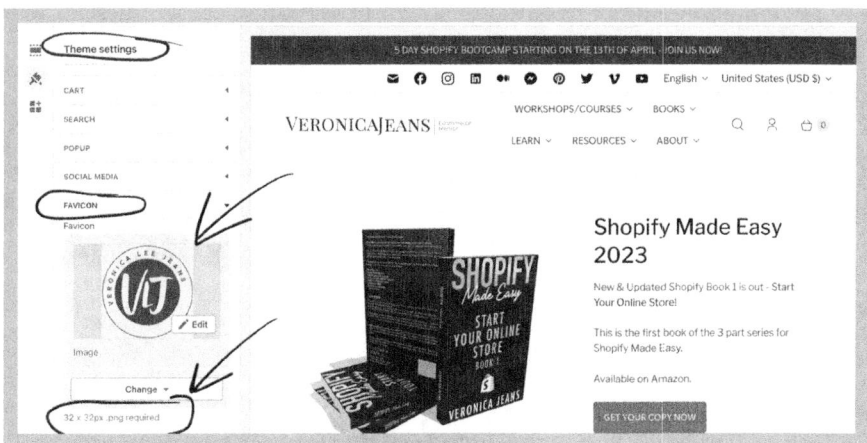

[2.12.65]

The favicon image will be automatically added to the browser tab.

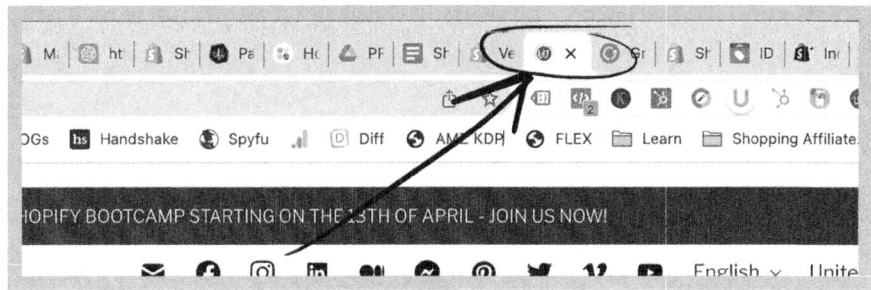

[2.12.66]

Currency Formats

You can choose to have product, cart, and checkout prices always show currency format.

Currency formats that are rounded are rounded up if the decimal number is 50 or greater, or rounded down if it isn't.

Some themes let you display the currency code along with the prices in your online store.

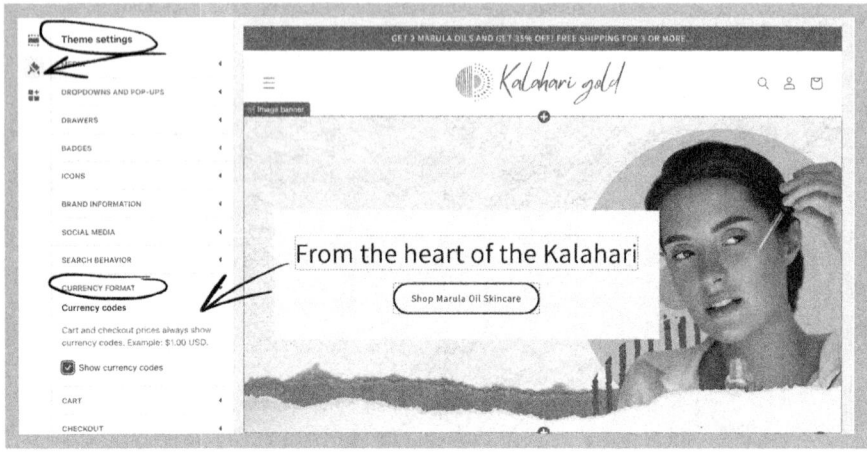

[2.12.67]

Your store's checkout always shows decimal places regardless of the currency formatting that you choose for your online store.

In the following image you can see the currency formatting options in Shopify.

Currency formatting options

You can show currency amounts in a few ways:

Money format	Rounded	Example
`{{ amount }}`		1,134.65
`{{ amount_no_decimals }}`	✓	1,135
`{{ amount_with_comma_separator }}`		1.134,65
`{{ amount_no_decimals_with_comma_separator }}`	✓	1.135
`{{ amount_with_apostrophe_separator }}`		1'134.65

[2.12.70]

Cart

You can change the style of the cart on your online store by adding different types of how the cart appears for the customer and add different options depending on your Shopify theme.

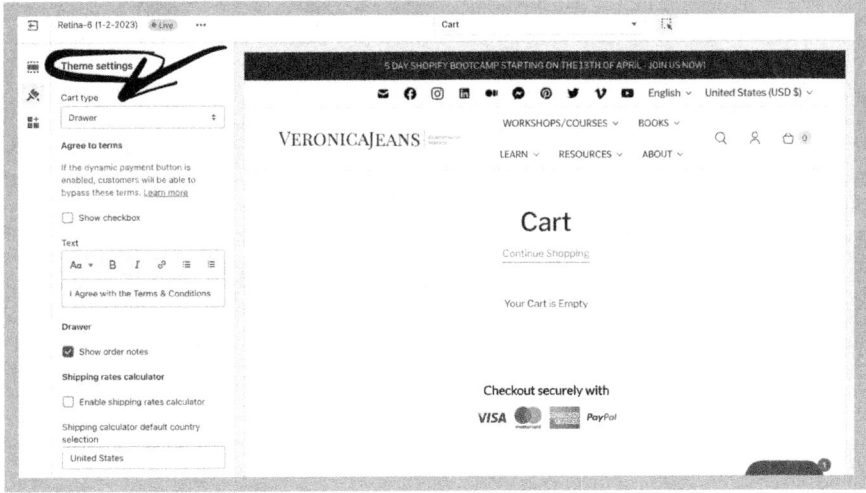

[2.12.68]

When a customer adds a product from your store to their cart, the cart can appear as a drawer, a page, or a pop-up notification. In the paid theme, you get more options for the cart.

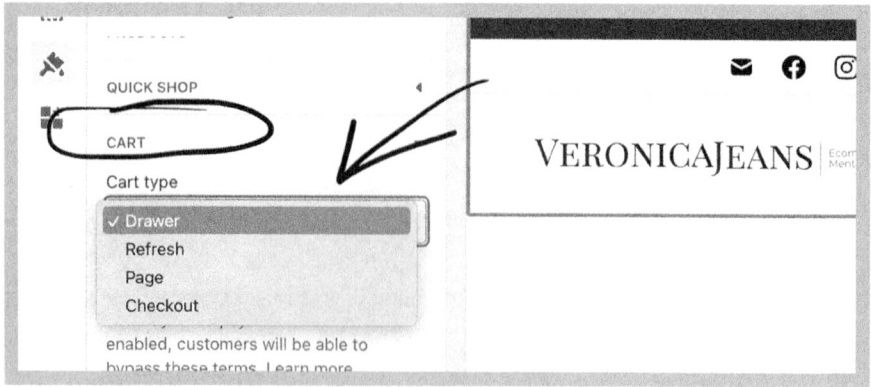

[2.12.69]

You can show the vendor and also a note text box for the customer to leave a note.

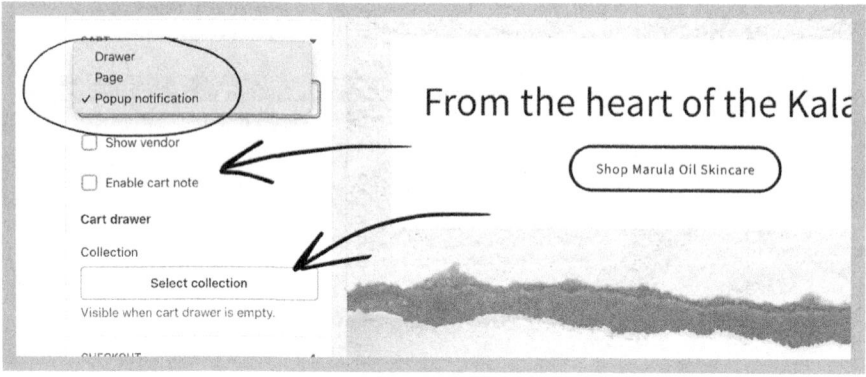

[2.12.71]

When the customer's cart is empty, you can display a featured collection on the cart drawer.

Checkout

This section lets you customize your store's checkout and see all the details in Chapter 4 - Store Information Pages.

Theme Style

A theme style is a collection of settings chosen by a theme designer. You can apply a theme style to your store to give it a polished look and feel. All themes have a theme style applied by default. When you customize a theme, you replace the theme style settings with your own. When you apply a theme style to your theme, you change your current settings, such as colors and typography.

APPS EMBEDS (3 SQUARES AND + ICON)

Once you have added Shopify Apps, you will be able to activate and add them to the different pages depending on the functionality of the app.

Apps can provide blocks that can be added as blocks in a section, and as sections in a template. This lets you add app functionality exactly where you want to use it on a page. App blocks can be added, removed, repositioned, and customized through the theme editor. App blocks might only be compatible with certain page types. For example, a size chart app might only be compatible with product pages.

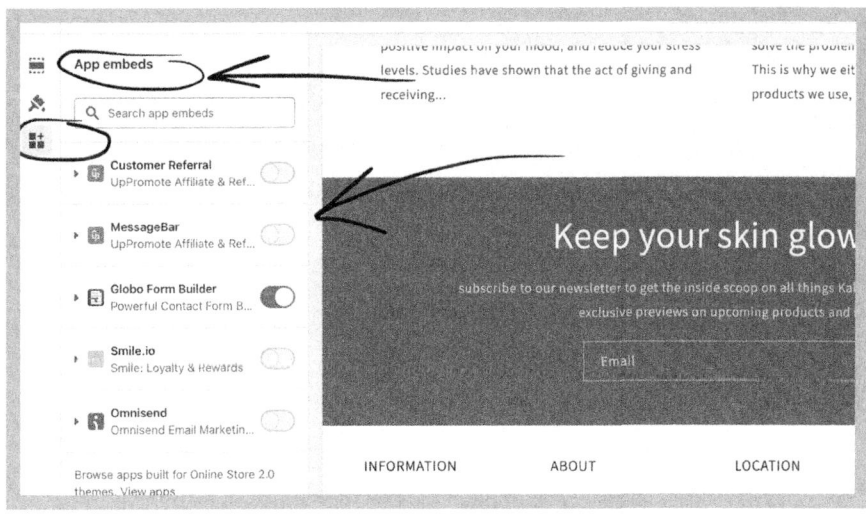

[2.12.74]

CHAPTER 11
VIRTUAL STORE FRONT

**WHERE TO FIND THIS IN SHOPIFY? ONLINE > THEMES > CUSTOMIZE

THE HOMEPAGE of an online store is like a virtual storefront. It's the first impression that customers have of your brand, and it sets the tone for their entire shopping experience. A well-designed homepage can increase conversions, boost sales, and help establish a loyal customer base.

Deciding on the most important features to place on a homepage is difficult, and there is no one-size-fits-all approach. The key is to continually test and learn from your audience's behavior.

It's important to adapt your content to suit the needs and interests of your visitors. Changing your content to see which one is more effective is a great strategy for engaging your audience and increasing conversions.

WHAT TO EXPECT IN THIS CHAPTER:

- *Create Your Homepage*
- *Customize Your Homepage*

WHY THE HOMEPAGE IS IMPORTANT:

First Impressions Matter - The homepage is the first thing customers see when they visit your website. This means it's the first opportunity to make a positive impression on your audience. A well-designed homepage can create a sense of **trust, credibility, and expertise**, which can help increase customer loyalty and repeat business.

Navigation and Usability - The homepage is also where your customers can access the **main navigation menu**, which guides them to other parts of your website. A clear and intuitive navigation menu can help customers find the products or information they're looking for quickly and easily.

Brand Identity - The homepage is an important space for communicating your brand identity to your customers. This includes your brand's logo, color scheme, and overall aesthetic. A consistent and cohesive brand identity can help build brand recognition and loyalty.

Product Showcase - The homepage is great for showcasing your products and highlighting your bestsellers or promotions. By strategically placing product images and descriptions on your homepage, you can entice customers to browse and make a purchase. **This can help increase sales and revenue for your ecommerce store.**

SEO Benefits - A well-designed homepage can also benefit your search engine optimization (SEO) efforts. By including relevant keywords and meta tags on your homepage, you can increase your website's visibility in search engine results pages (SERPs), which can drive more organic traffic to your website.

> Pro Tip: It can be helpful to learn from competitors and leading ecommerce sites, but the best way to know what works for your business is to adopt a test-and-learn approach. Continuously testing and making improvements to your homepage based on visitor behavior can lead to more sales.

CREATE YOUR HOMEPAGE

The homepage can only be created in your 'Customize' editor. Your homepage consists of all the parts that you have created, the branding tools, the information pages, the products, the collections, and the navigation menus.

In the chapter for Shopify Brand Settings, we created all the branding tools and options for your store.

Then in the chapter Shopify Theme, I showed you where to add more brand settings and options for your brand.

You have your colors, fonts, logo, favicon, description, and messages in the Brand settings.

Now we can access that information in the 'Customize' editor.

In your Shopify dashboard, go to 'Online store' and 'Themes' and click on the 'Customize' button.

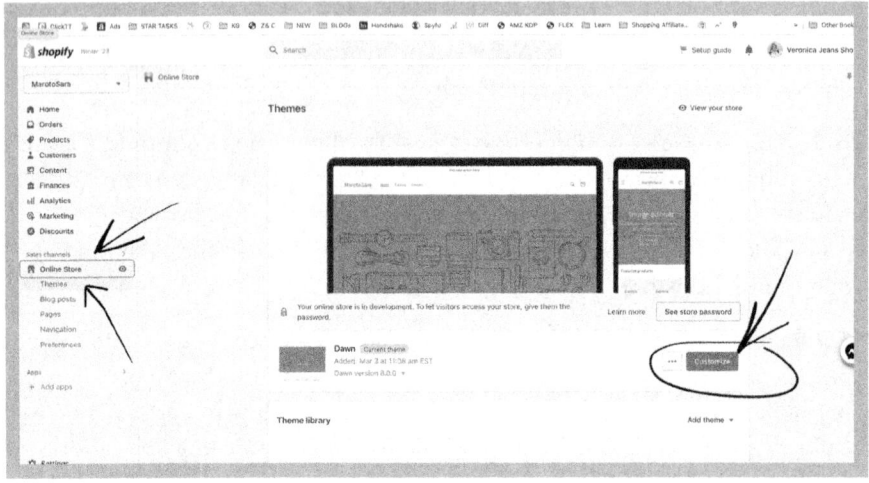

[2.14.1]

The home page is the default page in your 'Customize' dashboard.

CUSTOMIZE YOUR HOMEPAGE

The following image shows you the first view in your 'Customize' dashboard.

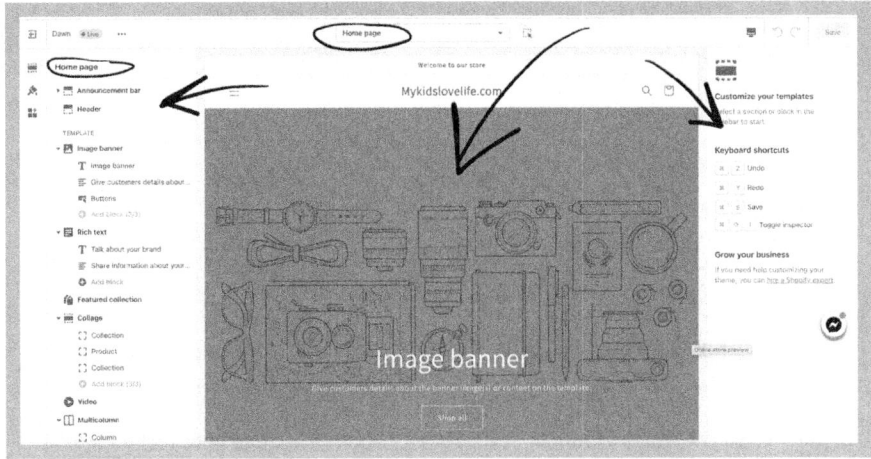

[2.14.2]

HEADER

Announcement bar section:

Step 1. Add the Announcement bar

The first section for the homepage is the 'Announcement bar'.

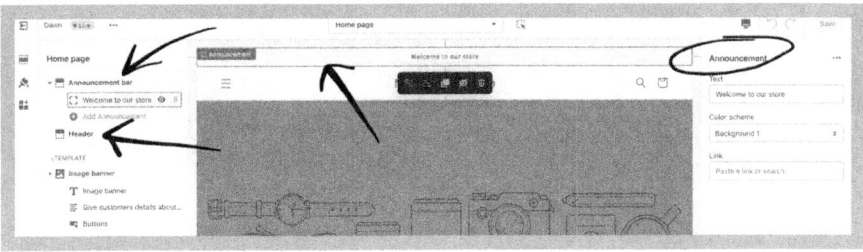

[2.14.1a]

The 'Announcement bar' lets you communicate important information to your customers on any page. The section has no settings on its own, but you can customize up to 12 different announcement blocks to display. You can add text, a color scheme, and a link to an announcement bar to make the text clickable for customers to a specific page. Offer free shipping or a money-back guarantee. This can definitely add to your sales conversions.

> Pro Tip: I would not add 3 announcement bars, because that would look extremely messy. I would limit them to 2 at the most.

Choose a **color for the background** of the bar to make sure it stands out but fits in the brand of your Shopify store.

Step 2. Customize your header

The header is one of the important areas of your Shopify store.

The header of your store will be repeated on every page. You cannot change the header for individual pages. The only time your header differs is on the checkout page. The only available section to add to the header is a 'Custom liquid' coding in the free Shopify theme.

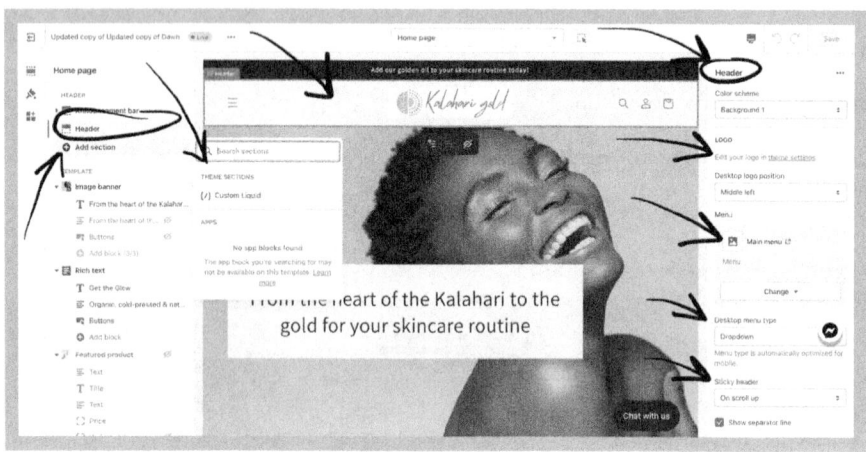

[2.14.3]

With a paid Shopify theme, the header also includes logo over transparent header and controlling the opacity of the header.

As seen the on the following image, my social buttons are directly under the 'Announcement bar' and not crowding the menu.

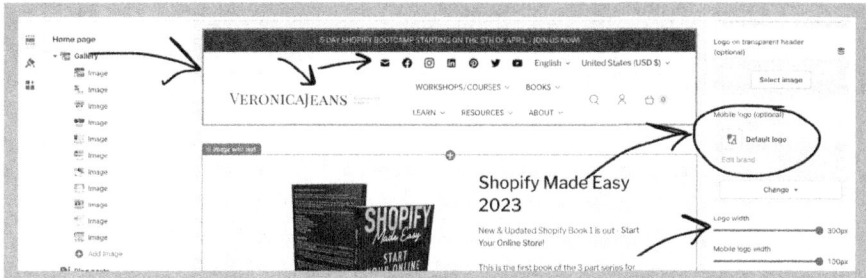

[2.14.5]

Every theme is a little bit different and the only way to know which one you like is to actually add it to your store and view the options and features in the 'Customize' dashboard.

Here are the options that need to be added to the 'Header' section.

Logo - The logo image can be changed in the 'Brand' or the 'Theme settings', depending on where you added your logo image. If your logo is in the 'Brand' settings, it will indicate as the **default logo.** The logo can be sized up to 300px in the default Shopify theme. If you have a paid Shopify theme, the logo can be increased to 800px depending on the theme.

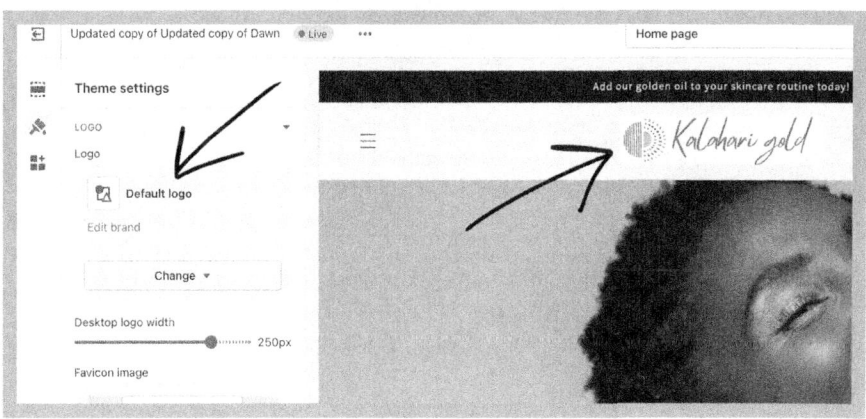

[2.14.4]

Main menu - Here you can add your choice of menu, either a dropdown or a mega menu.

Sticky header - This is exactly what it sounds like. Choose a **sticky header** option so the header stays in view on the browser window as the visitor scrolls up and down your website.

> *Pro Tip:* It's important to test both options and evaluate their impact on your website. Sometimes, a sticky header may obscure important product page information, in which case you may need to prioritize the product page and choose to forego the sticky header. Ultimately, the product page should be the primary focus as it's where customers make their purchasing decisions.

Mobile layout - this option is about the logo positioning in the mobile view. I generally do not add padding, but it depends on the information position when viewed in a mobile device.

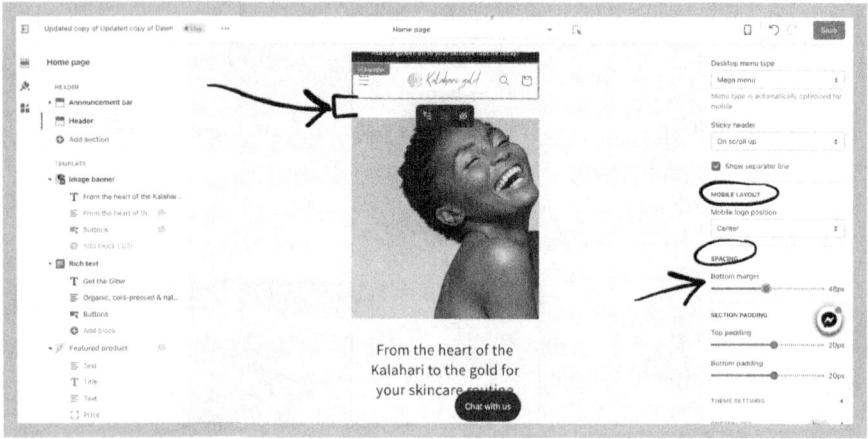

[2.14.6]

Section padding - as seen on the next image, the section padding is above and below the logo and menu.

[2.14.7]

> Pro Tip: It is nice to have add some space above and below the logo and menu, but I would suggest not too much, because this will push the important message out of view.

Color scheme – The color scheme for the header is one of the colors added in the 'Theme Settings'.

The colors can be changed in the 'Theme Settings'.

TEMPLATE

This is the body of the homepage which is called the 'Template' in the 'Customize' dashboard, all the different sections are added to create the homepage.

This is the only setting for the homepage setup.

Each page will be a different template and can be customized accordingly

In the 'Template', there are the different sections and blocks of the theme. Each theme will be slightly different.

The sections and blocks in the left sidebar, will be displayed in the 'Customize' editor in the middle of the dashboard. In the right sidebar will be features of each of the sections and blocks to choose different options.

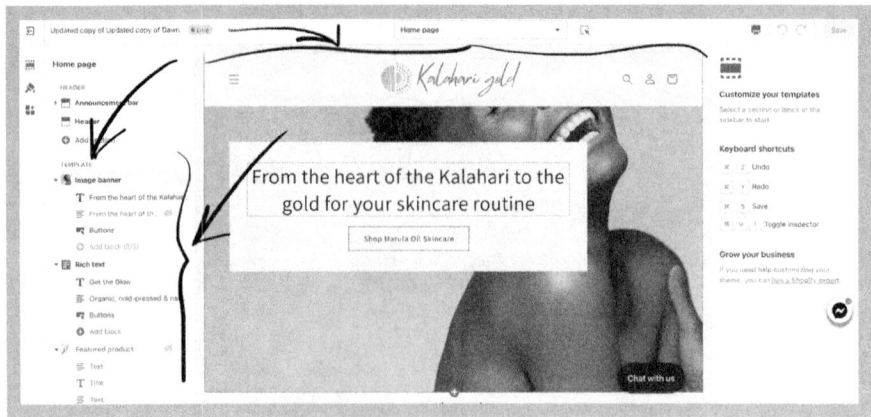

[2.14.19]

Step 1. Add brand message and promotion

Key marketing campaigns and brand messaging should be placed at the top of the homepage in the primary zone. Visitors need to immediately know what the store is about. What are you selling, or promoting and why should they buy. It must be a short and clear message. Add a button to your main **'Image with text'** to give your visitor an option to buy the product you are promoting.

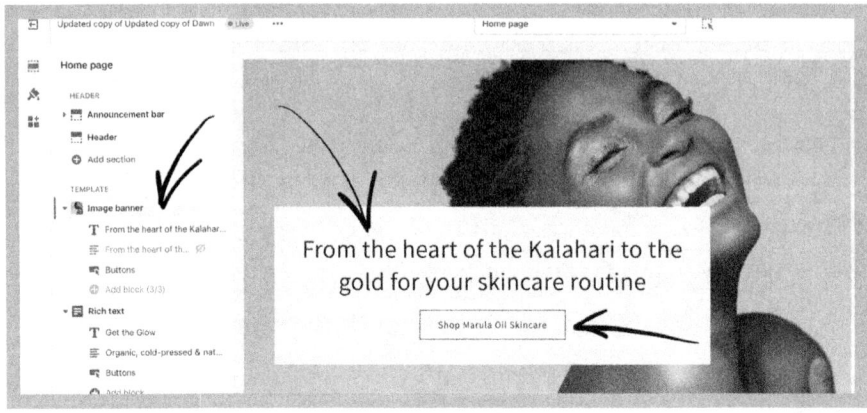

[2.14.8]

In this next image, themissingpiecepuzzle.com is promoting to engaged couples to create a personalized puzzle. Also notice the message which indicates what makes them different to other puzzle brands – 'arrives fast and made in America!'

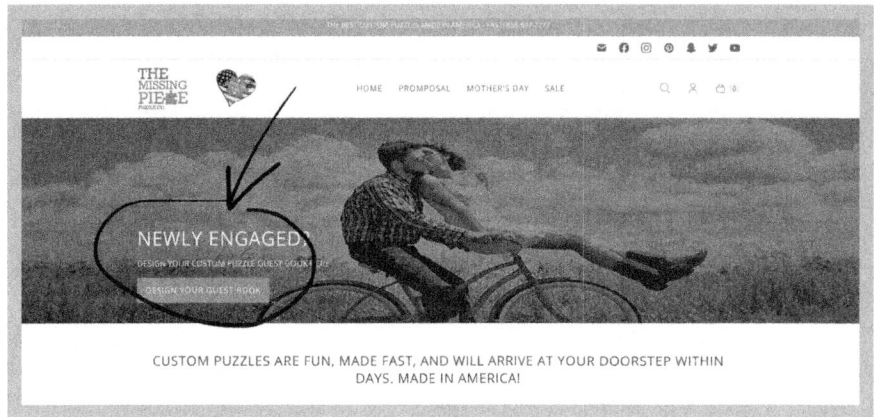

[2.14.9]

In the following image the message is very clear about what dustfumemist.com are selling.

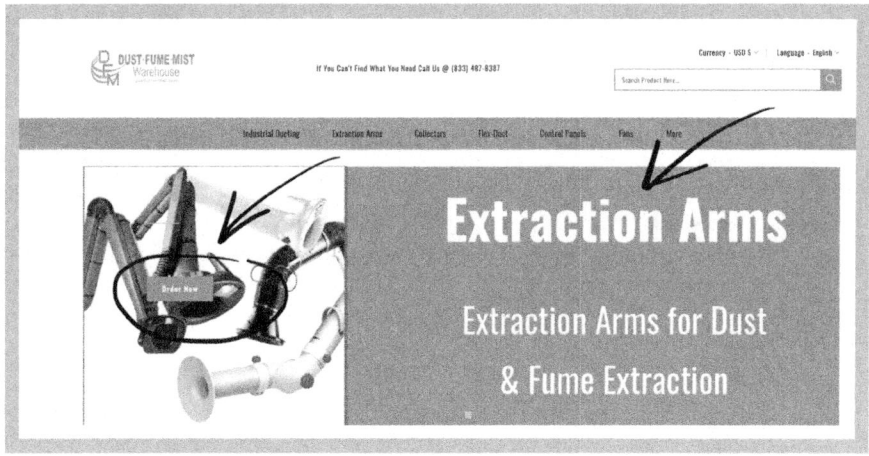

[2.14.10]

Although, the button needs to stand out so it can be noticed. See how in image 2.14.10, the button is the same blue color as the items in the image.

Step 2. Showcase your best-selling or most popular products

This can entice customers to explore your website further and encourage them to buy. On my website and store, I promote my new books and added more information about me. I used the **'Image with text'** section to add the media and information.

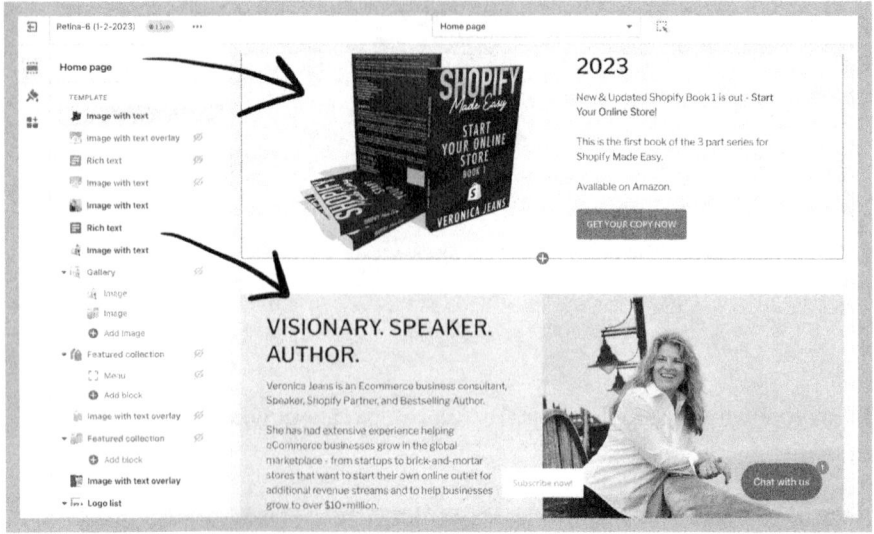

[2.14.11]

> 💡 Pro Tip: Visitors to your website or store do not buy immediately. Most of the time they need to see you online and visit a few times before they need or want your product. Giving them more information about who you are, goes a long way to increase the like and trust for any new visitor.

With Invicibleskincare.com, we encourage visitors to buy our products.

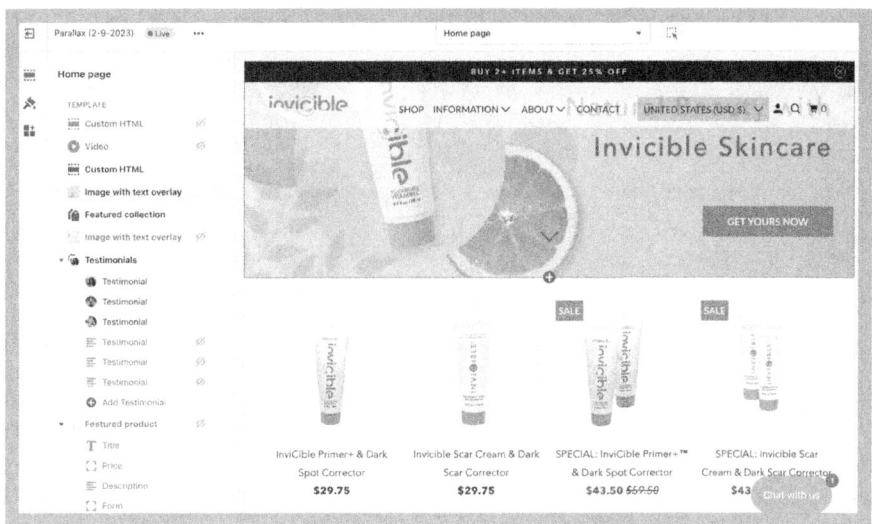

[2.14.12]

In the Industrialfarmco.com store, the most popular items are at the top of the page, right under promotion and message:

"20% OFF ORDERS OVER $250 & FREE SHIPPING IN THE USA FOR ORDERS OVER $35 - One-of-a-Kind Artisan Made Products"

[2.14.13]

Add your most popular collections if you have more than one collection. Rotate the collections with the promotions or best sellers. In themissingpiecepuzzle.com store, Donna the owner knows her customers look for puzzles by pieces, so she added the sidebar menu to her homepage.

[2.4.18]

> Pro Tip: Do not try to add all your collections or products on the page. Less is more. Rather, be strategic in creating your collections to make it easy for customers to find what they are looking for.

> Pro Tip: When you post links to social, be intentional about your posts.

Step 3. Use high-quality product images

High-quality images can help customers visualize the product better. Your visitors cannot touch, feel or smell your products, so giving them the best experience visually is imperative. Naughtygoodbites.com is a prime example of encouraging you to sample the delicious chocolates.

[2.14.14]

Sadly, I have seen too many store owners that do not make an effort to showcase their products with amazing images and expect to sell their products successfully.

Step 4. Include customer reviews and testimonials.

Customer reviews are part of your social proof that customer really like your products. This can help build trust with potential customers. Displaying reviews on your homepage can encourage customer engagement. Customers may be more likely to leave a review or share their experiences when they see that others have done that as well.

According to a study by BrightLocal, 91% of consumers read online reviews, and 84% trust reviews as much as personal recommendations.

[2.14.15]

On the hugpatrol.net we added reviews to the homepage and included photos of people. Not all customers want their faces on the internet, so we used generic photos from Shopify Burst.

[2.14.16]

The previous reviews look so much more appealing than the reviews that were on the homepage before as shown in the following image.

VIRTUAL STORE FRONT

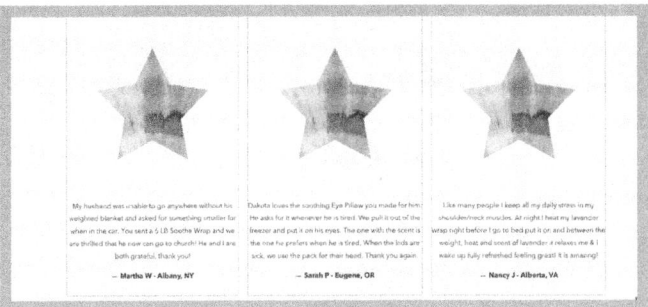

[2.14.17]

In the default Shopify theme, pick the **'Multiple columns'** section and add 3 **'Column'** blocks with images and text.

The rounded images with customer photos are created in Canva and then uploaded to the columns.

Step 5. Highlight any special offers or promotions

You worked hard to get potential buyers to your store. Don't waste the opportunity to offer them a sweetener. First, you need to create a discount promotion located in the 'Discount' setting on the main dashboard. Add all the details on the homepage with a **'Rich text'** section. In the following image I added the promotion text in the **'Title'** block and the code in the **'Text'** block.

[2.14.20]

Or add a special sales price in the product page. Although the discount price will only be for one product.

KALAHARI GOLD

Virgin Marula Facial Luxury Oil

~~$58.99 USD~~ $29.99 USD   Sale

Shipping calculated at checkout.

Pay in 4 interest-free installments for orders over **$50.00** with shop Pay
installments powered by **Affirm** Learn more

Quantity

— 1 +

Add to cart

Buy with G Pay

[2.14.21]

> Pro Tip: I prefer to use a discount code the customer has to add to the cart or checkout page. A few customers miss or forget to add the discount code and this gives you an opportunity to connect with your customer and make sure they get the discount. Which will get you a very grateful customer who will definitely come shopping again with a glowing review!

Step 6. Include social proof

Showcase any media mentions or awards to build credibility. TheMissingPiecePuzzle.com showcases all her media mentions on her homepage.

[2.14.22]

InvicibleSkincare.com has some mentions in magazines. Although they are using a paid Shopify Theme (Out Of The Sandbox). Here we used the **'Logo'** section to display the logos of the magazines.

[2.14.23]

Step 7. Display trust badges and security seals

Trust badges and security seals, and a money-back guarantee can help customers feel more secure when making a purchase.

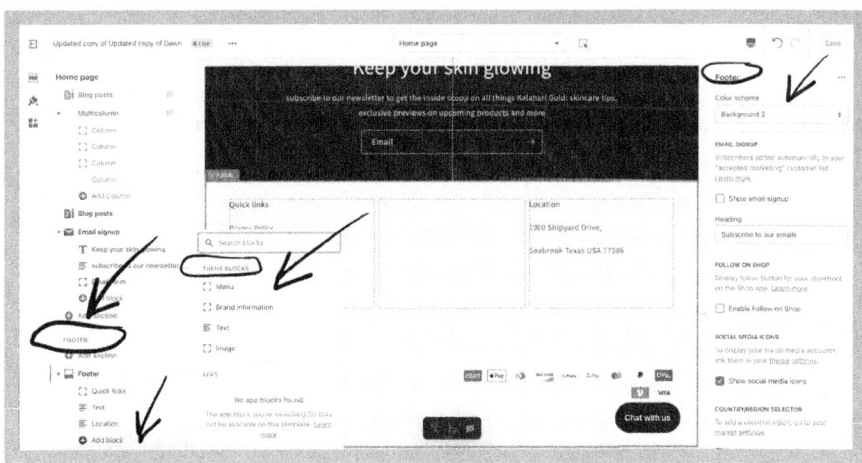

[2.14.32]

Step 8. Incorporate a search bar

This can make it easy for customers to find a specific product or category. In the following images you can see the different types of search bars. Dustfumemist.com show a half search bar above the top menu - (Paid Shopify Theme)

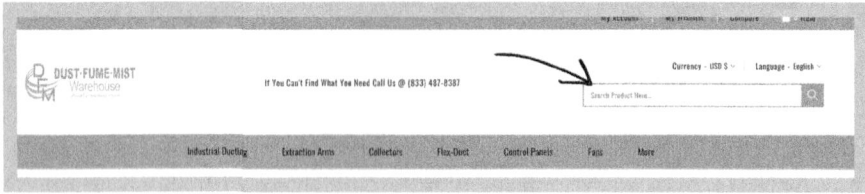

[2.14.25]

Itsabode.com shows a full search bar across the header (paid Shopify Theme - Out of the Sandbox)

[2.14.26]

Typically, the search function is shown with an icon whether it is a free or paid Shopify theme.

[2.14.28]

Step 9. Add an About Us section

It is a great idea to add information to the homepage that tells the story of your brand can also help build trust and credibility

This section is the '**Image with text**' and the image is added in the image block and the text is in its own block. You can add a button, but it depends if you have more information that leads your customer to the 'About Us' page.

In the following image you can see that I showcase some information about what differentiates me from my competition.

[2.14.29]

On the IndustrialFarmco.com store, we added the story about the family as seen in the next image.

[2.14.30]

Step 10. Include a clear and visible call-to-action

Encourage customers to take a specific action, such as making a purchase as soon as visitors land on the homepage. Your promotion should be at the top with a button to the product that you want to highlight.

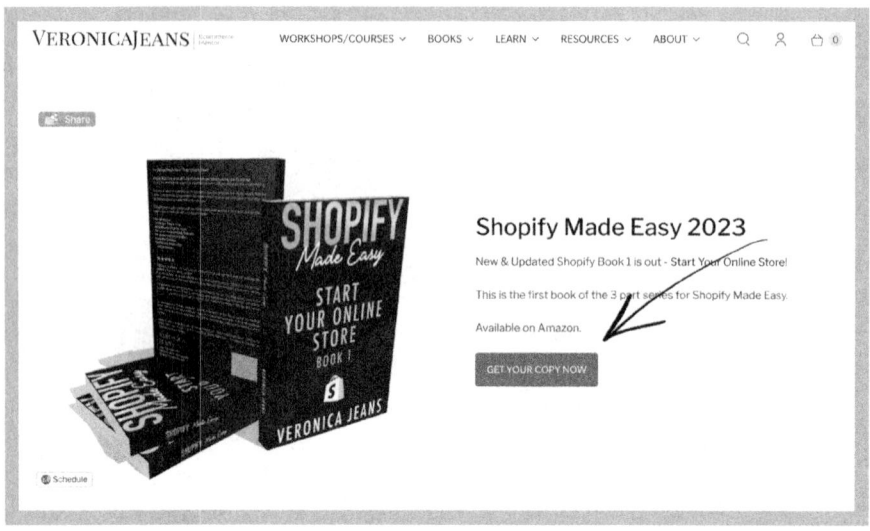

[2.14.31]

Here in Kalahari Gold store, we encourage them to check out and buy our product.

[2.14.32]

This is like a bill board for your visitors.

FOOTER

Your footer is the section at the bottom of your store pages. The purpose of a footer on your website is to add more information for your customer to navigate in your store. The information would be all your shipping, refund, returns, policies, about page, FAQ, sizing, and any other information that would aid your customer to use or buy your product.

[2.6.22]

The footer of your store will be repeated on every page. You cannot change the footer for individual pages. The only time your footer differs is on the checkout page.

Step 1. Add a newsletter sign up

It is always a great idea to collect email addresses from prospective customers. Unfortunately, this is an area that gets abused by spammers and bots. So not everybody that signs up is a prospective customer. To alleviate this problem, you can add more options for the signup, i.e., first and last name.

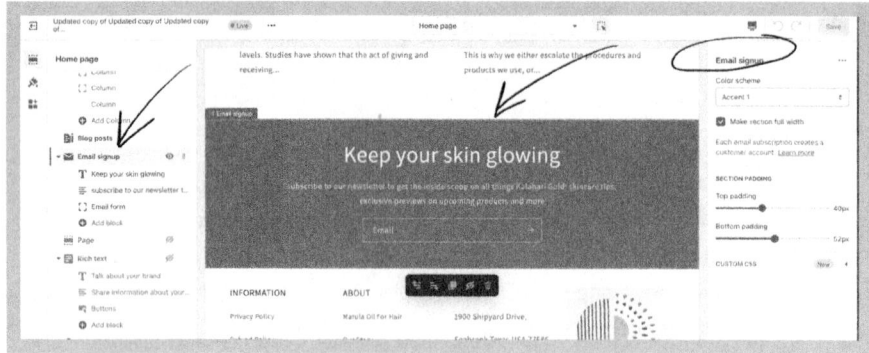

[2.14.36]

In the free Shopify theme, this is not possible. You can add your newsletter/email responder Apps to Shopify to help you in this endeavor. I will cover more about how to optimize your emails and forms in my next book: 'Optimize your Shopify Store'.

Here are some IDEAS to include in your footer:

Menus & Links:

- About Us
- Shipping
- International Shipping
- FAQ
- Privacy Policy
- Terms of Use
- Refunds & Returns
- Contact
- Your Mission
- Specials
- Associations and Memberships
- Press
- Testimonials

Text & Images:

- Business Hours
- Address
- Social Icons

- Email Signup (newsletter)
- Awards and Certifications

If you have a paid theme, you can be more creative with images and more text.

- Quick Links
- Talk about your business
- Newsletter

Quick Links are the menus you want to add to the bottom of your pages. You can add as many as you like.

In the 'Talk about your business' section, it is easy to just add the text, including a link.

I will also show you how to add a second footer menu or section to add information.

Step 1. Prominently display contact information

Contact information is added with the 'Text' block and should include a physical address, an email address and if possible, a phone number to show that you are a legitimate and accessible business.

[2.14.33]

💡 Pro Tip: If you don't have a physical address or you do not want to add your home address to the store, renting a UPS post box will give the option of a business address.

Step 2. Provide multiple payment options

This can help accommodate a wide range of customers and payment preferences are at the bottom of the footer and are added when you choose your payment provider. All the available credit card payment options will be visible.

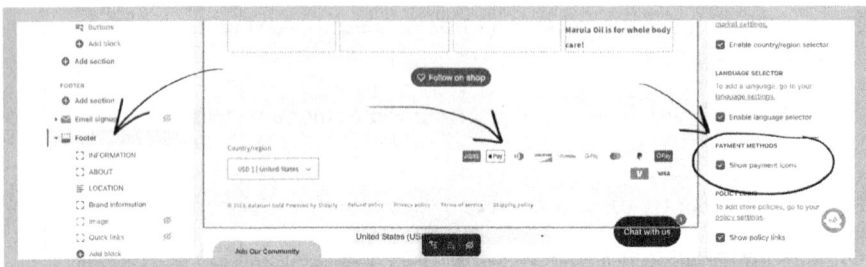

[2.14.37]

Step 3. Add footer menus

Add your policies and company information in the footer menu. Depending on your Shopify theme, you have varies options to add menus, text, logos, etc.

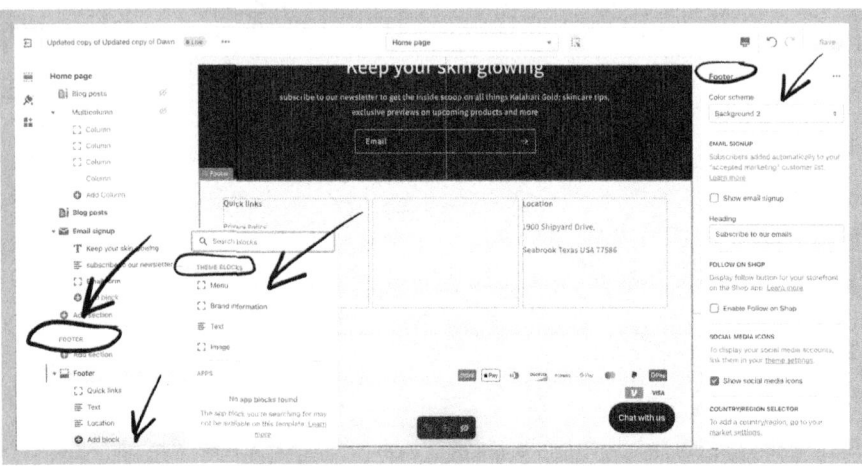

[2.14.32a]

CHAPTER 12
APPS & SALES

**WHERE TO FIND THIS IN SHOPIFY? APPS

FROM EDU.GCFGLOBAL.ORG: *"Simply put, an app is a type of software that allows you to perform specific tasks. Applications for desktop or laptop computers are sometimes called desktop applications, while those for mobile devices are called mobile apps. When you open an application, it runs inside the operating system until you close it."*

WHY DO YOU NEED APPS IN YOUR SHOPIFY STORE?

It helps to have Apps on any platform you create because no business is the same. Every online business has different requirements and different financial overhead capabilities.

Shopify provides you with the ability to host your online business. You decide what you need to improve and optimize your online business.

You decide which Apps you want to use with your store to make your processes more automated and enhance your customer's experience in your store. There are some free Apps and some paid Apps.

I have links for each App below that I recommend. All Apps I recommend have been used by either my clients or myself.

A lot of the Apps are going to have a monthly charge. Initially, you probably don't need anything expensive, depending on your product delivery. As you get busier, adding some tools to automate your process and make your life easier makes sense.

Don't forget to add all the added expenses of Apps to your business overheads.

What to expect in this chapter:

- *How to Add Apps to Your Store*
- *Recommended Apps*
- *Free Apps in Shopify*
- *Email Marketing Apps*
- *Option Apps*
- *Shipping Apps*
- *Migration App*
- *Migration or Import/Export App*

HOW TO ADD APPS TO YOUR STORE

Shopify will show you some examples to add if you want to. There are so many Apps for Shopify, but it is not a good idea to use too many. This will slow your store speed down, which is not what you want to happen.

Step 1. Download your Apps to your store

Click on the button at the top right to go to the Shopify App Store. Here you can download your Apps to your store.

Most Apps will load the requisite code in your store template when you follow the steps to activate the Apps.

For some Apps, you will need some help to load the code in the right places. Most apps offer this service for free, and I have had some great experiences and customer support.

The time delay usually is only a maximum of 24 hours, and some will add the code while you chat with them. Or you can hire a developer to add your code, but this will add costs for you.

Step 2. Test Your Apps

Always test the App and see if it works properly. For instance, if you are adding options, you will add your options in the App instead of the product page.

As I mentioned, most of the Apps' support is fantastic and will guide you through the setup.

RECOMMENDED APPS

I can recommend the following apps because I have used them for my clients and myself. But, as I said before, try out the Apps and see if they will work for you and your store.

Free Shopify Apps

Product Reviews - Adds product reviews feature (free) to your product page and collection pages. This app will allow your customers to add product reviews on each product page.

https://apps.shopify.com/product-reviews

Order Printer - Prints your labels, invoices, and packing slips (complimentary)!

https://apps.shopify.com/order-printer

Digital Downloads - If you sell digital products, you need this. Once you sell your digital product, a link will be sent to the customer to download the digital product they bought.

https://apps.shopify.com/digital-downloads

Marketing Apps

MailChimp & ShopSynch - This App is for newsletter sign-ups, abandoned cart emails, thank you emails, welcome emails, etc. (free up to 2000 emails a month)

Omnisend - Directly connected to Shopify and easy to use. And they now have Amazon analytics as well. And your email automation is super easy.

https://veronicajeans.online/omnisend

Klaviyo Email Marketing App - This app has better functionality than MailChimp. The flows or sequencing for your email campaign gives you triggers, conditions, and split conditions.

https://veronicajeans.online/klaviyo

There are more, but these are the marketing apps I have worked with.

Options Apps

Why do you need an Options App? If you have more options and variants than the Shopify restrictions, especially if the variants have a cost, you want to add to the product price.

Shopify only gives you three options and 100 variants.

Options in Shopify are, for example, your 'size,' 'color,' or 'length.'

Variants are 'L,' 'M,' 'S,' or 'blue,' 'yellow,' etc.

Apps that I have used are **Bold Options** and **Advanced Product Options (APO)**. I prefer APO because of the look on the product page. Most Apps come with a trial period. https://apps.shopify.com/product-options

https://apps.shopify.com/advanced-product-options

Shipping Apps

Shopify - Shipping in Shopify is pretty awesome, and the shipping pricing is very reasonable. If you are shipping from different shopping platforms, this will be the solution. For instance, if you had an Etsy store, Shopify, and another shopping platform.

Shipstation - This App will combine all the orders into one software and make life easier for your shipping requirements

https://apps.shopify.com/shipstation

Migration & Importing App

You are moving your information to Shopify from another website. If you move from another platform to Shopify, there are easier ways to migrate all your information instead of using Shopify import.

Free Shopify Store Importer - I have not used this app because it is a new Shopify app, and I have used the functionality of Matrixify blew me away, and I have not changed to another option because it is fantastic.

https://apps.shopify.com/store-importer

Matrixify - I have used the Matrixify app extensively to migrate all the information you need, from products, categories, pages, and blog posts to SEO. Images can be pulled into Shopify with a link from your old website as well, and you don't have to go down and upload all the photos. Moving or migrating your information to a new platform, you will have to port all your existing web page addresses to your new store on Shopify. This is necessary because if you have old links on the web, your customers won't get a 'Page Not Found,' but they will see the new page.

https://veronicajeans.online/matrixify

RESOURCES:

I update my Apps and tools for Shopify and marketing all the time. I add them to my tool page on my website.

Here is a link to my RESOURCES & TOOLS page:

https://veronicajeans.online/resources

WHAT IS NEXT FOR YOUR SHOPIFY STORE?

Shopify Made Easy Book 3 - Grow Your Shopify Business: *A Comprehensive Guide to Boosting Your E-commerce Sales and Growing Your Business*

This book is the second installment in a groundbreaking series created by Amazon.com Bestselling author, Veronica Jeans, to take you by the hand and walk you into the world of e-commerce.

Learn how to brand your Shopify store with Step-by-Step guides, lots of screenshots, and tips from a Shopify expert.

www.amazon.com/author/veronicajeans

Join my newsletters for Shopify & marketing courses, resources, and tools on my website: https://veronicajeans.online/resources.

QR Code for Resources

Please Kindly Review This Book

Thank you for reading Shopify Made Easy Book 1. Reviews are crucial for helping other readers discover new books that help them find their own freedom.

If you want to share the value of reading this book, help other readers know how useful this book was for you. I'd really appreciate it.

Recommending my book to others is also a huge help. Don't hesitate to shout out this book in your favorite social media group to spread the word.

APPS & SALES

QR code for Review on Amazon

Thank you so much!

ABOUT THE AUTHOR

Veronica Jeans is an eCommerce business consultant and Shopify expert who has coached entrepreneurs to build and negotiate all the intricacies of running an online store.

She has had extensive experience helping eCommerce businesses grow in the global marketplace - from startups to brick-and-mortar stores that want to start their own online outlet for additional revenue streams. She integrates her extensive knowledge in eCommerce and her international financial and tax expertise to offer up a playbook for generating income online.

Veronica lives on a yacht in Houston, Texas but is originally from Namibia. She lived with her hubby and sons in several countries before landing in Texas and has maintained she has landed in entrepreneur heaven.

Veronica is the author of the publications:

'Shopify Made Easy 2023' book series -

Book One: Start Your Online Business - A Step-by-Step Guide to Establishing a Profitable eCommerce Business with Shopify

Book Two: Build Your Shopify Brand - A Blueprint for Crafting Your Customer Journey to Maximize Sales

Book Three: Grow Your Shopify Business (or Grow Your Online Business) - A Comprehensive Guide to Boosting Your E-commerce Sales and Growing Your Business

Book Four: Optimize Your Shopify Store -

Companion Workbook & Checklist - Book 1 & 2.

Shopify Advanced series & *Content Marketing* series for Shopify coming soon September 2023.

'Shopify Made Easy 2022' book series - Build Your Ecommerce Empire, Brand Your Shopify Store, Optimize Your Shopify Store, Position Your Brand,

ACKNOWLEDGE

I want to thank everybody from the bottom of my heart to allow me to use our interviews and experiences in my book.

Printed in Great Britain
by Amazon